The Sociology of Education

The Sociology of Education

REVISED EDITION

OLIVE BANKS

SCHOCKEN BOOKS · NEW YORK

First published by SCHOCKEN BOOKS 1976

First edition published by SCHOCKEN BOOKS 1968

© Olive Banks 1968, 1971, 1976

Library of Congress Catalog Card No. 76-9137

Printed in Great Britain

Library of Congress Cataloging in Publication Data

Banks, Olive.
    The sociology of education.

    Bibliography: p.
    Includes index.
    1. Educational sociology. I. Title
LC189.B36   1976   370.19'3

Contents

1 Introduction

1 *The development of the subject*

The sociology of education, like the sociology of the family or of politics, is no more, but at the same time no less, than the application of sociological perspectives to one of the major institutions of society, and for this reason needs no special justification as the subject matter of a text for sociology students. At the same time the history of the subject, especially in the United States, has been unusual enough to warrant some account of its development as a discipline. Although depending for its advance upon the development of sociological concepts and research findings, the subject for many years remained outside the main stream of sociology, being conceived in the main as a part of the study of education. The interest of educationalists like John Dewey ensured the subject an early start, and it soon became a popular subject in colleges and universities in the u.s.a. Between 1910 and 1926 the number of colleges offering a course in educational sociology increased from 40 to 194, and 25 textbooks were published between 1916 and 1936.[1] Yet by the 1940s the number of colleges offering it had declined and the subject generally had fallen into disrepute.

Both Orville Brim[2] and Ronald G. Corwin[3] have analysed the weaknesses of the early attempts to develop the subject, and their arguments will only be summarized here, since in essence all the faults arise from the same source, its separation from the main stream of sociology. Many of the courses in the subject were developed in colleges or schools of education and few of those who taught them were sociologists by training. Some of the teachers undoubtedly had little knowledge of or interest in developments in sociology itself, and were interested in the subject primarily, if not indeed wholly, as an applied discipline. This tendency was further

1

encouraged by the predominance, amongst the students, of teachers in training. In consequence there was a strong emphasis on a programmatic and polemic approach. Research techniques remained at a primitive level, and there was a focus on a limited area of problems of interest to the practising teacher. Even in 1963 James Conant, making a plea that educational sociology should be taught by sociologists, was able to write: 'As to whether the present group of professors who consider themselves educational sociologists, should perpetuate themselves, I have the gravest doubts. I would wish that all who claim to be working in sociology would get together in the graduate training and appointment of professors who claim to use sociological methods in discussing school and youth problems.'[4]

The increasing disillusion with the old approach has in recent years been challenged by new developments in the subject which are bringing it back into departments of sociology, and this is symbolized by a change in nomenclature. It is now becoming customary to refer to the sociology of education rather than the old and now suspect terminology of educational sociology. On the whole, too, this new emphasis has come about because sociologists themselves have started to take an interest in education as a field of study. Significantly, also, a number of distinguished sociologists have recently made outstanding contributions in general theoretical sociology which have taken the form of studies in educational institutions.

As Brookover and Erickson have recently pointed out, the rapid increase in the quantity and quality of research during the past twenty years 'has been accompanied by a high degree of interaction and joint effort between sociologists and educators'.[5] They argue, too, almost certainly correctly, that the interest of sociologists in the field has itself been stimulated by the mass public concern for education since the Second World War. What caused the decline in the subject was not, therefore, its preoccupation with practical problems, but its isolation in departments of education away from the development of basic concepts and methods in sociology itself. It may be, too, that the nature of the problems which interested education at that time did not appeal to sociologists. Corwin, for example, has referred to the 'sterility of the questions that it asked'.[6] The difference between what educators and sociologists see as problematic is a fascinating topic in itself but one that unfortunately cannot be explored here.

This brief account of the early history and subsequent development of the subject in the United States does not, however, apply to Britain, where educational sociology failed to capture the interest of educationalists. Even after the Second World War it was rare to find it taught in either Teacher Training Colleges or University Education Departments. Only in the 1960s did it become recognized, on any scale, as a valuable part of a teacher's education.[7] In consequence the sociological study of education, in so far as it has existed at all, has taken place in departments of sociology rather than in departments of education.

Although Tropp[8] has traced its origins to the Royal Commissions and other educational reports of the nineteenth century it may really be said to have begun as a regular academic discipline in the research carried out at the London School of Economics in the years after the Second World War. The interest amongst this group of sociologists at this time was largely with problems of social structure and the economy, and they were fascinated, in Jean Floud's own words, 'by the spectacle of educational institutions struggling to respond to the new purposes of an advanced industrial economy'.[9] Consequently the early sociology of education was rooted very firmly in sociology rather than education, and this had a strong influence on the kind of problem it has concerned itself with. Another influence which has helped to shape its general direction has been its interest in educational policy. Williamson, for example, has pointed to the close links between the sociology of education and political decision-makers and the extent to which the research itself has been sponsored by official and semi-official agencies.[10]

More recently this approach has been challenged by what is sometimes called the 'new' sociology of education. It is interesting to notice that this new approach has been most successful amongst those who are training teachers,[11] and that the more traditional emphasis has been criticized as 'not primarily about education at all'.[12] The new sociology of education has turned away from a preoccupation with the social structure and sees itself as a part of the sociology of knowledge. Issues which were taken for granted by the old sociology of education, such as how knowledge is arrived at, and how it is transmitted in schools or classrooms, now become the major problem-areas of the subject. Although the merits and indeed the novelty of this approach can easily be exaggerated it is an important new development to which attention must be paid.

2 *The structural-functional framework*

It remains now to give a more precise definition of the scope of the subject as it is to be defined in this volume, and in particular to introduce some of the more important concepts around which it has been organized. The traditional conceptual framework in the subject is that of functionalism, and derives primarily from the writings of the French sociologist Emile Durkheim. The functionalist approach, as Durkheim used it, is to seek for the social function performed by an institution; that is to say the part played by the institution in the promotion and maintenance of social cohesion and social unity. All of the major institutions studied by Durkheim are conceived in this way and education is no exception. Its special task is defined by him as 'the methodical socialization of the young generation'. By this he means the development in the child of certain values and certain intellectual and physical skills 'which are demanded of him by both the political society as a whole and the special milieu for which he is specifically destined'.[13] Only in this way can the cohesion and survival of the society be assured.

This requirement is a basic necessity of all societies, however simple, and many anthropological studies have described the socialization process at work within primitive societies. The sociology of education, however, is more usually confined to studies of industrial societies, which offer certain distinctive and challenging problems. Most fundamental perhaps is the increasing importance in advanced industrial societies of specialized educational agencies which share with, and in certain circumstances replace, the pre-industrial socializing agencies, of which normally the family is the most important. Immediately, as Floud and Halsey have pointed out, this creates a fresh set of problems, since the specialized agencies themselves enter the situation as relatively independent factors, 'promoting or impeding change and producing unintended as well as intended, and dysfunctional as well as functional consequences'.[14] For example, there may be prolonged resistance to changes in curricula, teaching methods or entrance requirements, especially on the part of long-established institutions like grammar schools or universities, with consequences that may be disadvantageous for the economy. On the other hand, teachers can, and often do, act as a powerful pressure group to promote educational change.

At the same time the process of socialization itself becomes more complex. It is no longer simply a matter of the transmission of skills and values; the educational process itself must take on the role of the allocation and selection as well as the training of individuals for their adult role. Increasingly, in all advanced industrial societies, educational qualifications become important not simply as a sign or symbol of high status but as a necessary prerequisite of the majority of highly rewarded occupations. Indeed, the problems to which this gives rise have preoccupied the attention of sociologists in Britain and to a large extent also in the United States, to the almost virtual exclusion of the problems of social integration and social control with which Durkheim was so concerned.

One of the major strengths of the structural functional approach to education is the placing of educational institutions firmly in their relationship with the wider social structure. In any consideration of either the socializing or the selective function of education regard must be had to the context in which the educational institutions operate and the influences at work upon them. Of these, the economy is obviously of paramount importance, determining as it does the complexity of the skills required according to the level of technology. At the same time its differentiating and selective functions bring education inevitably into close relationships with the demographic aspects of society and with the stratification system. The controlling and integrating functions of education and its role in the transmission of values also necessitate close ties with the value system of society, with religious institutions and with the State itself as an instrument of control. Moreover, in so far as the educational process is a shared one, other socializing agencies, of which the family is the most important, must be recognized for the part they play, and their relationship with the more specialized educational agencies must be explored. Consequently, within the general framework of a structural functionalist approach the sociology of education has developed as a largely macrocosmic study of educational institutions.

Yet, as Floud and Halsey have pointed out, structural functionalism has certain methodological faults which have contributed to the weaknesses of the sociology of education. 'The structural functionalist is preoccupied with social integration based on shared values—that is, with consensus—and he conducts his analysis solely in terms of the motivated actions of individuals. For him, therefore, education is a means of motivating individuals to behave in ways appropriate to maintain the society in a state of equilibrium. But this is a difficult notion to apply to developed, especially industrialized societies, even if the notion of equilibrium is interpreted dynamically. They are dominated by social change, and "consensus" and "integration" can be only very loosely conceived in regard to them."[15]

Briefly, the structural functional approach tends to overlook not only the extent of differentiation in a modern complex society but also the fact that differentiation implies at least some degree, and often a considerable degree, of actual or contained conflict. It was one of the major errors of Durkheim to minimize the amount of conflict consequent upon the division of labour,[16] and this same error continues within the structural functional school. Yet even a brief glance at some of the educational controversies in our own society reveals that there is no common value system with regard to educational goals, but a series of opposing ideologies put forward by certain pressure groups which include, amongst others, the major political parties. The wider social structure in which the educational institutions are enmeshed must, therefore, be seen not as the result of any single or unified set of values, but as the expression of manifest or latent ideological conflict. The concept of ideology, including both its cognitive and evaluative aspects,[17] is indeed of fundamental importance in any understanding of the educational process, and it is unfortunate that it should have been so seriously neglected in the study of education.

Although it is often argued that the structural functional approach tends to neglect social change, this is not altogether a fair criticism since many of the major thinkers in this field have attempted to find a place for change in their theory. So far as education is concerned, however, there has been a very widespread tendency to treat it as a wholly adaptive institution. That is to say, change in the educational system tends to be seen as a response to changes in the other parts of the social structure. This contrasts with the prevailing viewpoint of educationalists like John Dewey, who have seen the educational system as a direct agency of social change, and who have enthusiastically looked to the schools to reform society. It is, of course, not difficult to prick the rather facile optimism of the educationalists who have sometimes hoped to produce major social reforms by simple changes in educational organization. Moreover, educational institutions have often been largely adaptive in their functioning, as can be seen in even a cursory examination of their response to the technological requirements of the economy in many advanced industrial societies. On the other hand, there is no evidence for any simple theory of technological determination. Educational institutions are shaped by many aspects of the social structure including the dominant value system. We need only consider in this context the ideological barriers to the development of technical education in Britain, and in particular the influence on the educational system and elsewhere of the support for the amateur rather than the expert.

Nor can it be asserted with confidence that education can never initiate change. There is an absence of concrete studies in this field but work is now being done on such topics as the part played by education in economic growth, and the effect of education in changing attitudes. It is clear, too, that education may well have unintended consequences of some importance as, for example, on the composition of new and old elites. Most important of all, in an age when change has itself become institutionalized, the pursuit of innovation rather than the maintenance of the social order becomes one of the major goals of the educational process.

At the present time structural functionalism as an approach is out of fashion. It is condemned on ideological grounds as conservative, or at best, tied to the 'reformist solutions of the Welfare State',[18] and on methodological grounds because of its association with with scientific positivism.[19] Underlying both these criticisms is the sometimes overt, sometimes covert determinism of structural functionalism and its tendency to reify society as something 'out there'. Peter Berger has used the analogy of the puppet to describe this view of man in society.[20]

Undoubtedly these arguments have uncovered some basic weaknesses in the traditional sociology of education. There has, for example, been an acceptance of a somewhat mechanical relationship between the educational system and the economy and a neglect of the activities and assumptions by which the two are actually related. On the other hand, by replacing the concept of man as social product by man as world producer[21] there is a danger in forgetting that man is both a determined as well as a determining being. As I have argued elsewhere, to ignore altogether the structural constraints on educational systems arising from particular technological developments or the ways in which educational systems are actually linked to occupational structures and the division of labour, may well be as harmful as to conceive of the relationship in an over-simplified way.[22] In this edition consequently I have tried to give weight to the argument of the critics while retaining what I think to be of value in the structural functional approach to the sociology of education.

3 The politics of education

One consequence of the interest in social stratification, social mobility and the division of labour has been the relative neglect by British sociologists of what may be called the politics of education. Most of the work in this area in this country has been carried out by political scientists or educational administrators and is not set in a sociological context. It may, for example, be mainly descriptive, or it may be concerned with exclusively administrative or managerial considerations. This is also true to a large extent in the United States, although the work of Neal Gross in particular has pioneered the sociological study of educational decision-making at the school level. There is also, in both countries, a growing literature on teachers as a professional group.

More recently, however, the reaction against structural functionalism has turned the attention of sociologists towards the politics of education. This is mainly because the new approach in sociology is one that places its emphasis upon control rather than order, and conflict rather than interdependence. For some sociologists at least this had led not only to a re-assessment of Max Weber but the discovery or rediscovery of Marx. The result is a new appreciation of the way in which educational development may reflect the struggles of competing groups rather than the 'needs' of society. Although the novelty of this approach may be exaggerated there is no doubt of its importance, not least perhaps in its powerful advocacy of the historical approach to sociology. It also provides a useful antidote to a mechanistic and 'over-determined' use of structural functional theory, although it too can fall into its own over-simplistic use of concepts, and a rather tendentious dogmatism. There are few empirical studies so far, particularly in this country, but it may well represent one of the important growth points in the sociology of education.

4 *The sociology of educational knowledge and the sociology of the classroom*

Although sociologists have by no means ignored the content of education, their attention in the past has tended to be focussed on the relationship between science, technology and economic efficiency, or between subject choice, educational qualifications and the occupational hierarchy. They did not, as Young has pointed out, take academic knowledge as something which in itself has to be explained, or ask what it is to be educated.[23] In other words Young is suggesting that sociologists should concern themselves with the fact that it is not only people, but also knowledge, that is processed in educational institutions. Ioan Davies similarly has argued that the central theme of the sociology of education should be what he calls the control and management of knowledge.[24]

Both Young and Davies are influenced largely by the Marxist tradition and are concerned primarily with the relationship between knowledge and power. This is also true of the French sociologist Bourdieu whose work has made a major contribution to a new realignment of the sociology of education with the sociology of culture and the sociology of knowledge.

Another important influence on the sociology of the curriculum is the phenomenological perspective associated with Schutz and Berger. Fundamental to this approach is the stress on intentionality and the social production of meaning through interaction, which itself gives rise to a distrust of the social survey and the closed questionnaire and a preference for participant observation and the tape recorder. In this respect the new approach looks back to the much older tradition of symbolic interaction which has always played an important part in the sociology of education in the United States through the work of Becker.

One of the major consequences for the sociology of education has been the interest in classroom interaction. This new sociology of the classroom must be distinguished in both method and intention from the work of the psychologists in this area, and indeed owes more to the social anthropologist particularly in its methodology. It is however still relatively undeveloped, although it is already producing some interesting case studies which indicate its promise for the future. Its weakness in so far as it attempts to be more than a limited branch of the sociology of education is its over-enthusiastic assessment of the power and independence of the individual teacher.[25] It does however add an interesting and important dimension to the sociology of the school.

5 The school as an organization

In 1958 Floud and Halsey in their 'Trend Report and Bibliography' had complained that 'too many sociological studies of schools are in fact studies of the social life of adolescents',[26] and in 1961 Jean Floud drew attention to the need for sociologists to explore 'the explicit and implicit demands of life in schools'.[27] In the United States, too, Gross in 1959 had complained that 'there have been few significant advances in our knowledge of the social and cultural structure of the school, and of the impact it exerts on the functioning of educational systems, since the publication of Waller's *Sociology of Teaching* in 1932'.[28]

Since then there have been a number of studies of schools and other educational institutions both in this country and in the United States. The growth of the field has not, however, led to an equal increase in our knowledge of schools and colleges as organizations. Davies, reviewing the field in 1970 argued that 'our ability to explain and generalize about how they work in any degree of depth is still limited by the shortcomings of organizational analysis itself and by the paucity of worthwhile empirical studies within education'.[29] He points, additionally, to the bewildering choice of theoretical approaches, reflecting the historical divisions within sociology, and the tradition of managerialism, which has focused attention on such issues as leadership style and morale.

Hoyle[30] has argued that two of the most widely used concepts in organization theory are authority and bureaucracy, both of which stem from Max Weber's treatment of authority. The question as to how far a school or an educational system can be described as a bureaucracy is still an open one, and the extent of bureaucracy in education, its causes and its consequences, have attracted considerable attention in the United States in recent years.

An alternative set of concepts also basic to organizational theory revolves around the concept of role which, as used by most sociologists, refers to a set of norms relating to a specific activity or relationship. Studies making use of the concept of role have centred largely on the teacher, although educational administrators have also figured prominently in research in the United States, and there is now a fairly extensive literature on the role of the teacher, both in the school and in the wider society.

With some notable exceptions, however, British research on schools has continued to focus, as Hoyle has recently pointed out, on the pupils.[31] Streaming and its consequences has been a dominant theme and a concern with pupil differentiation in one form or another has been a preoccupation with almost all the British studies of schools. This probably reflects the policy implications of these studies and their relationship to the comprehensive school debate. It is in this area in particular that the new sociology of the classroom would seem to have an important part to play.

6 *Aims and limitations*

In preparing this outline of the growing body of knowledge on the sociology of education, the needs of the sociology student rather than the intending teacher have been chiefly in mind. Consequently some familiarity with sociological concepts and, even more important, some knowledge of comparative social institutions has been assumed. The text, that is to say, is intended to follow on from an introductory course in sociology rather than to act as a substitute for it. This is to break away from tradition both in Britain and in the United States where until recently textbooks in this field have been aimed at the student of education rather than of sociology and the general slant of the subject matter has been to introduce sociology to teachers rather than to explore the sociological dimensions of educational institutions.

Even the best and most recent textbooks in this field tend to a very definite insularity in their approach. In particular American textbooks tend to give only a minimum of attention to other educational systems than their own. This is understandable enough in view of the enormous difficulties in the way of a genuinely comparative approach to educational systems which is at the same time sociological in its aims. Nevertheless it is the present writer's contention that, without some attempt to be comparative, it is very difficult to treat a number of important areas in the subject. Accordingly, although the main emphasis in this book is on the educational system in Britain, and indeed primarily in England and Wales, material from the United States has been introduced very freely, and wherever possible the United States and Britain are compared. In addition, information from a number of other European countries, and especially from the U.S.S.R., has been included from time to time. Unfortunately it has not been possible to include more than a brief reference to educational systems outside Europe and the United States, so that the place of education in developing societies has not been given the attention that the importance of the subject deserves.

The general plan of the book is to proceed from a consideration of education in its societal setting to a discussion of the sociology of the school. It begins therefore with a consideration of educational systems in their relationship to such major social institutions as the economy, social stratification, and social mobility. A consideration at this point of the effect of social class on school performance leads into the study of education and the family, and a review of research into the effect of home environment on the educability of the child. This is followed by a chapter on education in its political context. From here the focus begins to close more directly on the school itself although there is a preliminary chapter on the teachers as a professional group. This is followed by chapters on the sociology of educational knowledge, the school as an organization, and the sociology of the classroom.

The approach taken by the author is a somewhat eclectic one in that an attempt is made to do justice to both the older tradition in the sociology of education and the new directions that it has taken in recent years. Fortunately, there is now a greater appreciation of the continuities as well as the divergencies in the two approaches, and although it would be not only presumptuous but foolhardy to claim that anything like a reconciliation has been reached in these pages, it is hoped that it has in some respects paved the way for something of the sort.

This new edition, in trying to take account both of new empirical findings and new approaches to the subject, has been substantially rewritten. Although no major changes have been made in the overall structure, or in the order in which the material is presented, there are a number of minor rearrangements to meet the changing shape of the subject and criticisms of the earlier editions. The substantial increase in research in many areas has meant however that I have been forced to be even more selective in my use of sources, which should not in any sense be taken as a review of the available literature. I have tried instead to direct the reader to a representative range of sources and to indicate areas of disagreement and controversy. The particular approach to the subject which has guided the selection of both topics and sources is however a personal one, and no claim is made that is the only or even the best approach. It is presented as were the earlier editions in the hope that this particular version of the sociology of education will prove to be interesting to others besides myself.

2 Education and the economy

1 *The education explosion*

A consideration of the theoretical scheme outlined in the previous chapter makes it clear that in any society the educational system will be linked to the economy, in so far as young people must be trained in the skills they will require as adult members of the society. It by no means follows, however, that these skills will be taught wholly or even mainly within the school system, even where such a system exists. In pre-industrial societies all such skills are taught 'on the job' either within the family itself or at the work place. Even after industrialization, 'on the job' training has retained its importance, until recently, for many of the lower levels of industrial skill. What characterizes an advanced industrial society is the extent to which skills at all levels of the occupational hierarchy are increasingly acquired within formal educational institutions.

The new tools, new techniques and new materials which transformed nineteenth-century Britain, were only the start of a continuous process of technical development which has, in the twentieth century, accelerated rather than declined. Contemporary innovations, particularly in the field of automation, are so far-reaching that it is customary to talk and write of a second industrial revolution. At the same time innovation itself has become institutionalized, and research in pure science and in technology is harnessed to the needs of higher productivity. It is no wonder, then, that corresponding changes in the scope and the content of education are so often seen in terms of the needs of the economy. The purpose of this chapter will be to describe the relationship between these two aspects of society, and to consider in particular how far changes in modern educational systems can be explained in economic terms. Schelsky[1] has described the way in which science and technology have influenced the amount and kind of skill required of the labour force, and the changes which the future is likely to bring. He shows that the proportion engaged in manual work has declined and the proportion in white-collar and professional and managerial work has risen. Many new professional and semi-professional occupations have grown up, based upon the developing sciences and technologies. Within manual work itself the nature of skill has gone through many changes, as the traditional craft skills of a pre-industrial society gave way to new skills appropriate to new and changing technologies. Moreover, in recent years, especially where automation has been introduced, the traditional distinction between skilled and semi-skilled manual workers and clerical and technical staff is practically being obliterated. As a result of these changes the formal educational system of school and college, hitherto required mainly for an elite group of professional occupations, has expanded to provide for the needs, not only of a growing number of professional and semi-professional occupations, but also a skilled labour force which increasingly needs to be literate, adaptable and mobile.

The consequence has been what can only be regarded as an educational explosion. The establishment of universal literacy has been followed by a lengthening of school life, a widening and deepening of the curriculum and the gradual extension of higher education to a wider section of the community. This expansion of education has not followed the same pattern everywhere, and is considerably more advanced in some industrial societies than in others, but the general lines of the educational explosion can be traced in all advanced industrial societies.

Blau, for example, argues from both historical trends and cross-national comparisons that a society's technological development as indicated by energy consumption *per capita* is correlated with the level of education of its population, with the level of occupational differentiation and with the proportion of its labour force in professional work. The same is true of a society's economic development as indicated by gross national product *per capita*.[2]

At the same time the attitude to education has changed. An abundant and increasing supply of highly educated people has come to be regarded as the absolute prerequisite of social and economic development in our world, and increasingly, educational expenditure is seen as a vital investment in human beings.[3] A rapidly growing interest in the economics of education has produced efforts not only to reach a more precise measurement of the cost of education but also a more accurate estimate of the contribution that education can make to economic growth. Unfortunately, despite considerable research activity, no general agreement has been reached on this issue, and formidable measurement problems remain. It is particularly difficult, for example, to separate the effects of education from other factors which influence earnings, such as ability and social class.[4]

It would however be a mistake to see the educational explosion simply as a mechanical response to the 'needs' of the economy. Roberts for example has drawn attention to the way in which the influence of the economy is mediated through other institutions.[5] Since the financial resources required to enable education to meet the needs of an industrializing society have been mainly channelled through the state, government policies become of crucial importance, but these are by no means necessarily geared either to educational expansion or to the needs of industry. Indeed national differences in ideology can be shown to lie behind many of the variations in educational expansion both within Europe and between Western Europe and the United States. It is necessary therefore to look at ideological differences in some detail and to consider in particular some of the ways in which they may actually impede the response of the educational system to economic needs.

The ideological conflict between elitist and populist theories of education is found in all industrial societies and is the source of much current educational controversy. It can also be shown to have considerable influence on the rate of educational expansion. The elitist ideology, as its name implies, is traditionalist in its orientation, looking back to the time when education was the prerogative of a small elite. The attitude to education to which it gives rise tends therefore to be exclusive and emphasizes the needs of the few rather than the many. Such an educational philosophy can be seen very clearly in early nineteenth-century England, where the provision of free elementary education was made by charitable and religious bodies whose aim was primarily moral, and whose conception of the amount of education necessary for this purpose was of a very limited kind. The children of the poor needed to be taught Christian principles and to be able to read their Bibles, but writing was suspect and even dangerous. Moreover, although ideas on what was necessary grew gradually more liberal, the anxiety that the poor would be over-educated and made unfit for their station in life, continued at least until the end of the century. Indeed, in spite of the reforms of the early twentieth century which widened the curriculum and postponed the school-leaving age, the elementary system remained in being until 1944, providing a cheaper and more limited schooling for the children of the poor.

At the same time secondary education was conceived as a distinct system, providing for the needs of the middle and upper classes. Even the recognition by the end of the century of an educational ladder from the elementary school to the university did not really alter the conception of secondary education as a distinct system, linked to the elementary system by scholarships and free places, but separate from it administratively and socially. Moreover, attempts from within the elementary system to extend into secondary education were severely curbed.[6]

The 1944 Education Act, as is well known, abolished the elementary school and introduced free secondary education for all, and the secondary school became a stage in the educational process for every child. On the other hand in spite of the attempts to achieve parity of esteem between the different types of secondary education, the secondary modern school has retained at least some of the traditions of the old elementary system, and at the same time selection by ability has replaced, within the maintained grammar school, the right to entry on the payment of fees. An aristocracy of brains is not, however, any less of an elite than an aristocracy of birth, and in so far as the grammar school selects an able minority of children and prepares them for middle-class occupations it is still fulfilling an elite function and representing an elite philosophy of secondary education.

Evidence that the elite conception of education is out of line with the needs of the labour market is provided very graphically by Taylor's study of the secondary modern school. He shows how full employment and the creation of new jobs which require both a high level of skill and a good educational background have deeply influenced the direction of development of the schools. Not only has there been a widespread provision of extended courses of both an academic and a vocational nature, but the modern schools have been able 'to break the examination monopoly of other types of secondary school, and to participate in, rather than contract out of, the process of vocational competition and the promotion of social mobility through education'.[7] Developments within the secondary modern school since 1944 are therefore a particularly interesting example of the sensitive interplay between economic and ideological factors in educational change.

It is true, of course, that although the elite concept of secondary education has to a very considerable extent remained the dominant ideology in Britain, it has by no means gone unchallenged. The emergence of a genuine populist ideology can be seen very clearly as far back as the controversy over the high-grade schools in the 1890s. At the same time the need for skilled manpower, particularly for clerks and school teachers, made possible not only the expansion of secondary education, but the development of higher forms of elementary education. In the years between the two world wars, for example, many local authorities experimented with selective central schools, providing what amounted to a secondary education within the elementary system.[8] The effect after 1944 was a compromise in which the elite ideology, populist pressures towards equality, and the needs of the economy together produced an expansion of secondary education to include all children, but within the framework of an elite system.

More recently the elite ideology in secondary education has been severely challenged in Britain by the idea of the common secondary school, and it has been estimated that, by 1980, 75 per cent of the children in secondary education will be enrolled in comprehensive schools.[9] Similar developments are taking place in other countries in Western Europe and Sweden is already fully comprehensive. It seems that the selective system of secondary education will soon give way to some form of unselected school. If, however, we wish to see the effect on secondary education of an educational philosophy in which the populist ideology has long been the major influence we must look to the United States. The controversy between what have come to be called the Jeffersonian and Jacksonian principles of educational provision resulted in an early and almost complete victory for Jacksonian principles, which has expressed itself in the belief that education for all was essential in a democratic society, irrespective of social origins or even learning ability. This has been combined with strong popular support for the value of education.

Unlike the situation in Britain where the education of the masses has been imposed or withheld by powerful elite groups in Church or State, the common school in the United States was founded by 'relatively untutored farmers who established one-room district schools in rural neighbourhoods as they moved across the continent'.[10] In consequence, except in certain regions and neighbourhoods, there is a great deal of public enthusiasm for education, and parents on the whole are eager to take advantage of what the schools have to offer. As a result of this, not only is the common high school the normal type of secondary school in the United States, but graduation from high school at the age of 17 or 18 has now become the generally accepted level of educational achievement.

It is, however, in the field of higher education that we find the biggest consequences of differing ideological approaches to educational opportunity. The universities, as Halsey has pointed out, are 'intrinsically inequalitarian',[11] but this tendency is considerably enhanced when they are restricted to a very small section of the community. The symbolic value of the higher learning has always conferred high status on those who are admitted to it, and in addition it has had functional value, in so far as it has been a limited but possible avenue to positions of wealth and power in Church or State.

The effect of industrial development is to link the university to the economy through the market for professional and scientific manpower, and the benefits of higher education are inevitably extended to cover a higher proportion of the community. At the same time there are wide differences between countries in the actual amount of expansion, and the form the expansion takes—differences, moreover, which cannot be explained solely in terms of economic development. Anderson, for example, using data from a large number of countries in Eastern and Western Europe and the United States showed that, for males only, there is some relationship between a nation's type of economy and the rate of university attendance, but that this relationship is a limited one. 'The underlying factors explaining national contrasts must', he argues, 'be sought in values, customs and public educational policies.' Moreover, for women, none of the differences can be explained in economic terms.[12] Ben-David has also reached similar conclusions using, this time, a world-wide range of data. Even though there is some correlation between the production of graduates and the level of economic development, 'there still remain obvious and glaring exceptions'.[13]

Ben-David distinguished 'three influential academic systems, the European, the American and the Soviet, each of which produces different ratios and kinds of graduates. The positions of the other countries seem to be, at least superficially, the function of respective spheres of influence. The developing countries of the Middle East and Latin America whose academic traditions were imported from Europe, are situated close to and below the European countries, while the Philippines, which used to be an American dependency, are trailing the United States. The position of Canada and that of Japan reflect the replacement of European influence by American. Among the communist countries of Eastern and Central Europe there is a tendency to approach the U.S.S.R.'[14]

The European pattern of higher education has been strongly influenced by the dominant elite ideology. Only a very small proportion of the age-group entered any form of higher education, and the universities, at the apex of the hierarchically organized system, were particularly narrow in their recruitment. Table One below gives particulars from several countries in Western Europe for 1958-9, and shows that in spite of some variations, the general picture was fairly similar.

Since then higher education in general has expanded quite considerably both in Britain and in other countries in Western Europe, and it is no longer as accurate to describe it as an elite system. By 1967, for example, 14.3 per cent of the relevant age-group in England and Wales entered some form of full-time higher education, an increase of nearly 100 per cent in less than ten years. The universities were included in this expansion and by now catered for 6.3 per cent rather than 4.6 per cent of the relevant age-group.[15] It is clear however that most of the expansion in higher education has been outside in the universities, and this trend is likely to continue.[16] Indeed there is some evidence that the British university system will remain more elitist than its European counterparts. The Hudson Report has estimated that by 1980 'Britain will have a smaller university programme than any other Western country of similar size and economic structure'.[17]

In the United States in contrast higher education is open to a wide range of ability and to a very wide sector of the age-group. There is no attempt to restrict it to a minority of the population. Already in 1970 40 per cent of the age-group were at college, representing 66 per cent of those who actually graduated from high school and the early 1970s saw further expansion. More recently there has been a decline in college enrolments due to such factors as lack of employment opportunities and changes in the military draft law, and it may be that the U.S. is at last approaching a ceiling. Moreover, the actual numbers entering higher education are bound to drop in the 1980s due to changes in the size of the age-group.[18] On the other hand further expansion in the proportion enrolling in college can by no means be ruled out, especially from those groups, like blacks and women, who are under-represented. At the same time the distinctions within higher education are much less clear-cut than they are in Europe. In Britain, for example, there are clear differences between universities and other institutions providing higher education, and this is true of Europe generally. In the United States, however, there are no formal barriers between institutions and the system is 'in a state of constant flux. The Junior Colleges tend to develop into liberal arts colleges. Professional schools tend to develop general arts and science faculties. The liberal arts colleges themselves, if publicly controlled, seek to become State universities, and the latter soon begin to award Doctorates.'[19] The whole system indeed is one of open competition, an academic procession, as Riesman has called it, in which it is not always easy to decide on a single scale of rank or prestige.[20] This openness of the American system is an important element in the populist ideology and is one to which it will be necessary to return in more detail in the following chapter.

Table One[21]

Percentage of age-group entering higher education in selected countries, 1958-9

	Full-time courses only		*All methods of study*	
	Courses of British degree level %	All levels of higher education %	Courses of British degree level %	All levels of higher education %
Great Britain	4.6	7.7	6.6	12.4
France	8	9	8	9
Germany (F.R.)	4	6	4	8
Netherlands	3	7	3	8
Sweden	7	10	8	11
Switzerland	5	10	5	11

Some of the expansion of education in the United States can be shown to be linked to changes in the occupational structure, and particularly to the growth in the white-collar, professional and managerial work. On the other hand there is evidence that a large part of the rise in educational attainment has contributed simply to improving the educational level of existing occupations, and that this process is likely to continue. At the college level this educational upgrading has occurred for the most part in managerial and sales occupations. In the future, if these trends continue, 'the majority of the additional male high school graduates will be absorbed into the blue-collar occupations, while a majority of the additional college educated men will be absorbed by managerial, sales, clerical and some craftsmen occupations'.[22]

The extent to which the occupations involved either need, or indeed, benefit from, the process of educational upgrading has recently been challenged by Ivar Berg, who has marshalled a great deal of evidence to make the point that within a wide variety of jobs there are few signs that the better educated employees are in any sense more productive. Indeed, in certain areas, such as the selling of insurance, workers with less education but more experience perform better and earn more. Nor can the 'over-education' of much of the American population be viewed simply as the harmless extravagance of an affluent society. Berg points to the 'dissatisfaction resulting from unfilled and unfulfillable aspirations', as the educational coinage becomes increasingly devalued. At the same time, those who cannot, or do not succeed in the educational system are consigned 'to a social limbo defined by low-skill no-opportunity jobs'.[23]

To some extent, therefore, the expansion of education at both the secondary and the higher levels must be seen as a response to what might be called the structure of competition for mobility chances. As education becomes, and is seen to become, the avenue to better jobs, so the demand for educational qualifications grows, setting up an inflationary spiral in which educational requirements become even higher. Moreover, this process must be seen as a consequence not only of individual action but also of class and status struggles over the distribution of opportunity. Roberts, for example, sees the pressure for increased educational opportunity from the economically weaker sections of society as 'one of the driving forces behind the development of state secondary education in Britain'.[24]

The development of such an inflationary spiral is dependent upon many factors, including, as one of the more important, the nature of the links between the educational system and the market. In both Britain and the u.s.s.r., for example, the expansion of higher education is very largely dependent on government policy rather than on direct consumer demand. Consequently a pressure on places in higher education may, for a time at least, lead to a raising of entry standards rather than overall expansion. Similarly, where there is a differentiated system of higher education, as in both Western and Eastern Europe, the demand may be channelled into alternative and sometimes part-time forms of higher education. In the United States, on the other hand, the undifferentiated system of higher education is very sensitive to market forces, and there has been a continuous process of expansion to meet a variety of needs.

It is unlikely however that government policy can do more than delay the move from an elite to a mass system of higher education. The process is already underway on a world-wide scale, and, as we have seen, once started, it has its own momentum. At the same time it is by no means certain that the European system will be an exact copy of that in the United States. In the first place only an affluent society can afford such a system of higher education. In counting the cost it is not enough to estimate only the provision of buildings and the salaries of teachers; it is also necessary to include the cost of foregone earnings during the years spent at school and college when the student entry to work force is delayed, and the drain on skilled personnel that the provision of teachers represents. The quality of the educational provision is also a highly important aspect of its cost. It would for example be exceedingly difficult to maintain the teacher/student ratio customary in British university education if the proportions of the age-group entering it were to increase substantially.

Nor is it certain how far the highly differentiated European system will be modified. It is true that the differentiated system of secondary education is giving way all over Europe to the common secondary school, but the u.s.s.r., for example, manages to combine comprehensive secondary schools with a very highly stratified system of higher education.

2 *The content of education*

So far the discussion has been concerned with educational expansion, but any consideration of educational development must take into account changes in content as well as in scale. As the demands of the economy have required higher levels of skill, so the nature of that skill has changed, and with it the perception of the educated man. This is not the place to trace these changes in detail, but rather to indicate something of their general scope and direction.

It is sometimes argued that the changes in curriculum which have characterized the development of educational systems as a consequence of industrialization have been mainly a trend towards vocationalism. In fact this is true only in a very special sense. The process of education, whatever the agency that has charge of it, is always in part vocational, in so far as it must be concerned with the transmission of skills and values. This was no less true of the schools and universities of the past than of the schools and universities of today. Hofstadter and Metzger make this point very clearly when they write, of the universities of the middle ages, that their work 'was as relevant to the ecclesiastical and political life of the thirteenth and fourteenth centuries as the modern university is to the scientific and industrial life of our time. They provided vocational training for the clerical functionaries of church and state—for notaries, secretaries, legates and lawyers.'[25] This link between the formal educational system and the two great professions, the Law and the Church, has been of vital importance, determining as it has the content of schools and universities for many centuries.

If we are to understand the process by which the classical and literary curriculum—the traditional vocational training of the professions—became the very essence of non-vocational or general education, it is necessary to consider the extent to which the schools and universities have stood apart from the needs of the economy, focused as they were upon the needs of the Church and the State. Training in practical skills, at all levels, has traditionally taken place at home and in the work-place. Moreover, this tradition remained all but unbroken up to and indeed into the nineteenth century.

It is true that science had a place, if only a small one, in some schools and universities, but this had almost always been divorced from the practical processes of industry. So extreme indeed was the separation of the formal educational process from the development of the economy that Ashby could write that 'in the rise of British industry the English Universities played no part whatever'.[26]

The extent to which a modern industrial economy makes

demands upon the educational system is not in question. An advanced technology can no longer depend upon the traditional 'on the job' training. New and more complex skills require not only a literate work force but, in the higher echelons, a formal training in science and technology. At the same time the concomitant expansion in trade and commerce gave rise to a demand for commercial skills both at the practical and the more theoretical level. Finally the education explosion itself, with its need for more and more teachers, had a profound effect on the secondary and higher stages of the educational process.

On the other hand the extent to which these pressures are accepted or resisted varies very greatly from country to country. In particular, America and Russia have moved further and faster in this direction than Western Europe. Moreover the reasons for these differences are very complex, including not only the acceptance or otherwise of an elite ideology but the nature of the elite itself. In addition, as Ben-David points out, the rate of expansion of educational provision is itself related in several important ways to changes in educational curricula. For this reason it is necessary to look in some detail at the social processes involved in harnessing the educational system to the needs of the economy, and in particular to the means by which these processes have been delayed.

A number of studies have shown how the development of scientific and technical education in Britain has been handicapped by the association of the universities with the training of a particular elite. 'University education was a matter of luxury, part of the way of life of the upper classes. Originally the clergy was the only profession for which people were trained at universities. Higher civil service and secondary school teaching were added to this during the second part of the last century. All these professions, or important parts of them, were closely connected to the upper class, or were upper-class callings.'[27] As a result, a university education was in itself a powerful status symbol, indicating membership of the community of the educated, and giving the rank of gentleman.

Rothblatt, in his account of nineteenth-century Cambridge, has shown in detail how the aristocratic and clerical heritage of the ancient universities was incorporated into the education of the professions. The dons strongly emphasized high ethical or altruistic standards as the predominant characteristic of a professional man and this was 'sharply brought to bear against the Victorian businessman'. Professional men, and this included the civil service at home and overseas, 'began to see themselves as in a special sense the descendants of the landed aristocracy and the new gentlemen of English society'.[28]

Moreover, the Industrial Revolution, as Ashby has pointed out, was not accomplished by the educated classes. 'Men like Bramah and Maudsley, Arkwright and Crompton, the Darbys of Coalbrookdale and Neilson of Glasgow, had no systematic education in science or technology. Britain's industrial strength lay in the amateurs and self-made men: the craftsman-inventor, the mill-owner, the iron-master. It was no accident that the Crystal Palace, that sparkling symbol of the supremacy of British technology, was designed by an amateur.'[29] In consequence for a long time technical education in Britain was seen as appropriate to the artisan and foreman level, rather than at the level of higher education, and there was little appreciation of the practical application of science to industry.

Cotgrove, in his study of the development of technical education in England and Wales, has attempted to explain the late start in the nineteenth century and the slow progress in the inter-war years largely in terms of 'the 50 years or more of industrial pre-eminence which had established industrial traditions in which science and research were absent'.[30] This long period of pre-eminence induced a mood of complacency among British industrialists and businessmen which has lasted, to some extent, until recent years.

A second factor, which Cotgrove also believes to be of considerable importance, is the lack of scientific and technical qualifications on the part of the proprietors and managers in industry. Either they had risen from the ranks with only a modicum of elementary education or they had been educated in the mainly classical and literary tradition of the middle-class secondary school. Consequently they were not themselves in a position to appreciate the potential value of a scientific or technical education to industry and might even be prejudiced against it. As a result there has not been, until recent years, a demand for men with scientific or technical qualifications, and in much of top industrial management the arts graduate has been preferred.

The same points have been made by Musgrave in a study of the British and German iron and steel industries, and their relationship to the labour force. He, too, lays stress on the cleavage between industry and higher education which arose partly out of the tradition of the self-made man, partly because of a belief in the practical rather than the theoretical approach. The general belief was that 'every workshop or factory in the kingdom' was a technical school in which trades could be 'learned with far more efficiency than under the most learned professors'. At the same time the dislike of science and industry on the part of the upper classes and the universities meant that 'many able men were diverted from industry to politics, the professions and the Civil Service'.[31]

Musgrave contrasts the situation in Britain with that of Germany, where science was given a very high place, both in secondary and higher education, and in industry itself. Consequently, by 1900 German boards of management in large firms consisted of highly paid specialists, who were constantly watching for scientific discoveries helpful to their business; under them was a large staff of men trained to university level to develop such discoveries. In the iron and steel industry, mainly large integrated firms, the salaries of such experts ran into thousands of pounds. As a consequence, Germany's technical and scientific development was rapid and, in spite of her late start, was able not only to catch up with Britain but even in some instances to surpass her.

Landes too has made a telling comparison of British and German educational achievements in the nineteenth century. He cites four kinds of knowledge, the ability to read, write and calculate, the skill of the craftsman, the training of the engineer, and high-level scientific knowledge. Each of these has its own contribution to make to economic performance and 'in all four areas, Germany represented the best that Europe had to offer; in all four, with the possible exception of the second, Britain fell far behind'.[32]

Like Cotgrove and Musgrave, Landes stresses the distrust of technical and scientific education, the development, in many trades, of a mystique of practical experience, and the lack of opportunities for graduates in science and technology. No wonder, he concludes, that gifted young men followed the traditional liberal curriculum to careers in the civil service, or to the kind of post in industry or trade 'that called for a gentleman and not a technician'. In Germany by contrast 'an effective system of scientific and technical training was the foundation and promise of wealth and aggrandizement'.[33]

This is not to suggest that there had been no change in higher education in Britain. The new university colleges founded at the end of the nineteenth century were much more utilitarian in their outlook than were the ancient foundations at Oxford and Cambridge with their elitist traditions. Indeed, representing middle-class rather than aristocratic attitudes, the provincial universities and university colleges were willing enough to accept the task of training for the newer technological professions as well as for the growing needs of the secondary-school teaching profession. Sanderson,[34] for example, has argued that from the middle of the nineteenth century innovation in a large range of industries began to depend increasingly on a more theoretical knowledge. In the absence of suitable scientifically trained graduates, industry in Britain began to import chemists from Germany, and it was this which gave impetus to the movement to create new universities and to link them with industry. Oxford, and to a lesser extent Cambridge, as well as the Welsh and Scottish universities, stayed aloof, and there is even evidence that Cambridge, for example, tended to move sons of businessmen away from a business career.[35] The new civic universities, on the other hand, were distrustful of the idea of a liberal and supposedly non-vocational education. They emphasized science and technology because of the industrial nature of their financial support, and because of the background of their students.[36] Another important factor must have been the absence of any aristocratic or clerical tradition.

The First World War brought a closer involvement between industry and the universities, and new industries in particular were 'avid absorbers of graduates from the beginning',[37] but progress was still relatively slow. In the inter-war years much of industry continued to be apathetic towards the graduate, and at the secondary level the grammar and central school-leavers found better opportunities in clerical occupations. This was partly because of the higher status of the clerk, but partly too because industry was still organized to recruit elementary school boys at the age of 14, even for apprenticeships.[38]

Only since 1945 has there been any real willingness to provide money for expansion, and a demand from industry for the large-scale employment of science and technology graduates. Government plans have included the expansion of science and technology faculties at the universities, the setting up of new technological institutions, including technological universities, and the provision of more advanced work in technical colleges below university level.[39]

Nevertheless, in spite of a period of rapid development in the facilities for higher scientific and technological education, the rate of expansion is still much less than in the United States and in Russia. Nor it is claimed has the rate of change been sufficient to meet the increasing demands of the economy. The Swann Committee concluded in 1968 that both industry and the schools needed a 'much greater injection of scientists and technologists, and that for most of the 1960s the pattern of employment of graduates in this field, particularly of the most able, has been at variance with this need'.[40] Graduates in science prefer to stay in the universities, to enter government research establishments, or to go abroad. The same is true, to a lesser extent, of graduates in technology. Rudd and Hatch[41] explain this, in part, as the failure of industry to make itself attractive to graduates, in part to the desire of the graduate for a working environment that will provide freedom and independence. They found graduates employed in industry less satisfied with their work than other graduates.

In the secondary schools, the years after the war saw a major swing to science in maintained boys' schools and a similar, though smaller swing in independent and direct grant schools. Since 1962, however, the proportion of both boys and girls taking A level science courses has declined. In 1962 the proportion in all schools taking A level science was 56.1 per cent for boys and 23.5 per cent for girls, but by 1967, after a steady fall the proportion had dropped to 45.8 per cent for boys and 16.8 per cent for girls. Since 1964, moreover, the *numbers* of Sixth Formers taking science courses has declined, in spite of the considerable overall expansion of Sixth Forms during those years.[42]

A number of reasons have been suggested for this swing away from science, including the shortage of good science and mathematics teachers in schools. The Dainton Report,[43] for example, showed that substantial proportions of science and mathematics teaching was done by teachers without qualifications in their subjects. Although these teachers are used mainly to teach the younger pupils, it is at this stage that the decision to specialize is usually made. The nature of the science curriculum in secondary schools has also been suggested as a factor, and this is supported by a number of studies of school children, reported by Pont,[44] which emphasize the amount of work required, the difficulty of the work, and boredom with the subject. Further work on pupils' attitudes to science is currently in progress.[45]

There are clear signs, also, that technology as a career does not enjoy the prestige of pure science—a reflection almost certainly, of its very recent admission as a full academic discipline, and its still uncertain social status as a profession.[46] Two s tudies by Hutchings[47] have suggested that boys have a low opinion of technology as a career. Moreover the brightest boys in the schools he examined tended to opt for pure science, and technology was a second best for those who could not get their first choice. A further study of undergraduate students of science and technology from Oxford Cambridge, Imperial College, Leeds and Bradford reinforced this picture.[48]

The concept of a swing from science is not, however, without its critics. McPherson[49] for example has argued that the use of the word swing is misleading since it diverts attention away from changes in the composition of the population in secondary and tertiary education, which may provide a better explanation for the slower rate of growth of science studies than the examination of possible changes in individual preferences. Moreover to look for reasons in the science curriculum or in examinations reform is, he argues, to overlook differences in the opportunities which are perceived to be offered to arts and science subjects for pupils to realize their educational and occupational aspirations. Nor does McPherson believe that the fault lies with the pattern of early specialization typical of the English grammar school in the years since the war. On the other hand Neave,[50] on the basis of his study of university entrants from a wide sample of comprehensive schools, suggests that certain features of comprehensive school organization may be producing a swing *to* science. He found that entrants to university from comprehensive schools were more likely than other entrants to opt for science, and less likely to opt for the social sciences and technology. Neave believes that the mixed subject pattern at both O and A level, and in particular the open Sixth Form which allows students to catch up on O level subjects, are responsible for this apparent swing to science. McPherson, however, warns that we must distinguish between factors which merely 'qualify' and factors which actually 'predispose' pupils to study in higher education. Moreover it is difficult to assess the significance of Neave's figures without taking into account entrants from both comprehensive and other schools into polytechnics. It may be for example, that the polytechnics have a special appeal for the comprehensive school Sixth Formers interested in engineering, which would explain the swing away from technology.

Another aspect of the shortage of scientists to which attention has recently been directed is the unpopularity of science and mathematics with the majority of girls. Evidence collected from ten countries[51] revealed distinct sex differences in the attitude to mathematics and science, with boys showing greater interest in all the countries studied. They were also more likely to specialize in both mathematics and science. The main purpose of the study, however, was to test achievement, and here again clear sex differences were recorded in both subjects. On the other hand there were very marked variations between countries in the magnitude of the differences. In both Finland and Sweden, for example, there was less tendency than in other countries for science to be a male study, whereas in the Netherlands, Belgium and the Federal Republic of Germany the tendency was particularly strong. Clearly these differences must be explained in terms of cultural variations in the attitude to sex-roles as well as in the opportunities for women in the labour market. Girls would therefore appear to be a likely source of recruitment to mathematics and science if traditional attitudes to the employment of women begin to change.

At an even more fundamental level Gannicott and Blaug have claimed that the argument for a shortage of scientific manpower on which both the Swann and Dainton Reports are based, is itself 'totally devoid of economic content'. In fact, Gannicott and Blaug argue tellingly that the swing away from science and also the 'brain drain' are both indications that the apparent shortage is in reality a surplus of scientists and technologists. 'If', they argue, 'the curriculum really does produce narrow specialists imbued with the ideal of pure research and biased against employment in industry, one wonders why the bias apparently disappears when contemplating employment in America'.[52] The essence of their criticism is that Dainton and Swann have ignored the operations of the labour market, and based their calculations not on demand as the economist understands it, but on a rather vague assessment of needs which 'turns out on examination to be nothing more than an assertion of a value judgement that more scientists and technologists would benefit the country.'[53]

The argument of Gannicott and Blaug provides us with a salutory dash of cold water and points out the acute problems involved in any essay in manpower forecasting.[54] On the other hand, we cannot dismiss out of hand what they call 'the special pleading of a science and engineering lobby'. British industry, as we have seen, has traditionally been prejudiced against the university graduate and preferred the man trained on the job. As a consequence there may be a very wide range of qualifications within an occupational group like managers or technologists, many of whom may well be without any formal qualifications at all.[55] The extent to which this attitude is harmful to the efficiency of British industry today is still not clear, although we have already noted the arguments by Cotgrove, Musgrave and Landes to the effect that it has been harmful in the past. Collins however in a recent study has found that high educational requirements for employment appear to be related most strongly to a strong emphasis on a 'public service image'. Next in importance came organizational prominence measured either by organizational size or national orientation. A rapid rate of technological change was also related to educational requirements, particularly within market organizations and within small organizations. Moreover each of these three variables appears to have an independent effect on educational requirements.[56]

The British preference for a mixture of learning and earning has influenced the whole new range of technical and professional employment opened up by changes in industry in the twentieth century. To meet the needs of these students a profusion of part-time courses have developed, leading to a variety of qualifications ranging from a predominantly craft level, like the City and Guilds courses, to the National Certificate Courses catering for largely non-manual occupations such as draughtsmen, quantity surveyors and similar occupations. The whole recruitment and training policy in many industries has also been geared to these part-time qualifications. Such firms have preferred an early entry, at or about the statutory school-leaving age, followed by on-the-job training, and part-time study. These courses have consequently been the route not only to technician level but even, for the determined and lucky student, to full professional status. This part-time route to professional employment has been an important one in Britain in the history of the professions and has indeed in some cases provided a good proportion of its recruits in the past.[57] Even now many engineers have learned their skill by some form of apprenticeship with part-time further education, and only about half are graduates.[58] There is some evidence, however, that those who achieve professional status by this route are at some disadvantage, at least in financial terms.[59] Moreover, even the successful achievement of a Higher National Certificate does not necessarily lead to commensurate promotion. Cotgrove, for example, cites a government enquiry which found that 48 per cent of those obtaining Higher National Certificate in 1952 were in posts in 1958 which did not require H. N. C. as a necessary qualification.[60]

Since the war there has been considerable dissatisfaction with the present structure of technical education. In particular, criticism has focused on the part-time route because of the lack of time it allows for study, even when evening classes are supplemented by periods of day release. Wastage is high and is not necessarily related to ability, the attitude of the firm and the motivation of the individual student being perhaps the most important factors.[61] Consequently there have been moves to provide more full-time courses in both polytechnics and technical colleges. On the other hand, part-time education is still an important stepping stone to technical qualifications.

In the United States, in contrast, the expansion of secondary and higher education has included a radically different approach to professional and vocational courses. 'In Europe students pursued more or less the same kinds of study in the thirties as they did in the early years of this century, and the variety is still limited. In the United States, on the other hand, growth of higher education took place through a process of constant differentiation. Fields of intellectual and occupational interest which elsewhere remained outside the academic framework became academic subjects in the United States.'[62] It must also be borne in mind that in the United States there is not the sharp distinction customary in Europe between universities and òther institutes of higher education. 'In American universities, besides the liberal arts and sciences and the traditional professional schools of law, medicine and theology found in Europe since medieval times, there appeared schools of journalism, librarianship, business methods, nursing and later, practical arts, home economics, physiotherapy. In Europe few, if any of these schools are to be found in universities, but usually in separate institutions of sub-university standard.'[63]

Undoubtedly this variety in higher education has been of vital significance in making possible the high rate of expansion in the United States. If, as in Europe, the scope of higher education tends to be restricted to the traditional subjects, expansion on any scale is impossible without overcrowding in the traditional professions. This overcrowding did of course actually occur in many European countries in the inter-war period and is a feature of twentieth-century India and China.[64] The outstanding feature of the system in the United States is the way in which this overcrowding has been averted. Under the influence of pragmatic and equalitarian ideologies the original elitist conception of higher education has been transformed. Universities and colleges in the United States are essentially middle-class rather than aristocratic in their outlook, serving the needs of the new professional middle class created by the economy.

The situation in the U.S.S.R. is sociologically even more interesting. The traditional elites have been destroyed and the new power group, the Party, has deliberately attempted to fashion the educational system as an instrument for social and economic change. 'The role of Soviet education is to assist in the building of a communist society, in shaping the materialist world outlook of the students, equipping them with a good grounding in the different fields of knowledge and preparing them for socially useful work.'[65] This aim is pursued by the central authority, the Party, consciously and deliberately. Educational policy is shaped with the 'building of a communist society' constantly in mind, and policies which do not appear to be in keeping with this achievement are ruthlessly scrapped. The degree to which the system is consciously guided is heightened by the very high degree of centralization and the degree of uniformity which is enforced throughout the whole of the U.S.S.R. 'From ministerial level command is passed on to provincial or city departments of education, then to district departments, and finally to school directors and teachers. The farther down the chain one goes, the greater the amount of detail laid down for the conduct of the schools. By the time it comes to the teacher, the area of personal discretion is very small. Not only basic policy, but the content of the curriculum, schemes of work, teaching methods, and the like are prescribed for the teacher in considerable detail.'[66]

As part of the drive for economic development the educational system is geared very deliberately to the needs of the economy. The first of the aims of higher education as set out in the Statute of 21

March 1961 is 'the training of highly qualified specialists brought up in the spirit of Marxism-Leninism to be well skilled in the developments of recent science and technology, both in the u.s.s.r. and abroad and in practical matters of production, who should be able to make use of modern technical knowledge to the utmost and be capable of themselves creating the technology of the future.'[67] Accordingly a greater emphasis is placed on science and technology in higher education, even than in the United States, and this bias towards scientific and practical subjects extends back into the secondary schools.[68] In addition there is an attempt to direct labour for the first three years after graduation, in order to ensure that trained personnel go where they are most needed. This attempt is not always successful and there are plenty of cases of evasion and wire-pulling,[69] but it demonstrates the extent to which individual preferences are subordinated to economic needs.

3 *Education and underdevelopment*

It is clear from a comparison of these three very different educational systems that the economy, although it may set limits on the variations in educational provision, by no means accounts for all of the differences that we have found. Indeed, because the relationship between the two is mediated by other institutions, which affect the nature of the relationship in important ways, there is room for considerable controversy not only over the extent to which educational systems can be explained in economic terms, but also on the part played by education in economic development. In order to illustrate this further it is instructive to look briefly at the relationship between the economy and education in some of the 'developing' countries of the world.

There has long been a widespread faith in both academic and government circles that education is the main determinant of economic growth. This belief is reflected, for example, in the increasing proportion of the United States Technical Cooperation Programme devoted to educational assistance.[70] In fact, however, planning policies which have given priority to investment in educational expansion have often had disastrous consequences, and increasingly the simple view of the primacy of educational institutions in economic development has lost ground.[71] It is interesting, therefore, to consider why education has been deemed to be of such overriding importance.

One of the reasons, undoubtedly, is the misleading analogy with highly developed and rapidly growing economies. 'It should be noted', Hoselitz has pointed out, 'that those who have stressed the productive aspects of education have, on the whole, drawn their examples and their empirical evidence from such countries as the United States or Western European nations.' These are all countries with, amongst other relevant factors, 'a high degree of specialization in many occupations and hence with a substantial need for elaborate training programmes for many of the skilled occupations. Hoselitz goes on to point out that these conditions apply only to a limited extent, if at all, in many developing countries. Consequently, although some returns from investment in education may be expected at all stages of economic development, investment in educational facilities may produce much lower returns at certain earlier stages of economic growth than the application of equal amounts of investment in other forms of capital.[72] For example, the development of roads and power stations may yield higher returns in terms of economic development than an equal investment in education. Comparative studies of education and economic development also illuminate the complexity of the problem. Thus, although Bowman and Anderson[73] found little economic development in countries with less than a 30 per cent literacy rate and a literacy rate of over 90 per cent in those countries with the highest *per capita* income, there was no correlation between literacy rate and *per capita* income for those countries falling between the two extremes. More recently, Aran, Eisenstadt, and Adler in a comparative study of ten developing countries found that similar educational developments have apparently different results in different social situations.[74]

This is not to suggest that literacy is not important for a developing economy. Cipolla has suggested that England, and later Prussia and Sweden, already had a large reserve of literacy when they started on the road to industrialization and that this provided 'the basic intellectual and cultural humus for the germination of a vast number of mechanical and organizational innovations'.[75] Dore, too, has claimed that a high literacy rate in the 1870s was an important factor in the swift development of Japan as a highly industrialized nation.[76] At the same time, it has been argued that 'efforts to accelerate basic literacy by simply imposing elementary schools on a sector of society that has not yet begun to change has often borne little fruit in underdeveloped societies'.[77] That this may also have been true in Europe is strikingly illustrated by Thabault's account of the development of primary education in a French village. At first, before 1850, attendance at the village school was poor. The peasants, Thabault argues, had little respect for learning. 'Neither from the point of view of personal dignity, nor for daily practical use could they see the necessity of learning to read or write'.[78] Later, by the 1880s, the situation had changed. Easier means of communication had raised the standard of living, and new openings for employment were being created by developments in government service in industry and commerce. In consequence the development of the school accelerated sharply. Thabault thus sees the influence of the school as 'at all times dependent on the economic and social status of the commune and on the attitude of mind of the people'.[79]

There are also many examples of developing countries where the investment in education has outstripped the comparatively limited growth in the economy. 'The result, now a commonplace, is a vast and nearly uncontrollable increase in the number of unemployed and under-employed school leavers, whose political orientation toward the policy is marked by disaffection and alienation.'[80] This discontent arises primarily because education has become linked with the expectation of elite status. This is particularly likely to occur in ex-colonial territories where education has been given an exaggerated importance, and where social advancement has been closely tied to educational achievement. At the same time the speed of the educational expansion has undoubtedly made the adjustment harder to make.

The content of education is also seen as relevant to economic growth, and the traditional literary education inherited from colonial days is contrasted sharply with a more practical and scientific approach. In higher education in particular, but also at the secondary level, there has been an emphasis on the humanities, law and arts subjects rather than on science and engineering. A number of reasons have been put forward to explain this, including the lower cost of liberal education, the continuing influence of the European tradition, and the attraction of the civil service. In Africa, for example, 'not only did the civil service continue to enjoy the high prestige it had had in the colonial period, but independence meant that many new posts were opened up to young Africans. For ten years or more, the new universities were able to look forward to a period during which abundant employment opportunities were available to their liberal arts graduates'.[81] A number of developing societies have, accordingly, attempted to move towards a more practical education and African educational schemes in particular are 'full of provisions for manual work, especially agricultural, for all, and specialized technical education for as many as can be afforded'.[82]

To a large extent, this move away from traditional arts subjects is necessary, particularly if secondary and higher education is to be expanded. In Egypt, for example, 'about 70 per cent of the university enrolment is in the Faculties of Art, Law and Commerce, and for the vast majority of these graduates there is no demand; there is meanwhile a pressing need for scientists, doctors and engineers and the 20 per cent enrolment in these fields absorbs the best student talent'.[83] On the other hand, the swing towards science and technology carries its own dangers. It is just as easy to overestimate the demand for scientists and technologists as it is for lawyers, and it is even more expensive. Foster, for example, has suggested, taking Ghana as his example, that there is a real danger that technicians will be produced before they can be made use of by the economy.[84] Nor is it enough to provide training programmes if students do not choose to undertake the training, or if they do not make use of it afterwards. Whether or not they do so will depend ultimately upon their perception of the opportunities provided by different types of career. Only if technical and scientific employment can compete with law and administration in terms of social and economic rewards is it likely to appeal to the college graduate.

Moreover, as Hurd and Johnson point out, the same argument applies at lower levels of the educational ladder. 'School graduates, whether prepared as general farmers or as agricultural technicians, have proved unwilling to return, so equipped, to the land of their fathers, or to the land of anyone else's fathers for that matter. It is argued that this unwillingness stems from the content of education in many under-developed societies, which stresses an elitist attitude towards manual work of all kinds, thus prejudicing students against farming life. It is true that a prejudice against manual work may exist, but in a number of societies it has been observed that such school graduates are more willing to face urban unemployment or accept labouring jobs in the city than return to the villages.'[85]

Foster [86] too, has suggested that in Africa rejection of vocational training is a reasonable response to a situation in which the rewards continue to go to those with an academic education.

Nor is this problem confined to Africa. In Turkey, where efforts to expand technical education and to modernize the curriculum of vocational schools were part of the modernizing process, the results have been disappointing. According to Kazamias this is because 'the rewards after graduation from vocational schools are not so enticing or so great as those accruing from attendance at other schools'. Indeed he reports that trained Turkish technicians have been emigrating to West Germany for higher pay.[87] In part too the attitude towards careers and the occupational hierarchy is influenced by the 'traditional Ottoman disdain' for careers in business and industry.[88]

On the other hand it may also be argued that to concentrate upon the relationships between education and occupation is to overlook the possible significance of changes in attitudes and values. From this point of view education is seen as introducing the developing society to new needs, and new expectations, and even to the idea of change itself. In short, education helps to wean the developing society away from the old, and towards the new; it inspires a belief in progress, in efficiency, in achievement and in rationality. Inkeles and Holsinger have recently made a study of what they call the modernization syndrome and 'modern man'. They argue that education makes a difference not only in cognitive content but also in cognitive style, that is, the way the individual reasons'.[89] Even more subtle are the differences which education may bring about in individual attitudes and values. They bring together considerable evidence from several countries that formal schooling does indeed have an effect on 'modernity' even when other factors like parental background, residence, factory experience, living standards and exposure to mass media are all controlled. They argue that it is not just the exposure to cognitive learning which produces the modernizing effect but integration into a large-scale organization and the ability of formal schooling to confer status.

In a rather different context Michael Katz has described the way in which the American school handled the transformation of an agrarian into an industrial society. This involved an emphasis on precision and promptness, and on professionalism and system. He argues that 'a newly industrialized people must learn to reward a man for what he can do rather than for what he is'.[90] It may be, therefore, that it is in the transmission of appropriate values rather than particular skills that the educational system is drawn into relationship with the economy.

3 Education and social mobility

1 *Education and occupation*

Throughout the previous chapter emphasis has been laid on the way in which the system of social stratification mediates between educational institutions and the economy. One of the main reasons for the crucial role played by social stratification is the link, in contemporary society, between educational qualifications and the occupational hierarchy on the one hand, and occupation and social stratification on the other. One of the main features of a modern industrial society is the extent to which entry to a large range of occupations is increasingly dependent on the acquisition of the necessary educational qualifications. Although one can easily exaggerate its extent, the movement from status ascribed by birth to status achieved through education remains accurate as a very general description of important tendencies within modern industrial societies.

The use of the educational system as a means of social and economic ascent is not of course new. The system of scholarships for poor and able boys has a long history and is by no means confined to Western Europe. Nevertheless opportunities for such ascent were rare, and could not be other than rare when the occupations open to the educated man, whatever his social origin, were limited to the learned professions and their ancillaries. Only with the unprece- ◄ dented expansion in the professions and quasi-professions and in technical and commercial employment does the opportunity arise on any but the smallest scale for social and economic ascent through educational achievement.

Blau for example has pointed out the growing relationship in the United States between occupational differentiation and the growth of educational qualifications. Moreover, data 'on more than sixty countries similarly show that a society's occupational differentiation exhibits substantial positive correlation with the level of education (.73) and with the proportion of the male labour force in professional and related occupations (.55).'[1]

This is reflected in close links between educational qualifications and occupational level so that those at or near the top of the occupational structure have more education than those at the bottom. For example, in the United States, as Table Two indicates, professional and kindred workers have had the most education, as a group, and labourers the least.

Table Two

Per cent of white males 35 to 54 years old in the experienced civilian labour force who have completed specified levels of school, by major occupational group: 1961[2]

Major occupational group	Less than 5 years at school	High school graduates	College one year or more
Professional, technical and kindred worker	0.2	91.3	74.5
Managers, officials, and proprietors except farm	1.0	68.0	35.4
Clerical, sales and kindred workers	0.8	65.6	28.0
Craftsmen, foremen and kindred workers	3.0	36.4	8.0
Farmers and farm managers	6.1	32.5	7.5
Operatives and kindred workers	5.7	24.9	4.0
Labourers, except farm and mine	12.3	17.2	2.8
Farm labourers and foremen	29.2	12.1	2.7

Although not presented in the same form, and using slightly different occupational categories, Table Three shows that the same pattern, although with some important variations, also applies in Great Britain.

It will be seen that not only is there a general relationship between education and occupation in both countries, but that the pattern of the occupational hierarchy, with the exception of farmers and agricultural workers, is also very similar. The main difference lies in the greater range in the United States. The column in Table Three giving the median years of schooling shows that the differences between the socio-economic groups are smaller in Great Britain.

Table Three

Age of leaving school of male population by socio-economic grouping, Great Britain, 1961[3]

Socio-economic group	Percentage leaving school			Median years of schooling
	15 and under	16, 17, 18	20 and over	
Professional	22.1	40.6	37.2	12
Employers and managers	60.2	32.2	7.2	10
Intermediate and junior non-manual	60.3	32.8	6.9	10
Farmers	76.7	19.8	3.5	9
Agricultural workers	92.0	7.4	0.6	9
Foremen and supervisors	92.1	7.3	0.5	9
Skilled manual	92.1	7.7	0.5	9
Semi-skilled manual	94.2	5.3	0.5	9
Unskilled manual	96.4	3.2	0.3	9

Studies of social mobility have also demonstrated the important part played by education. For example, Glass's study in Britain[4] showed quite clearly the advantages of a grammar school education for those of working-class or lower-middle-class origin. They were much more likely to be socially mobile than those who had received no more than an elementary education. Similar findings have been reported for the United States.[5] In both these studies, although the detail varies, the pattern is substantially the same; within lower status groups a child is more likely to be socially mobile if he has a superior education, and at the same time a superior education lessens the possibility of downward mobility for those in the higher status group. More recently Blau and Duncan, in a major study of the American occupational structure, have argued not only that 'educa-

tion exerts the strongest direct effect on occupational achievements'
but that 'most of the influence of social origins on occupational
achievements is mediated by education and early experience'.[6]

Several observers have also argued that the links between educational and occupational achievement will grow very much closer
over time. Both Havighurst and Husén, for example, see the year
2000 in terms of a more meritocratic system. 'The industrial and
democratic society of the year 2000', Havighurst has predicted, 'will
be even more open and fluid than the most highly industrialized
societies today, so that education will be the main instrument for
upward mobility, and lack of education or failure to do well in one's
education will be the principal cause of downward mobility'.[7] Similarly, Husén looks forward to the time when 'educated ability will be
democracy's replacement for passed-on social prerogative'.[8]

The evidence for a tightening bond between education and occupation has not, however, gone unchallenged. Anderson for
example argues that 'while education certainly influences a
man's chances to move upward or downward, only a relatively
modest part of all mobility is linked to education'.[9] Using data
from Glass's social mobility study as well as other similar studies,
he shows that there is far more mobility than can be explained in
terms of education, both in terms of mobility upwards on the part
of those with a low level of education, and in a downward movement
of those with a high educational level. In none of the three countries
for which data exist does lack of education necessarily prevent
mobility any more than a good education necessarily prevents a fall
in status. He does suggest, however, that education is more closely
linked to social mobility in the United States than in Sweden or
Great Britain.

Boudon has also drawn attention to the capability of people to
resist downward mobility, and for this reason argues that the study
by Blau and Duncan probably overestimated the effect of education
on social mobility.[10] Jencks too claims that 'while occupational
status is more closely related to educational attainment than to anything else we can measure, there are still enormous status differences
among people with the same amount of education'.[11] Similarly, he
found that although income is related to educational background, so
that those who had done some graduate work were making 2.7 times
as much as those who had not finished elementary school, education
does not in fact explain very much of the variation in men's incomes

overall. This is in part at least because, although schooling provides access to highly paid occupations, disparities within occupations are greater than disparities between occupations.[12]

Jencks' findings have not gone unchallenged[13] and it may be that in the final analysis it will be seen that he has underestimated the effect of education on both occupation and income. On the other hand, as Miller has pointed out, the 'concern of Jencks and his colleagues to "explain" total variance rather than to focus on statistically significant differences'[14] may be the key to the surprising nature of their findings. Without denying the influence of education on occupation Jencks is interested, like Anderson, in its limitations as an explanation of differences in occupational achievement.

The strength of association between education and occupation will obviously depend upon the extent to which formal educational qualifications are a necessary requirement for positions of high status. In so far as status can be achieved in other ways, whether by training 'on the job' or by the possession of special talents, as in the world of sport or entertainment, the importance of education as a factor in mobility is reduced. An advanced industrial economy increases the importance of formal educational qualifications but it has by no means succeeded in imposing them universally.

Another vitally important factor is to be found in the distribution of schooling in relation to the occupational structure. One of the consequences of industrialization is, as we have seen, an increase in the proportion of middle- and upper-level jobs. Where this is combined, as it frequently has been, with a low fertility rate in the middle and upper classes so that they fail to reproduce themselves, there is plenty of room at the top and conditions are favourable for considerable social mobility. If at the same time the educational system, as in pre-war Britain, provides few opportunities for the children of working-class families to receive more than a basic elementary education, then we are faced with the kind of situation Anderson describes, in which a great deal of upward mobility occurs irrespective of education.

Industrial management in Britain today provides us with an extremely clear example of precisely this type of situation. Unlike professional occupations it has not been closely tied to formal educational qualifications, except for certain specific technical functions. Promotion from the shop floor has in the past been an important avenue of recruitment. At the same time it has been a rapidly expanding field of employment, providing frequent opportunities for social mobility. Studies of the educational background of managers reflect this general situation quite clearly. The Acton Society Trust,[15] for example, showed that even in the large firms which they examined, 53 per cent of managers had been to an elementary or an ordinary, i.e. non-grammar, secondary school. This is not to suggest that education at a grammar or public school is not an asset in reaching management status. Forty-seven per cent of the managers had been to public or grammar schools, and the authors of the report estimated that, comparing these figures with the general population, grammar school boys have had twice the average chance of becoming a manager, and public schools boys about 10 times the average. Nevertheless we are still left with a very large proportion of managers who have reached their position without a grammar school education.[16] On the other hand it would be equally mistaken to assume that such managers had necessarily been socially mobile. Lee has suggested that the chances of promotion 'from the ranks' were always greater for the middle classes and those with more education, and that 'if more men in the past appeared to reach management or the professions without the benefits of extended full-time education than do so at the present time, this trend could be, at least in part, explained by the fact that the proportion of young who voluntarily stay on at school has increased faster among the middle class than elsewhere'.[17]

It is almost certain however that the picture of management qualifications given us by this and other studies is becoming out of date. There is a growing tendency to recruit managers with professional and scientific qualifications, rather than to promote from the lower ranks in the firm. Recent years have seen an expansion in the requirement of graduates, and a proliferation of student apprenticeships and other training schemes designed to attract the more highly educated entrant. At the same time changes within the educational system itself are providing a considerable increase in the number available to industry with higher qualifications. Such changes include an expansion in higher education generally and in technical education at all levels. Some of these changes are new, others have been operating for some time and have already produced differences of some magnitude between older and younger managers. For example, younger managers in the Acton Society Trust study are more likely to have a degree or some kind of professional qualification. They are also more likely to have had a grammar or public school education.

On the other hand, it is also possible for higher education to become so general in the population that it no longer differentiates sufficiently to act as a criterion in itself for occupational selection. Indeed, it has been suggested that the relationship is already declining in the United States as the proportion with a college education goes on increasing.[18] Under such circumstances it is likely that more subtle distinctions will operate, including the prestige level of the individual college or university, and personality or social status differences. At the same time, although a college degree may no longer be a sufficient qualification for an elite occupation, successful graduation from high school may be a necessary qualification for anything other than unskilled work, or even, in some places, for any work at all. In such circumstances, too, graduate work increases in importance as a qualifying device, and so we have the enormous expansion of graduate education in the United States since the war.

Yet a further factor of vital importance determining the part education plays in social mobility is the nature of the selective mechanism within the school system. The more efficient this is in predicting school and vocational success, the more closely, that is to say, that educational achievement is related to 'ability', the less likely will it be that ability will operate as a factor independent of schooling, and so serve as a separate factor in social mobility. The study of social mobility is in consequence bound up with the analysis of selective mechanisms and their operation. But before we can begin to consider the question of how efficiently the schools select, we must examine the different mechanisms of selection used in different educational systems.

2 *Strategies of selection*

Turner's well-known ideal-type analysis of modes of social ascent, with their accompanying strategies of educational selection, is a useful framework of analysis for studying education as a process of selection. Turner distinguishes two modes of ascent: sponsored mobility and contest mobility, both of which are founded upon quite different ideological positions and also different elite structures.[19] Sponsored mobility, compared by Turner with sponsorship into a private club, is characterized above all by early selection, followed by a clear differentiation of those singled out from the rest, usually in quite separate institutions. The process that follows has the nature of a special preparation for elite status, and covers not only special skills, but an indoctrination in the standards of behaviour and the value systems of the elite group.

The English educational system of the late nineteenth and early twentieth century was a very close approximation to the ideal type of sponsored mobility. The system of elementary education for the children of the poor was quite distinct from the system of education for the middle classes. Transfer between the two systems was possible, but it was not likely, and was reserved for the working-class child of exceptional ability who showed promise of successful assimilation to the middle classes. The Education Act of 1902 and the Free Place Regulations of 1907 between them destroyed the exclusive hold of the middle classes over the secondary system. Increasingly, after the First World War, working-class children entered the secondary schools until, in certain areas at least, all places were free,[20] and in some schools the majority of children were from working-class families. Nevertheless certain essential characteristics of sponsored mobility remained, notably the stress on early selection and a considerable degree of segregation. It was customary to select children for free places at the age of 10, and to transfer them to the secondary school at 11, leaving the great majority of children in the elementary system. Those who were transferred went to schools with a higher rate of grant, better-paid and better-qualified teachers, and the chance to acquire the formal educational qualifications which were, as we have seen, a great advantage in the transition to or maintenance of middle-class status.

With the 1944 Education Act the elementary system came to an end, and for the first time secondary education became a stage in the education process, rather than a special type of education appropriate to the middle classes. Even so, however, Turner was still able to characterize the English system of education as one of predominantly sponsored mobility because, within the new system of secondary education, there was a distinction between types of school, with the new secondary grammar schools carrying on almost unchanged the secondary school tradition. The old scholarship examination was replaced by the 11-plus, which although undoubtedly more efficient performed precisely the same function. The new secondary modern schools were, certainly, an improvement on the old senior elementary schools, but the fact of selection and segregation remained. It is true, also, that all secondary education became free, and that success in the 11-plus was the only way to get into the grammar schools, but this is to emphasize the significance of the selection process rather than to diminish its importance. To focus on the grammar schools, however, is to ignore the vital part played in English education by the independent, and particularly the so-called public schools. These still remain as a segregated middle- and upper-class system[21] with important links to elite status, either directly, or through their relationship with Oxford and Cambridge. The English public schools played an important sponsorship role in the nineteenth century when they were used by *nouveaux riches* manufacturers to enable their sons to achieve elite status. Today, however, Halsey suggests that, except for a tiny handful of pupils they have little to do with mobility, but a great deal to do with status differentiation.[22]

The alternative system of selection is based on the ideology of contest mobility, likened by Turner to a race or other sporting event, in which all compete on equal terms for a limited number of prizes. The chief characteristic of contest mobility is a fear of premature judgement and not only is early selection avoided, but any open selection is, as far as possible, avoided altogether. The competitors may drop out of the game of their own accord, but they will not be barred from the competition, as occurs under sponsored mobility. Moreover, in order to allow everyone an equal chance, segregation is avoided or postponed or in some way minimized to avoid giving anyone or any group an unfair advantage.

Turner used the United States system of education as an example of contest mobility, although he is careful to point out that existing systems are only an approximation to the ideal type. There are few overt mechanisms of selection in the United States and certainly nothing corresponding to the 11-plus. Although there are specialized high schools, corresponding to the English grammar schools, the common or comprehensive school is the normal pattern in the United States. Moreover, although there is increasing opportunity for students of different ability to take different courses, there is no sharp separation between students of different ability levels.

Entry to higher education in the United States also runs true to the principles of contest mobility. Although private colleges can be, and often are, highly selective in their choice of students, those colleges which are supported by public funds often encourage relatively unlimited entry, at least by British standards, and it has been estimated that 'high school graduates of all levels of ability can gain admission to some institution without going very far from home'.[23] At the same time those American colleges which practice 'open door' admission policies protect their standards by means of a heavy failure rate which may be as high as one in eight in the first term and continues at a high level throughout the course. There is a remarkable degree of unevenness in the drop-out rate between institutions, but the overall attrition rate is high. Estimates vary, but it has recently been claimed that 'already 6 out of 10 students who enrol in American universities and colleges fail to get the ultimate degree to which they aspire', an overall drop-out rate of about 60 per cent.[24] Some of these drop-outs will, however, return later, or will transfer to another college, so that failure need never be seen as absolutely final.

Another approach is that of the two-year junior or community college. Unselective, and tuition free, the junior college takes those students wanting to go to college who are not judged to have sufficient academic ability to manage the four-year senior college course. Such students are channelled into the junior college, which provides not only a one- or two-year programme of vocational or semi-professional training for those students who do not aspire any higher, but the possibility of transfer to the senior college for those who can reach the required standard. A recent study has shown that the great majority of students are enrolled in transfer courses and aspire to go on to a four-year college or university.[25] Although only about 1 in 3 students succeeds in achieving a transfer the four-year college standards are protected and the 'open door' policy is maintained although only at the cost of subventing the vocational goals of the colleges.[26]

Higher education in Britain follows the general pattern of sponsored mobility. All forms of full-time higher education have high admission standards and this is particularly true of the universities.[27] Wastage rates are correspondingly low and, although subject to fluctuation, are currently estimated at 16 per cent.[28] As in the case of the United States this overall rate conceals considerable fluctuation between institutions with on the whole the highest wastage rates at the technological universities and the lowest at Oxford and

Cambridge. This almost certainly reflects the high wastage rates in applied science and technology, which are double those to be found in arts and social science.[29] Nevertheless it is in the field of further education, with its tradition of part-time study, that we find wastage comparable to the American pattern, and here too we find 'open-door' admission policies which allow entrance to all students who meet the minimum entrance requirements. The Crowther Report survey of wastage in part-time technical courses made it plain that the forces operating at this level are those of contest rather than sponsored ability.[30]

In general the European tradition is in line with sponsored rather than contest mobility. The U.S.S.R. is, however, a major exception in that it approaches the pattern of contest mobility to a much greater extent than has been customary in Europe. Soviet schools are, with few exceptions, completely comprehensive. Indeed, not only do the Russians refuse the early selection of an elite, but they reject the whole theory of innate abilities upon which so much elite thinking is based, and argue that, within certain limitations, abilities are learned rather than inborn. Mental testing is 'not merely characterized as theoretically unsound but also, and as a consequence practically misleading',[31] and it is generally held that if children are slow to learn it is the teaching which is at fault. Accordingly educational psychologists in the U.S.S.R. are concerned not with devising tests for the measurement of ability but rather with the 'study of human learning, and, particularly, learning under the conditions of organized teaching in schools, under planned educational influences'.[32]

Within the schools, comprehensive principles are carried to much greater extents than are commonly found even in the United States. Not only is there a complete avoidance of streaming and setting, but there is an emphasis on all children covering the same course at the same level.[33] This contrasts with the American system, which allows for considerable individual variation within the comprehensive framework. A great deal of emphasis is laid on bringing up the weaker members of the class, and the brighter members of the class are encouraged to help those who are slower with their work, rather than to push ahead with their own studies. Those children who fail to meet the required standards have to repeat the grade. There is some evidence that a fairly high proportion each year do in fact have to repeat the work, although the proportion will vary from place to place. Nigel Grant reports that 'according to the Assistant Director of Education in Leningrad, 16,000 out of a total of 450,000 school children in the city were repeating the year's work during the school year 1962-3'. Since Leningrad is better off than most places for teachers and school buildings, the national proportion is probably a good deal higher. In addition, some of the obviously mentally backward children will be placed in special schools and there are various unofficial ways of getting rid of very unresponsive children, including sending them to a school with lower standards or allowing them to leave school before they reach the statutory leaving age. On the other hand, and in spite of a very formal approach and a highly academic content, Nigel Grant concludes that 'more children make the grade than would be thought possible by those conditioned to the values of a selective system'.[34]

The comprehensive principle does not, however, extend right through secondary education. At the age of 15 there is differentiation into three quite distinct types of school, which correspond quite closely to the three sides of the English tripartite system, except of course that the selection takes place at a much later age. The Russian version of the grammar school is the three-year 'general education secondary school' leading to the school-leaving diploma, which entitles its owner to apply for admission to higher education. Some 20 to 25 per cent of the age-group are in schools of this kind. Secondly there is the technicum, which also takes up to 25 per cent of the age-group. Although it is possible to stay on at the technicum and obtain a school-leaving diploma, most of its students do not go on to higher education, at least for the time being. The remaining 50 per cent do not continue in full-time education at all. They are, however, required to attend at afternoon or evening classes of approximately 15 to 18 hours a week, for one, two, or usually three years. The ablest of these pupils are encouraged to go on to the technicum, so that the door is never completely closed, but this part-time route does not by itself lead to the school-leaving diploma.[35] It can be argued, therefore, that there is considerably more selection in the Russian system than in the United States.

Although in theory all who complete the school-leaving diploma are eligible for higher education, in practice the competition is so keen that all kinds of higher education can be highly selective. The institutions themselves have their own entrance examinations, and there are variations in standards, in spite of the theoretical equality of status. Thus it is harder to get into a university than into a pedagogic institute for teacher training. The proportion of applicants accepted also varies according to the popularity of the universities concerned, but nowhere is there room for more than a fraction of those who apply, and extensive use is made of part-time courses to relieve the pressure. As in the case of Britain, however, this part-time route leads to high drop-out rates. Moreover an attempt to give preference to those who had done some practical work in industry or agriculture has now fallen into disuse.[36] It is not easy therefore to categorize the educational system in the U.S.S.R. as either sponsored or contest mobility.

Moreover, although it can be argued that in Britain, and indeed in Western Europe generally, the predominant tradition has been one of sponsored mobility, the modern trend is clearly away from a differentiated secondary system and towards the comprehensive school.[37] This trend is still slow and uneven and in Britain for example there is still a long way to go before it extends to the whole secondary school population. Nevertheless it has been calculated that by 1980 75 per cent of children in this country will be in comprehensive schools.[38]

In an attempt to extend the scope of Turner's model, Hopper has recently constructed a typology for the classification of educational systems, based upon the structure of their selection processes.[39] Although retaining certain aspects of Turner's own typology, and indeed to a considerable extent building on it, Turner's presentation is both more complex and more systematic if not indeed formalistic. Like Turner, he is interested in *when* pupils are selected, and makes this a major aspect of his schema, and also in *how* they are selected, but he adds a new dimension, the degree of centralization and standardization of the system. It is in his more detailed treatment of ideologies of selection that he differs most from Turner. He distinguishes between *ideologies of implementation,* which specify the principles on which institutions should be organized, for example, elitist or egalitarian, and *ideologies of legitimation,* which justify these institutions by reference to goals, values and legitimizing symbols. There are four ideal types of legitimation: aristocratic and paternalistic, which are both essentially elitist in their implementation, and meritocratic and communistic, which are both egalitarian. The United States is classified by Hopper as having a low degree of early formal differentiation and specialization, and a meritocratic ideology, whereas England has a medium degree of standardization, a high degree of early formal differentiation and specialization, and primarily a paternalistic ideology. The u.s.s.r. on the other hand, has a communistic ideology and a high degree of centralization and standardization.

There is no doubt that this more elaborate and flexible schema makes it possible to classify societies, like the u.s.s.r. for example, which do not fall neatly into either sponsored or contest mobility. Nevertheless Hopper's typology has been criticized on a number of grounds. Perhaps the most radical critique is that of Davies,[40] who condemns Hopper for his concern with selection and his neglect of the transmission of culture, or what Davies calls the management of knowledge. In other words, he is denying that selection is a central function of education even in industrial societies, and therefore that it is inappropriate as the basis of a typology of educational systems. As Smith[41] has argued, however, Davies himself has failed to recognize the significance of selection processes for the management of knowledge.

While defending Hopper against some of Davies's criticisms,[42] Smith himself examines a number of problems in the application of Hopper's categories. 'In achieving a high degree of parsimony', he argues, 'Hopper has tolerated ambiguity.'[43] There are, for example, problems of what Smith calls 'concealed multidimensionality', as, for example, in the concept of degree of centralization.[44] Both Smith and Davies also criticize Hopper for ignoring the source of ideologies manifested in the system, and so under-emphasizing the conflict between groups for control of the system. This is particularly important in the analysis of the processes of change.

Smith himself has categorized education as a distribution process in which educational knowledge is distributed among different categories of students and along a number of different educational routes. Moreover, this process takes place within and is affected by a system of power relationships which control both selection and the transmission of knowledge. In this way he has attempted to reconcile Davies on the one hand and Hopper on the other.

3 Equality of educational opportunity: myth or reality?

It is legitimate to ask whether different types or modes of selection differ at all in their consequences. Do they, for example, select for different characteristics, or do the same kinds of people reach the top whatever the system of selection? In general, when sociologists have asked this kind of question they have phrased it more specifically in the context of equality of educational opportunity. Above all they have wanted to know how efficient selection strategies have been in matching opportunities to ability. A great deal of work has been done in this area in recent years, and since it is easily accessible only a brief review will be attempted here.

The usual approach to this problem is to attempt to measure specific inequalities in educational opportunity as they apply to different sections of society, and the most fruitful area so far has been the study of social-class and educational differences. Social class is not a particularly straightforward concept, and there are in fact many differences in the precise definition or classification employed in different studies. This makes comparison difficult especially when international differences are involved. On the other hand, there are sufficient common factors to allow rough comparisons to be made, provided it is remembered that the basis of classification is often not identical. It is usual, for example, to take father's occupation as the main basis of classification and to group the manual occupations as 'working class' and the non-manual occupations as 'middle class'. Most classifications are sufficiently close to this pattern to make it workable, provided all the limitations are kept in mind.

On this basis a few general patterns emerge clearly from a number of national studies and international comparisons. When secondary education is of different types, working-class children can be shown to be less likely to enter the more academic schools and, once there, to be more likely to leave early. Table Four, which is adapted from an article by Little and Westergaard,[45] shows clearly the class differential at entry to the school, and the increase in the differential as a result of early leaving, as they occurred in England and Wales.

In other Western European countries the general pattern would appear to be of a very similar kind. Working-class children are less likely than middle-class children to enter the more academic types of secondary education and even if they do so they are less likely to complete the course. A recent survey by the O.E.C.D. has demonstrated, across a wide range of societies in Western Europe, not only the extent of social class inequalities of this kind but their persistence over time.[46]

Table Four

Proportions obtaining education of a grammar-school type among children of different classes born in the late 1930s

Father's occupation	At ages 11-13	At age 17
Professional and managerial	62	41½
Other non-manual	34	16
Skilled manual	17	5
Semi-skilled manual	12	3
Unskilled	7	1½
All children	23	10½

There are also considerable social class differences in access to the universities. These have recently been demonstrated by Halsey[47] in an anticipatory glimpse of the findings from the current study into social mobility at Nuffield College. He shows that, in spite of some improvement in the position as a result of the post-war expansion, children of the upper middle classes are three times as likely as the lower *middle* class to reach a university, and the lower *working* class have less than half the chance of the lower middle class. There is evidence too that in some countries the position for the working-class student is even less favourable. Whereas in Britain 25 per cent of university undergraduates are from working-class homes it is only about 8 per cent in France, and 6 per cent in Germany.[48]

There are also social class differences *within* higher education. School leavers from the working classes are not only less likely to reach Oxbridge or other of the high status universities but are more likely to go to the technological universities.[49] Watts argues that this is largely because technology faculties in general have a larger proportion of working-class students and a comparison, for example, of technological universities with technology faculties in the provincial universities shows little difference.

The non-university sector of full-time higher education, along with part-time education in the technical colleges, is often seen as an 'alternative' and perhaps even more congenial route by means of which the students of working-class origin can attain a measure of social mobility through educational qualification. In fact, however, we find the same pattern of social class differences as for the more orthodox route through the grammar school and the universities. This has been well documented by Hordley and Lee[50] who show that it operates at both the lower and the advanced levels. Children from middle-class families tend to be found in the courses leading to higher rather than lower qualifications,[51] and in full-time rather than in part-time courses.

One of the more striking features is the way in which the alternative route provides for the children of non-manual families who fail to achieve the entry requirements of universities. This is strikingly illustrated by Donaldson's study of Enfield College of Technology. He showed that the proportion of students from the working class was well within the range of university undergraduate populations for all subjects, and even included a higher proportion of students from independent schools than such universities as Essex and Lancaster.[52] At the Open University, too, students in middle-class occupations have been in a majority, with teachers taking a heavily disproportionate share of the places. Moreover, the system of exemptions means that those who already hold educational qualifications, and teachers in particular, can gain a degree much more quickly.[53]

There is also some evidence that recent trends in higher education are making it increasingly difficult for the working-class student. A paper by Couper and Harris, for example, describes the increase in the proportion of middle-class students over a four-year period as a College of Advanced Technology changed into a university.[54] Burgess and Pratt have drawn attention to the role played by the establishment of formal entrance requirements, the shedding of part-time and low-level work and the aspirations of the staff.[55] In a later study the same authors have made the same charges against the polytechnics.[56] It may be that they have somewhat overstated their case, but Donaldson has demonstrated the extent to which the middle-class A level holder has invaded at least one College of Technology. Moreover, since competition among qualified applicants is much greater in humanities and social studies than in science and technology, there are strong pressures towards changes in the subject of study away from technology, and this may further reduce the proportion of working-class students.

On the other hand, Hordley and Lee strike a warning note when they point out that we do not, in fact, know whether the percentage of working-class children who benefit from the alternative route is decreasing or increasing over time. They suggest, for example, that it is easy to exaggerate the extent of opportunity which existed in technical education in the past, and that genuine opportunities for working-class boys were rare. Consequently opportunities since the war may actually have increased. Moreover there is evidence that it may have been a route of some significance for the working-class boy who was an 'early leaver' from the grammar school. Whatever the trend over time, however, there seems to be little evidence that the alternative route goes very far in mitigating social class differences in educational opportunity.

In the United States, too, the pattern of class differences is much the same as in Europe, in spite of differences in the organization of secondary education. Dropping out of school before high school graduation is more characteristic of low status families, measured in terms of income, and of father's occupation.[57] Relatively more children from lower status families are also scholastically retarded.[58] Consequently high school graduation is itself related to socio-economic status in the United States. However, it is after high school graduation that the largest number of young people leave the educational system and it is at this point that estimates of talent loss in the United States are concentrated. Table Five illustrates the relationship between socio-economic background and college entrants for high school graduates only, based upon a national survey.

Table Five

The percentage of High School graduates who went to college the following year by socio-economic background and sex: 1960 [59]

Socio-economic Status

Sex	Low	Low Middle	Middle	High Middle	High	Total
Boys	24	40	53	65	81	49
Girls	15	24	32	51	75	35

A more recent survey has shown that the relationship between college attendance and family income is still very high in spite of the expansion of the 1960s. Only 15 per cent of the college age-group attend from very low-income families as compared with 56 per cent of those from families in the highest income bracket.[60]

Sewell, in a longitudinal study of Wisconsin high school seniors, has also demonstrated the way in which there is a progressive worsening of opportunities for the student of low socio-economic status at successive stages of the educational process. He found that a student from a high status family had almost 2.5 times as much chance as a student from a low status family of continuing in some kind of post-high school education, but an almost 4 to 1 advantage in access to college. At the postgraduate level the advantage was as high as 9 to 1, since the student of low socio-economic status was more likely to drop out of college and less likely to go on to graduate or professional education.[61]

One of the reasons for this progressive worsening of opportunity is that students from low status families are less likely to go to a highly selective college and more likely to go to a two-year junior or community college. It has been estimated, for example, that students who go straight to four-year colleges are from two to three times more likely to graduate than those who start at a two-year college.[62]

The two-year colleges as a group attract a larger number of lower and lower middle socio-economic status than do the four-year colleges. One survey showed that whereas nearly two-thirds of the fathers of four-year college students came from professional or managerial occupations, this was true of only one-third in the two-year colleges.[63] In this sense they serve to widen opportunities for working-class students. On the other hand there is also evidence that, like some of the polytechnics in this country, they may be almost as important for the middle-class student of low ability who would otherwise be excluded from higher education. A study of one college in California showed that it was in fact dominated by students from the middle income groups and admitted very few from really poor families. Moreover, students from lower income groups had *higher* ability on both verbal and quantitative tests than those from the middle income groups.[64]

In spite of somewhat fragmentary data, a number of Russian empirical studies indicate that the same pattern of differences between social grouping is to be found in the u.s.s.r. Drop-out rates from secondary education seem to vary with the occupational level of parents, and technical schools have a lower proportion of the 'intelligentsia' than the schools leading to higher education.

Children of the intelligentsia also appear to have more chance of being accepted for higher education, and there is some evidence that children who do reach the level of the intelligentsia achieve this via engineering and management rather than careers in science, medicine or higher education.[65]

In Poland, too, the children of the intelligentsia have a much greater chance of entering higher education than the children of workers and peasants in spite of a system which allows extra points for social background. There is also considerable differentiation by choice of subject. Thus the children of peasants are likely to enter a college of agriculture and the children of industrial workers a technological university. The teacher training colleges and academies of theology also recruit heavily from the children of the working classes and the peasantry.[66]

Apart from these differences between social classes which seem to persist in very different societies there are also very widespread variations between regions, and particularly between urban and rural areas. Fiszman, for example, has described the situation in Poland where most of the unskilled labour force 'is recruited from the villages where many of the youth fail to complete even the first six grades'.[67] In the U.S., similarly, Sewell has shown that there are considerable differences in the college plans of rural and urban boys and girls even when intelligence and socio-economic status are controlled.[68]

Nor are these the only kind of regional differences. In the United States, differences both between and within States are very great. A recent report of the Carnegie Commission on Higher Education has documented in detail the enormous variation between States in the proportion of the age-group attending college.[69] There are also sharp differences between suburban and metropolitan areas.[70]

Regional differences in this country have been tellingly illustrated by Taylor and Ayres, with the North revealed as underprivileged on a wide range of indices of educational achievement, in comparison to the very favourable position of the South. To a large extent this is a reflection of the difference in material prosperity of the two regions, but the analysis as a whole suggests that this is not the whole explanation. The Midlands, for example, although comparable in many respects to the South in its general prosperity is closer to the North in length of school life.[71]

There are also several important recent studies which explore differences at the level of the local education authority.[72] Boaden, for example, has surveyed the educational provision of a number of county boroughs in England and Wales and reveals a complex pattern of interrelationship between needs, resources, and what he calls the 'disposition' of the local authority.[73] Using a different approach Eileen Byrne has examined in depth the policies of three local authorities since the war, and their effect on the allocation of educational resources.[74]

Yet another important source of educational inequality in the United States is found amongst distinctive minority groups. A study of school achievement levels showed that although whites and oriental Americans achieved at comparable levels, other minorities were considerably lower.[75] The dropout rate from school is also higher for particular ethnic groups, for example only 73.1 per cent of Negro youth were still at school by the age of 16 to 17, compared with 88.6 per cent of all white students. Moreover the ethnic factors in school retention become even more selective with advances in school level. Only 41 per cent of Puerto Rican males and 47 per cent of the females who had completed the ninth grade went on to graduate from high school. For Indians in the same age group the figure was about 50 per cent and for Negroes and persons of Mexican origin, between 50 and 60 per cent.[76] Not all ethnic groups are similarly disadvantaged however; Japanese and Chinese Americans have levels of achievement which are higher than white Americans,[77] and 'a Jewish boy is more likely to graduate from college than is a Gentile of equal ability'.[78]

During the 1960s the position of ethnic minorities improved and they began to enter college, particularly the two-year college, in greater numbers. On the other hand they are still seriously under-represented in the colleges and universities. It has been estimated that ethnic minorities made up 24 per cent of the national college-age population but they comprised only 5 to 6 per cent of the total college enrolment in 1971.[79]

The final area of inequality to be discussed is that between the sexes. The Robbins Committee on Higher Education[80] was very much aware of the wastage of girls' ability that occurs at the level of higher education and in the senior forms of the secondary schools. Girls were less likely to get O levels than boys and less likely to go on to higher education. Only 7.3 per cent of the age group entered full-time higher education in 1962 as compared with 9.8 per cent of the men.

Moreover, as is well known, there has long been a tendency for girls to be channelled into colleges of education rather than universities. Thus, whereas in 1962-3, 40 per cent of students in all forms of higher education were girls, they represented only 28 per cent of university students.

Since Robbins there has, however, been a steady and considerable expansion in the number of girls taking both O and A levels, and, in the case of A levels in particular the percentage increase is very much higher than for boys. Moreover girls are now entering universities in much greater numbers. By 1973, 36 per cent of all university students in Britain were women and there are indications that the proportion is still rising.[81]

In the United States, although many studies have demonstrated that girls tend to get better grades than boys while they are at school[82] a lower proportion go on to college. As in this country, however, the position is changing fairly rapidly. Between 1960 and 1971 women's share of undergraduate enrolment rose from 38.5 per cent to 44 per cent, and it is still rising. Although this compares favourably with Britain, it should be remembered that it includes all forms of higher education, including teacher education where, as in this country, women outnumber men. There is also a very considerable wastage at graduate level. Although women comprise 37 per cent of postgraduates only 14 per cent of those receiving doctorates are women.[83]

In Europe universities are still largely a male preserve.[84] There are however very big variations between countries, dependent partly on the position of women in the employment market, partly, as in the comparison between Britain and the U.S., on the nature of the system itself. In the U.S.S.R., for example, men and women enter higher education in roughly equal numbers.[85] Indeed, a recent study[86] suggested that women students currently outnumber men. There is some evidence however that women tend to predominate in certain kinds of higher education rather than in others. They are, for example, less likely to go on to postgraduate education, and less likely to study science. They also go on to teaching in very large numbers.

Finally, we may note the way in which socio-economic background and sex interrelate one with the other. This has been well documented by Sewell in the follow-up study of 9,000 Wisconsin high school students to which reference has already been made. Although the educational chances of males were found to be greater than those of females at every educational level, the male advantage is greatest in the lowest socio-economic categories and least in the highest.[87] Similarly in this country, as Little and Westergaard point out, 'the disparity between the sexes widens as one goes down the social scale', until at 'the extreme of the scale, an unskilled manual worker's daughter has a chance of only one in five or six hundred of entering a university—a chance a hundred times lower than if she had been born into a professional family.'[88]

Although this review of educational opportunity in societies with very different strategies of selection has revealed a consistent and persistent inequality on a number of fronts, it has also shown important variations in the pattern as well as the degree of inequality. It is important therefore to consider the extent to which alternative educational structures and different ideologies of selection do in fact distribute educational chances differently, even if they all fail to distribute them equally.

One of the most obvious ways of distinguishing between strategies of selection, and one which plays an important role in the typologies of both Turner and Hopper, is the age at which selection occurs. We can distinguish between systems which separate children early on into quite different educational routes and those which postpone formal selection by means of the comprehensive or common secondary school. Although the evidence available is by no means satisfactory it does seem that these alternative structures of secondary education differ not only in terms of how and when they select, but also, although this is more debatable, whom they select. There is, for example, a good deal of evidence that the comprehensive system encourages more pupils to stay longer at school, and so raises the proportion of pupils qualified to go on to forms of higher education. The reasons for this are complex, but are associated with the ability of the comprehensive school to provide a greater range of courses, with better facilities than the majority of non-selective schools in a selective system.[89]Comprehensive schools which do not provide these opportunities do not appear to encourage pupils to stay on at school.[90] The more flexible organization of comprehensive school sixth forms may also be an important factor. Neave, for example, has pointed to the importance of the 'open' sixth form which allows pupils to 'catch up' on missing O levels.[91]

63

The comprehensive school therefore serves as a quite powerful vehicle of educational expansion. What is less clear is the extent to which this expansion, in itself, benefits working-class and other disadvantaged pupils. Early research on comprehensive schools in this country tended to show that they did little more than underline existing class differentials in educational opportunity.[92] These findings however derive from a very small number of schools which are not necessarily typical of more recent developments. Later research by Neave[93] on 969 university entrants in 1968 from 163 comprehensive schools revealed a somewhat different picture. Thirteen per cent of his sample were '11 + failures' and these tended to come from homes where there was less sustained encouragement and support than in the rest of his sample. They were also slightly more likely than the rest to be working class. Neave therefore expects the comprehensive school gradually to improve the chances of the working-class child to get to university.

At a somewhat different level of approach there are also wide differences of opinion on the extent to which educational expansion has in itself produced greater equality of opportunity. Boudon[94] in a highly complex analysis of the issue has however concluded that over time there has been a steady and slow decline in inequality of educational opportunity. In an ingenious argument he points out that, for individuals, the chance of attending grammar school in England has actually increased much *more* rapidly for lower-class boys. Only one per cent of boys in this group born before 1910 attended such schools, compared with 10 per cent of those born after 1930, an increase of *ten times*. For the children of the professional and managerial group the rise was from 37 per cent to 62 per cent, not even twice as many. But, as he goes on to point out, it is easy to overlook this improvement in individual chances, since an increase of 10 times 1 still only represents 9 *more* working-class boys, whereas for the professional and managerial group the increase represents 25 more boys. Since the same process can be seen at work in higher education as well, a small increase in the number of working-class students and a large increase in the number of middle-class students can actually mask an improvement in educational opportunity for the working-class boy.

Both this country and the United States have tended to rely on educational expansion as the main method of increasing opportunity in higher education. An alternative approach to the problem is illustrated by the quota system, which fixes the proportion of children from various social backgrounds. Used fairly extensively in communist societies they appear to have had a large part to play in the comparatively low level of educational inequality in these countries. More recently attempts have been made to introduce them into higher education in the United States in order to improve the position of women and black students. On the other hand, such schemes face many difficulties.[95] They do not for example, in themselves, solve the problem of the student who is not adequately prepared for higher education, or is poorly motivated, so that, unless the institutions involved are prepared to accept a double standard, they must provide remedial teaching or face a high wastage rate. They may also run into opposition from university teachers, or from students excluded by them. Consequently they are often short-lived in practice.

On the other hand, even if we can demonstrate that inequality of educational opportunity is, as Boudon has argued, showing a slow but consistent decline we still have to consider to what extent this materially affects the chances of working-class children and other disadvantaged groups for social mobility. We have already examined in some detail in an earlier chapter the problem of educational devaluation which seems to be an inevitable accompaniment of large-scale expansion. The result, all too often, is that the value of higher education in terms of social mobility is depressed by the very processes which bring working-class and other disadvantaged students into it in large numbers. At the same time, such students tend to be concentrated in shorter courses, or less prestigious institutions. They are also less likely to go on into graduate education.

There is also some evidence that educational achievement does not necessarily eliminate differences in social background. Thus a Swedish longitudinal study showed that within groups of similar educational background there were differences in income by socioeconomic origin, and those in group 1 averaged twice as much in earnings as those in group 4.[96] In this country Halsey has demonstrated that the administrative class of the civil service recruits disproportionately from middle-class graduates in comparison with both university teachers and the scientific civil service.[97]

This may be less true in the United States, where Boudon for example argues that 'the weight of social heritage relative to meritocracy is likely to be smaller'.[98] On the other hand, it has been estimated that the economic return for a given amount of schooling is smaller for blacks than whites in the United States,[99] largely because of racial discrimination.[100] Women, moreover, both black and white, are not able to convert their educational attainments into earnings nearly as effectively as their husbands.[101] Inequality of educational opportunity is therefore only part of the pattern of inequalities in social opportunity.

As many observers have been quick to point out, a society based on strictly meritocratic principles would not necessarily be a more equal society. Barbara Wootton has argued that 'a rigid class structure is not incompatible with a considerable measure of individual mobility',[102] and both Jencks and Boudon have argued, although in different ways, that the way to equality of economic opportunity is through a more equal society, rather than through equality of educational opportunity.[103] This is an important issue and one to which it will be necessary to return in later chapters. For the moment we must remain in the mainstream of the sociology of education and look at the attempts to locate the reasons for inequality of educational opportunity in the family background of the child.

4 Family background, values and achievement

1 The family, social class and educational achievement

The advance of industrialization has had, as one of its most important consequences, the progressive removal from the family of its educational function. Formal educational institutions have taken over from the family not only the teaching of specific skills, but much normative training as well. The school, that is to say, has become the focal socializing agency,[1] at least for those years during which the child is full-time within the educational system. Yet, even in the most advanced industrial economy the school cannot and does not take over completely from the family. The first five or six years of life are crucial foundation years, and even after starting at school the child normally continues to live with his parents and to be deeply influenced by their behaviour and attitudes. Moreover it is not only that the family shares in the socialization process alongside the school and, indeed, other agencies as well. It is also true to say that the family exerts a profound influence on the response of the child to the school. For this reason educational sociologists have turned to a consideration of this influence, and in particular to attempt to describe the family environment which is most likely to encourage a favourable response to school, and a good academic performance.

At the same time, the increasing weight of the evidence pointing to the persistence of social-class inequalities in educational performance, in spite of the democratization of educational provision, has made it inevitable that studies of family background should be closely related to considerations of social class. The consistent tendency of working-class or manual workers' children to perform less well in school, and to leave school sooner than the children of non-manual workers, calls for explanation, and it has seemed reasonable to look for that explanation in the working-class family.

It would, however, be far from the truth to conclude that the attention paid by sociologists in recent years to this problem has taken us very far towards a solution. We have many studies into the relationship between social-class background and educational achievement, and many different aspects of that background have been suggested as casual factors in the link between home and school, but up to now we have very little knowledge of the precise way in which these different factors interelate to depress intellectual performance. It is necessary therefore, to preface an account of the present state of research in this field with a brief indication of why this particular research topic should have proved so difficult to handle.

Perhaps the most important of the several reasons that underlie all the problems in this area of study is the enormous complexity of the concept of home environment or home background. Not only are there many different aspects of family life which appear to be important, but these are themselves frequently hard to pin down into suitably operational terms. This is particularly true where, as is often the case, the researchers are attempting to include such factors as child-rearing practices, speech and thought patterns, and fundamental value orientations. In addition, it can be shown that these factors do not operate independently but are closely related to each other and may well have a cumulative effect.[2] Under such conditions it is almost impossible to discover the precise way in which a particular family background operates to produce under- or over-achievement. Nor, of course, are there such things as working-class or middle-class families in any absolute sense. The households defined as working-class in terms of fathers' occupation contain very many heterogeneous elements, and so do those similarly defined as middle-class.

In addition to problems of this kind, similar difficulties surround the attempt to relate the concept of achievement to a particular educational context. Although the tendency of the working classes to under-achieve is a very consistent one, it cannot be assumed that it is always produced by the same combination of factors. Parental interest, for example, may be more important in one kind of school system than in another, and achievement motivation may count for more in one kind of teaching situation than in another. It follows that we cannot infer from one educational system to another, or indeed, even from one school to another, without prior study.

The concept of under-achievement itself presents us with a considerable range of problems, since there is no way of measuring potential as distinct from actual ability. As Vernon has pointed out, we must 'reject the notion that any tests can reveal the innate components of mental aptitudes', for these are 'non-observable and non-measurable'.[3] Intelligence tests therefore, do not measure genetic potential or capacity, although there are grounds for believing that they are a better indicator than attainment tests.[4] Moreover, although it is now generally agreed that there is a genetic component in human ability, so that some individuals 'have more favourable genes for the aquisition of cognitive schemata than others',[5] the extent to which group differences can be explained in genetic terms is the subject of considerable controversy.

Jenson, for example, has argued[6] that racial and social class differences in measured ability are mainly genetic in origin and that only extreme environmental deprivation can keep a child from performing up to his genetic potential. This view has been seriously challenged[7] and would seem to represent an extreme view. Vernon for example believes that the genetic component in intelligence test scores cannot be estimated accurately because 'the relative importance of the environmental factors clearly varies with the range of environmental differences.'[8] The dispute is unlikely to be resolved until we have a much greater knowledge of the way in which abilities develop in interaction with the environment.

On the other hand there is a great deal of evidence that socio-economic status has a considerable effect on academic achievement *even when measured ability* is controlled. In the u.s., for example, a national follow-up of 1960 high school seniors showed that while about 90 per cent of high school graduates in the high ability, high socio-economic quintiles attended college, this was so for only about 69 per cent of the boys in the high ability, low socio-economic quintiles and only 52 per cent of the girls in this grouping. Moreover about 40 per cent of even the low ability, high socio-economic quintiles went to college, but only about 10 per cent of both boys and girls in the low ability, low socio-economic quintiles.[9] Even more remarkably, the same study showed that even amongst those who went to college, those of high ability and high socio-economic status were more likely to graduate from college, and much more likely to go on to enter a graduate or professional school. Thus of those in the highest socio-economic quintile, 41.9 per cent of the men and

20.1 per cent of the women enrolled in some form of graduate study, and only 24.5 per cent of the men and 8.2 per cent of the women in the lowest socio-economic quintile.[10]

Parallel findings are reported from the follow-up of Wisconsin high school students studied by Sewell and his colleagues. Dividing the cohort into quartiles, for both socio-economic status and ability, they found, for example, that in the top quarter of students in ability a student from the lowest socio-economic category was only half as likely to attend college as a student from the highest socio-economic category. At the level of graduate study, the odds were 3.5 to 1 in favour of the high socio-economic status students over the low socio-economic status students even in the high ability category.[11]

Data collected by both the Crowther Report and the Robbins Report show a similar pattern of relationships between measured ability, socio-economic status and educational achievement. In a survey of National Service recruits, the Crowther Committee found wide social class differences in the age of leaving school, even at the highest level of ability.[12] Moreover information collected by the Robbins Committee showed that social class differences are not eliminated even at I.Q. levels of 130 and above.[13] Table Six shows that within this very able group, children from manual families were not only less likely to go on to higher education of any kind, but were also more likely, if they did follow a course of higher education, to do so outside the universities.

Table Six

Higher education of 'able' children of different classes, born 1940-1

I.Q. at 11	Father's Occupation	% obtaining higher education of the following kinds			
		Full-time degree level	Other full-time	Part-time only	Total
130+	Non-manual	37	4	10	51
	Manual	18	12	10	40
115-129	Non-manual	17	17	4	38
	Manual	8	7	9	24

Whatever the final outcome on the nature/nurture controversy, therefore, there is abundant evidence that genetic factors are unlikely to explain more than a part, and even a relatively small part, of social class differences in educational achievement.

2 The material environment

'Until 1945, roughly speaking, the problem of social class in education was seen, by social investigators and policy-makers alike, primarily as a *barrier to opportunity*. The problem was an institutional one; how to secure equality of access for children of comparable ability, regardless of their social origins, to institutions of secondary and higher education designed for, and still used in the main by, the offspring of the superior social classes.'[14] Indeed, one of the most interesting features of an educational system organized on elitist principles is the belief that the working classes do not need more than a minimum of education, and would not, in any case, be capable of making use of it. Once it is accepted that there should be a greater measure of educational equality, and once the major institutional barriers have started to give way, attention can be focused upon the more subtle ways in which inequalities in educational opportunity are preserved.

There is, however, one environmental factor of considerable importance which has been seen for many years as a serious handicap to some working-class children; that is, the effect on school performance of extreme poverty, whether this is due to low wages, unemployment, a large family or the loss of a breadwinner. There are several ways in which extreme poverty might be expected to exert an influence on school performances. Malnutrition and poor living conditions are bound to have an influence on the health of the child, and so directly or indirectly on his ability to learn. Indeed, the early realization that this was so was a factor in the development of such school welfare provisions as free meals and free milk to children in need, and the development of the school medical services. Pre-natal damage may also occur to the child as a result of inadequate pre-natal care. Poverty can also have an influence indirectly, by limiting the family's ability to forego adolescent earnings. Under such circumstances scholarships and free places will be refused unless there is a generous provision for maintenance. Poor housing and overcrowding can not only seriously impede the child's home-work but even his opportunity for reading or constructive play.

There is little doubt that before the Second World War the economic circumstances of working-class life gave little incentive to look elsewhere for reasons for their under-achievement. Since 1945, however, the general improvements in the economic standard of working-class life, and the maintenance of full or nearly full employment, have led researchers to doubt whether it is any longer possible to think of poverty as the only, or indeed as the major factor, in working-class under-achievement. Instead attention has focused on poverty as only one influence amongst many others, and one which may be relatively unimportant. This is true both in this country and in the U.S.

For example, a study of the growing up of a whole age-group in a Mid-Western city in the United States found that only five per cent of the school drop-outs gave clear evidence of having to leave school for financial reasons. Seventy-five per cent of them stated quite clearly that there was no financial necessity for leaving school. Furthermore, it was possible to compare the drop-outs with their socio-economic controls who were still in school, on the extent to which they contributed to their own support through jobs, payment for board and room, clothing purchases and the like. When the two groups were compared on these items, it was found that 70 per cent of the controls were mainly self-supporting, whereas only 55 per cent of the drop-outs were mainly self-supporting.[15]

The relative paucity of grants to attend college would seem likely to be an important factor in the wastage that occurs in the United States between high school graduation and entrance to college. Moreover, although the current tendency is to increase financial aid, the amount is still small,[16] and parents are by far the most important source of finance.[17] Moreover students themselves often give financial difficulty as the reason for failing to attend, or to drop-out from, college.[18] Yet in general the emphasis in American writing on the subject is to stress the motivational factors, and parental attitudes. For example Berdie, in a study of 25,000 Minnesota high school seniors found that only one-third of those who were planning not to go on to college said they would go to college if they had more money.[19]

The Crowther Report attempted to discover the part played by financial circumstances in early leaving from grammar and technical schools. They showed that such early leaving 'was negligible if the father's income exceeded £16 a week'.[20] At the same time the proportion of young people mentioning the desire to earn money as a reason for leaving school declined as the father's income increased. However, we have no means of knowing how far poverty was the causal factor at work here, or how far parental and children's attitudes were the decisive factor. Since the same study showed that 'even in the lowest income group approximately 30 per cent of children had stayed at school beyond the age of 16',[21] it is clear that poverty is not necessarily a handicap if other circumstances are favourable.

More recently the Plowden Report has made an ambitious attempt to differentiate the effect of what it calls home circumstances from parental attitudes and from the effect of the school. Its definition of home circumstances was very much wider than the definition employed by Floud, Halsey and Martin since it included not only the physical amenities of the home but number of dependent children, father's occupational group and, very surprisingly, parents' education. Nevertheless, even with this very wide and indeed heterogeneous set of variables, it was able to conclude that 'more of the variation in the children's school achievement is specifically accounted for by the variation in parental attitudes than by either the variation in the material circumstances of parents or by the variation in schools. Secondly, the relative importance of the parental attitudes increases as the children grow older.'[22]

A special survey of children in the Manchester area directed by Stephen Wiseman for the Plowden Committee also came to substantially the same conclusion: 'When we think of the problem of material and cultural deprivation, we see it as a problem affecting the "submerged tenth", the slum dwellers, the poverty-stricken. We tend to assume that it affects only the tail-end of the ability-range as well as the tail-end of the income-range. Both of these views are wrong, and the second is even more radically wrong than the first. Educational deprivation is *not* mainly the effect of poverty; parental attitude and maternal care are more important than the level of material needs.'[23]

Nevertheless, in acknowledging the force of this kind of evidence it is important to recognize that poverty, poor housing, overcrowding and other slum conditions still affect a large number of children in ways which are likely to depress their educational performance.

Thus, on the basis of a national survey of primary school children in 1964, it was found that the households in which they were living were overcrowded in as many as 25 per cent of the cases.[24] Yet both Douglas in his major follow-up study of a national sample of children, and the Kellmer Pringle National Child Development Study based on 11,000 seven-year-old children have demonstrated a relationship between overcrowding and school achievement.[25] There is also evidence that children from poor homes are handicapped by poor attendance and higher rates of sickness. The Newsom Report for example showed not only that the average reading age of fourth-year pupils in schools in slum areas was 17 months worse than the average for secondary modern schools, but among third-year pupils in such schools, as many again as in secondary modern schools generally, missed more than half a term's work.[26]

Also bearing on the same problem, some striking findings from the Kellmer Pringle National Child Development Study demonstrate the extent to which unskilled manual workers' children suffer disproportionately from physical deficiencies, such as squints and stammers, and behaviour problems such as bed-wetting and nail-biting. At the same time children from such families were less likely to be immunized and to attend clinics, and the report draws attention to the way in which those sections of the community which in general have most need of the statutory services tend to use them least.[27]

In Britain, one of the most influential post-war studies on the effect of the material environment has been the research by Floud, Halsey and Martin into the 11+ examination in south-west Hertfordshire and Middlesbrough. They showed that in south-west Hertfordshire where 'virtually everyone enjoys an adequate basic income and good housing', the material environment of the home was of less importance in differentiating between the successful and the unsuccessful child than differences in the size of the family and in the education, attitudes and ambitions of the parents. In Middlesbrough, on the other hand, where incomes were lower and housing conditions less favourable, 'the successful children at each social level were distinguished by the relative material prosperity of their homes'.[28]

Yet, even in studies on the slum child, we find an emphasis on factors other than material deprivation. Most of the work on educational under-achievement in recent years has been into those more subtle areas which touch upon the role of values and motivation. This is particularly true of those studies which have attempted to understand the underlying causes of under-achievement, or which have tried to develop a theoretical framework. Indeed one of the basic weaknesses of all the studies of material deprivation has been the lack of any theoretical scheme which attempts to explain the manner in which the material environment handicaps a child. We have already noticed the disparate and heterogeneous indices which characterize many of the studies in this field, and which betray at once the lack of any systematic attempt to develop theory. Yet if we are to understand the part played by material factors in school achievement we need to know how they operate. This is particularly important in this area because obviously they do not in themselves influence school performance directly. In consequence the true indices of material deprivation are not poverty and housing as such but school absence through illness, neglected homework and the inability to pay fees or take up a scholarship.

At the same time there is obviously a close relationship between material deprivation and the whole way of life of the family. Poverty can make a parent less willing to keep a child at school; can make it difficult for him to afford books and toys, or expeditions which help a child to learn; can enforce housing conditions which make the whole family strained and unhappy or make it almost impossible for parents and child to talk or play together. Moreover, even when these conditions are no longer present, the fact that they have existed in the recent past, or were a feature of the parents' own childhood, may exert an influence on attitudes, values and aspirations for a generation or even more. It is for this reason that it is sometimes suggested that school achievement should be related not to isolated factors in the environment but to family life as a whole. We shall consider this point more fully after a consideration of the other aspects of the home environment which have occupied the attention of sociologists in recent years.

3 The achievement syndrome

Sociologists have long been interested in the existence of differing value systems and value orientations which can be used to explain differences in behaviour as between different groups in society.

Moreover, studies of social class differences in beliefs and values can be shown to have considerable relevance for the explanation of class differences in educational performance. These differences centre upon the emphasis each sociaclass characteristically places upon achievement. Hyman, for example, has drawn attention to the extent to which the beliefs and values of the lower classes actually reduce 'the very *voluntary* actions which would ameliorate their low position'. Using American data Hyman showed that working-class parents tended to place less value on formal education; they were, for example, less anxious for their children to stay on at school, or to go on to some form of higher education. They were also less likely to be ambitious either for themselves or their children.[29] Children of working-class parents also tended to have lower aspirations than the children of middle-class parents even when I.Q. was controlled.[30] A more recent study by Sewell and Shah has pointed up the importance of parental interest and encouragement in a most striking way. They studied a randomly selected cohort of 10,318 Wisconsin high school seniors and found that where parental encouragement was low, relatively few students, regardless of their intelligence or socio-economic status levels planned to go to college. On the other hand, where parental encouragement was high, the proportion of students planning on college was also high, even when socio-economic status and intelligence level were relatively low.[31] The senior author, in a later article,[32] argues that encouragement from parents, teachers, and friends, as well as the youth's own perception of his ability, act as mediating variables between socio-economic status and ability, on the one hand, and aspirations on the other.

Several studies have also drawn the same conclusions from English data. The greater interest shown by middle-class parents in the education of their children was exemplified, for example, by Floud, Halsey and Martin in their study of Middlesbrough and south-west Hertfordshire.[33] Douglas also found comparable results in his national sample. 'The middle-class parents take more interest in their children's progress at school than the manual working-class parents do, and they become relatively more interested as their children grow older. They visit the schools more frequently to find out how their children are getting on with their work, and when they do so are more likely to ask to see the Head as well as the class teacher, whereas the manual working-class parents are usually content to see the class teacher only. But the most striking difference is that many middle-class fathers visit the schools to discuss their children's progress whereas manual working-class fathers seldom do.'[34] More recently the Plowden Committee found similar social-class differences amongst the parents of a national sample of primary-school children. Middle-class parents were more likely to want their children to stay at school longer and more likely to prefer a grammar school, and, as in the Douglas study, middle-class fathers were more likely than working-class fathers to take an interest in their children's education.[35]

The conclusion, that the working-classes are less ambitious for their children, and that the children are less ambitious for themselves, has not however gone unchallenged, and some studies have stressed the importance of relative rather than absolute measures of ambition, or what Turner has called the ladder model of mobility. According to this model, mobility is measured by the number of 'rungs' an individual moves up the ladder. 'Each individual starts from a given rung, and the unskilled labourer has as far to climb in moving up two rungs to the skilled labour category as the small business owner has in moving up to a managerial position in a large business. On the other hand, the son of a large business owner or official has nothing more to do than to "stay put" in order to remain in the same category, and requires no more ambition to do so than the semi-skilled labourer's son who becomes a semi-skilled labourer himself.'[36]

Boudon, too, points out that the choice of a particular school or course might involve a high probability of social demotion for an upper-class child but the possibility of social promotion for a child from the lower classes. At the same time the cost of an advanced course might well be high for the working classes, not only in monetary terms, but also in terms of separation from peers and loss of family solidarity.[37]

Turner concludes that neither the ladder model nor the race model are in themselves adequate representations of mobility in modern society, because the educational system itself has to some extent blunted the influence of family background. He found that although the boys of higher social background had the higher aspirations they were in fact less ambitious in relative terms.[38] Empey too in a study of high school seniors found that although lower-class boys had lower occupational aspirations than those from a higher class their ambitions were by no means limited to their fathers' status, and in relative terms they were as ambitious if not more so than boys of higher status.[39] Although, by excluding early drop-outs, these studies may have somewhat overestimated the level of ambition of working-class pupils there is plenty of evidence that such pupils and their parents have higher aspirations than a simple ladder model would predict. Thus a cross-sectional study of third to twelfth grade pupils in a large metropolis in the United States found that 64 per cent of working-class elementary school children and 69 per cent of working-class senior high school students were found to desire middle-class occupations above the clerical and sales level.[40] A number of British surveys have also demonstrated that, although there are consistent class differences in the level of ambition, the aspirations of even unskilled working-class parents for their children can often be surprisingly high. Thus the national survey for the Plowden Committee found that 36 per cent of unskilled manual workers wanted their children to stay at school until 17 or over, and 30 per cent of them hoped their children would go to a secondary grammar school. Although these aspirations are low in comparison with those in non-manual and particularly in professional occupations, they are certainly higher than the subsequent achievement of these children. Thus only 7 per cent of the children of unskilled workers actually went on to grammar school, compared with 52 per cent of the children of professional fathers. In the case of skilled manual workers 48 per cent of the parents hoped their child would go to grammar school, compared with only 18 per cent who actually achieved their aim.[41]

Other writers have suggested that there is no genuine differentiation in the values attached to success, and that the working classes put less emphasis upon it only because they perceive the obstacles in the way of its achievement. Several studies in recent years have found that there is little difference between the social classes in the importance they attach to 'getting ahead', and that if anything it is the working class to whom occupational success is the most important. They are also, however, much more likely to see the path to occupational success closed to them.[42] Moreover, a number of studies comparing aspirations and expectations have shown that the discrepancy between the two is higher for the working class. Stephenson, for example, in a comparison of British and American studies found that in both countries it is the working-class pupils 'who lower most their aspirations when it comes to considering plans or expectations'.[43] More recently Caro and Pihlblad reached the same conclusion in a study of male high-school seniors in the United States.[44] Turner's study, already referred to, found no relationship between confidence in occupational choice and social-class background, but this may be because of his particular sample of working-class boys. The findings of Caro and Pihlblad are of particular interest because they show that the size of the aspiration-expectation disparity was related not only to social class but also to academic aptitude. This suggests strongly that one of the obstacles to opportunity perceived by working-class boys is their lack of achievement at school.

Evidence for the influence of achievement on the aspirations of both boys and their parents is provided by a longitudinal study of school success and school failure in three English secondary schools.[45] The aspirations of the boys and their parents were high in each of the schools studied, although they were highest in the traditional grammar school and lowest in the comprehensive school. Expectations were also high, although, generally speaking, lower than aspirations. When expectations and aspirations were related to achievement, however, it was found that the difference between them was much greater for unsuccessful than for successful boys. A comparison of the change in aspirations and expectations between the second and third year carried out in one of the schools showed that unsuccessful boys had lowered both their expectations *and* their aspirations. It is suggested that parental aspirations must be seen not simply as a cause but also as a consequence of success at school. This is revealed in the interviews with parents, who were clearly expressing not only their perception of the relative value of different types of higher education but also its relevance for their own child.

The way in which school success or failure seems to 'feed-back' into both aspirations and expectations provides an empirical grounding for Hopper's conception of the regulation of ambition. He argues that 'at every level and through every route within its total selection process, an educational system must strive, on the one hand, to "warm-up" some of its students, and, on the other, to "cool-out" those who are rejected for further training'.[46] Thus all societies are faced with a dilemma which they attempt to resolve in different ways. Hopper also suggests that, in an educational system characterized by sponsorship and elitist ideologies, ambition is more likely to follow than to precede some sign of educational success;

whereas in an educational system with contest and egalitarian ideologies the reverse is likely to be true.

Certainly in a system where there is overt selection there is evidence that both aspirations and expectations are likely to be influenced by the allocation procedure itself. Passing the 11 + is often taken as a sign by parents that they have a 'clever' child, whereas allocation to the secondary modern school has a depressing effect on aspirations.[47] There is reason to believe that working-class parents are more sensitive to these signals than middle-class parents, who are more confident both in their own judgment and in the abilities of their children.[48] On the other hand a longitudinal study by Himmelweit found that the type of school attended was a better predictor of both the aspirations and the occupational history of the pupil than either his ability or his social background. Although in both grammar and secondary modern schools boys of middle-class background did better than those of working-class background such differences were small compared to the very large differences between boys going to different types of school.[49] Similarly, Neave, in his study of university entrants from comprehensive schools argued that upwardly mobile working-class children and their parents are far more likely to rely on school assessment of their abilities and aptitudes than middle-class students and that for the working-class family 'good O levels raise for the first time the question of a conscious decision'.[50]

An interesting comparative study of schools in the United States and Denmark throws further light on Hopper's argument. In both countries the great majority of students planned to go to college when their parents, as measured by questions to the mother, had college aspirations for them, while few whose mothers did not want them to continue, actually planned to do so. On the other hand, enrolment in a pre-college or academic course or programme was also strongly related to college plans in both countries. However, when the two countries were compared it was found that whereas in the United States family plans and school programmes each seemed to have an equal influence, in Denmark the influence of parents seemed to be much the stronger. Thus in the United States, but *not* in Denmark, enrolment in a college programme seemed to override any parental influence *not* to go to college. The authors explain this in terms of the greater cultural support for college in the United States, where the majority of parents and students aspire to college.[51]

Thus this study suggests that a contest and egalitarian ideology, far from increasing the influence of family background as Hopper suggests, actually provides cultural support for the able adolescent to continue his or her education.

Further evidence for this conclusion is given by a comparison of high school students in the United States and Norway. A large number of high schools were included although all were in predominantly rural areas. In this study a scale of perceived parental interest was used which was wider than parental aspirations. The same kind of relationship between social class background, parental interest, and college plans was found in both countries, with academic achievement acting as an important intervening variable. There were however important differences between the two countries which parallel the findings from the study of the United States and Denmark. Only in the case of American boys did academic performance have any appreciable influence in reducing class bias.[52] The authors suggest that a superior performance record in high school may function as a 'family involvement catalyst' for working-class parents, a conclusion which is substantially the same as Neave's findings in the English context. We may assume therefore that, even in the absence of early selection into a differentiated school system, other measures of school achievement have a similar effect on the aspirations of pupils and their parents.

An alternative approach to the concept of ambition is to see it not simply in terms of educational and occupational aspirations but as a complex set of interrelated value-orientations which aid in the achievement of educational and occupational success. Value-orientations in this sense are 'complex but definitely patterned . . . principles . . . which give order and direction to the ever-flowing stream of human acts and thoughts, as these relate to the solution of common human problems.'[53] It is argued that there are five such problems, which are universal in the sense that they face everyone, everywhere, and which are also essentially philosophical in that they are all concerned with meaning. Moreover each problem has a limited number of possible solutions. Accordingly, societies and individuals can be classified in terms of the kind of answer they give to each of these problems. Since there are five problems, and a number of possible solutions to each problem, the varied combinations of answers can give rise to considerable variety, although in practice it appears that there is a certain amount of clustering amongst solutions so that a preference for one answer to a problem will also to a large extent imply the answer to several of the others. Table Seven outlines the five 'problems' and the postulated 'solutions'.

Table Seven

Problem	*Possible solution*		
Human nature	evil	a mixture of good and evil	good
The relationships between man and nature	subjugation to nature	harmony with nature	mastery over nature
An evaluation of the past, the present, and the future time	an emphasis on time past	an emphasis on time present	an emphasis on time future
An evaluation of the meaning of activity	an emphasis on being	an emphasis on being in becoming or development	an emphasis on doing
Significant relationships	individuality	collectivity	

The preferred choice, and so the whole pattern of value orientations, will vary not only between whole societies but within societies, both between sub-groups and classes and between individual persons. Moreover, it is anticipated that value orientations will operate on both a manifest and a latent level, since the degree of consciousness individuals have of the value orientations which influence their behaviour, will vary from the completely implicit to the completely explicit.

As developed by Kluckholn this concept is, of course, intended as part of a general theory of social action but it is clear that it has great relevance for our understanding of differences in the level of achievement orientation. Kluckholn herself has pictured the dominant American value orientation as held by the middle classes as emphasizing human nature as a mixture of good and evil; the relationship between man and nature as one of mastery; the time orientation as future-directed; the activity orientation as doing; and the relational orientation as individualistic. Thus belief in man's mastery over nature encourages a perception of the world as something to be used or manipulated which contrasts strikingly with the belief that man's fate is determined. It provides a world-view, that is to say, which sees human achievement as possible. The doing-orientation, which Kluckholn sees as chacteristically American, is important because it emphasizes what the individual can do rather than what he is. It is, therefore, close to the concept of achieved rather than ascribed status. Kluckholn defines it as 'a demand for the kind of activity which results in accomplishments that are measurable by standards conceived to be external to the acting individual'.[54] The relational orientation is also important for achievement, in so far as the dominant American preference is for lineal or individualistic rather than collateral or collectivist relationships. The consequent freeing of the individual from kinship ties is seen as an important ingredient in social mobility. It is, however, in the concept of future-time orientation that we have the most striking of the Kluckholn orientations. Its chief characteristic is a high evaluation of the future, rather than the past or the present. The concept of future orientation, therefore, overlaps with the concept of deferred gratification developed by Schneider and Lysgaard.[55]

Although Kluckholn's value orientations are frequently used in discussions of educational achievement, we do not have many attempts to measure the actual extent of class differences in the value orientations she has described. Many of the attempts to do so were summarized by Kahl in 1965. He concluded: 'Each of the field studies reported here had its own purpose, and accordingly devised its own measurements. Samples included high-school boys, adult men, and adult women. Yet the studies all came from the same theoretical stance, and their results proved to be comparable and parallel. Simple attitude items were devised to measure abstract values about certain social relationships and behaviour connected with achievement orientation, and they produced scales that "worked" in two senses; the same items clung together to define given scales, despite the distances of time, geography and language that divided the field studies; and the correlations of the scales with an outside variable, socio-economic status, were stable.'[56]

The concept of deferred gratification has also been studied in relationship to social class, and many of the findings have been summarized by Murray Straus.[57] He is critical of most of the work in this field, chiefly owing to its methodological limitations. As he points out, 'most of the literature is at the theoretical and case study levels of empiricism, and relatively few studies report quantitative data'. There is also a certain amount of confusion between the adolescent's deferment of gratification and the parent's demands for deferment on the part of the child. On the basis of his own study of adolescents he suggests that in fact there seem to be two deferred gratification patterns rather than one, willingness to defer material needs, and willingness to defer inter-personal interaction needs such as sex, aggression, and affiliation. Although he found that the willingness to defer material needs was related to socio-economic status, this was not so for inter-personal interaction needs. However, since his sample virtually eliminated the 'lower-lower' class, this finding does not necessarily apply to the working class generally.

More recently Turner has also sounded a note of warning with respect to the findings on class differences in value orientations. He points out that the relationships found have often been quite modest, and often 'indices composed of several items conceal the fact that some of the items are not themselves related to stratification'.[58] His own study of Los Angeles high-school seniors found no relationship between willingness to defer gratification and social-class background and few differences with respect to other value-orientations, although the absence of the school 'drop-outs' is likely to have influenced his findings. Turner also introduces the interesting concept of *value-relevancy*. There is, he points out, 'a difference between accepting a value and translating it into a goal in one's own behaviour'. He hypothesized, accordingly, that social strata 'would differ more in the values they accepted as goals for their own behaviour than in the values they would endorse in less personal contexts'. Moreover his data provided 'impressive support for this view', at least in the case of his male pupils.[59] The implications of this argument are of great interest, and suggest that the expectations and perceptions both of themselves and of others, held by working-class parents and their children, have perhaps been neglected as a subject of study.

Scanzoni, in interviews with nearly 1,000 families in the Indianapolis area, has recently attempted to throw further light on the concept of value-orientations. His study included middle- and working-class families, both Negro and white, but did not cover the 'lower lower-class'. Scanzoni found that high aspirations and a belief in 'mastery over nature' were fairly uniformly distributed over the class structure, and indeed that the working classes were slightly *more* likely to stress mastery values and the 'American Dream'. On the other hand, working-class families were more likely to stress passive rather than active value-orientations. That is to say, they tended to stress caution, to de-emphasize risk-taking and to encourage adjustment to rather than manipulation of the opportunity structure. They also had less self-esteem and fewer expectations of success. Scanzoni concludes that working-class children 'find themselves in an ambiguous situation of conflicting orientations'. Indeed, in 'their desire to have children become socially mobile these kinds of parents put substantial pressures on them to try very hard (perhaps even "too hard"). Yet in curious and paradoxical fashion, with perhaps both parents and children being unaware of it, they paint a bleak picture of the child's actual chances to "make it" as an individual.'[60]

The attempt to find class differences in value orientations is clearly an interesting and promising approach to the problem of under-achievement, even if, as this brief review has indicated, much more needs to be done in the way of empirical testing. On the other hand, we need to know not only whether there are differences in the patterns of basic value orientations between social classes, but how these different patterns of values actually relate to achievement. Consequently, the most useful studies are those which hold social class constant, and attempt to relate measures of value orientations directly to achievement.

An example of this kind of study is the Harvard Mobility Project. This study, using a questionnaire distributed to boys in public high schools in eight towns in the Boston metropolitan area, found that 'the I.Q. scores of the boys and the occupations of their fathers turned out to be of practically equal utility as predictors of the boys' educational ambitions. Most boys with high intelligence or from high status homes planned a college career, whereas most boys with low intelligence or from low status homes did not aspire to higher education.'[61] Within the middle and most populous part of the status hierarchy however it was much more difficult to predict college aspirations. 'Thus a boy from the top quintile of intelligence whose father was a minor white collar worker or a skilled labourer had almost a 50-50 chance of aiming at a college career.' A later follow-up study also showed that most of the boys planning a college career actually did go on to college.

In order to discover more about the aspirations of boys in the lower middle range of the status hierarchy, 24 boys were chosen for interview. 'They fell into two groups; 12 boys were in the college preparatory course, had marks in the top half of their class, and definitely planned to go to a regular academic college after high school. The other 12 were not in the college preparatory course and did not plan to go to college.' The boys all had I.Q. scores in the top three deciles of their school, and all came from petty white-collar, skilled or semi-skilled workers. Both the boys and their parents were interviewed at length, and from the interviews emerged a picture of two very different basic value orientations which appeared to be related to the different aspirations of the boys. Eight of the 12 boys with college aspirations and only one of the 12 boys without them came from families who believed in what Kahl in his description of the interviews describes as 'getting ahead'. Such parents 'used the middle class as a reference group that was close enough to have meaning, though far enough away to be different'. They were aware of their own failure to get on and felt themselves, in part at least, to be failures. Consequently they did everything they could to get their sons to take school seriously and to aim to get to college.

The other parents 'accepted the scheme of things and their own place within it'. Living for the present rather than the past or the future, the children were encouraged to enjoy themselves while they were young. The value of 'doing what you like' was applied to school work, to part-time jobs and to career aspirations.

These parental attitudes were matched very closely by those of the boys' who had learned to look at the occupational structure, the school, and college, from their parents' points of view. Only a few boys differed from their parents. Kahl concluded that only boys who had internalized what he describes as the 'getting ahead' values were sufficiently motivated to overcome the obstacles which, as lower-middle- and working-class boys, they had to face in school.

Kahl's study does not refer specifically to Kluckholn's scheme, but it is clearly related to it, and indeed Kluckholn was one of those involved in the direction of the research. Moreover, although not intended as anything other than exploratory, it does at least suggest that parental value orientations may well be a most important factor in the boy's own attitude to school. A later study by Rosen, however, has attempted to relate various measures of value orientation to the school achievement of high-school boys in a more systematic way. Items were constructed to cover three of Kluckholn's orientations, active-passive, present-future and familistic-individualistic. Those responses which indicated an activistic, future-orientated, individualistic point of view were classified as reflecting achievement values and a score was derived for each boy by giving a point for each achievement-orientated response. Achievement value, using this measure, was related both to social class and to educational aspirations, but not actual achievement as measured by school grades. Of particular interest, however, is his finding that over-aspirers, i.e. those with higher aspirations than the norm of their social class, tend also to have higher-value scores, while under-aspirers tend to have lower-value scores than the norm of their social class.[62]

Rosen's findings, however, conflict to some extent with those of Straus in his study, already referred to, of the deferred gratification pattern. Straus found that his measures were related both to achievement, as measured by school grades, and to occupational aspirations, although they were not, except for material deprivation, related to social class. It is not clear whether this difference in the findings is due to the nature of the two samples, or the use of a different instrument.

In Britain a number of studies have been made, using Kluckholn's general theoretical framework, and here too the results suggest that this particular approach is worth-while. Swift, for example found that, in the lower-middle classes, the mobility-pessimism of the father was associated closely with 11 + success.[63] This may be compared with Kahl's findings with respect to his 'common-man' boys and their parents. There have also been studies using a modified form of the instruments devised by Rosen. Jayasuriya, for example, has related the value orientations of secondary-school boys to their father's occupation, and found a class difference not only for the instrument but for its three separate elements, active-passive, present-future, and familistic-individualistic. However, as soon as he holds I.Q. and school constant, the social-class differences disappear.[64] There is, that is to say, an approximation to middle-class norms by working-class boys in grammar schools. More recently Sugarman, using similar questions in four secondary schools, has found that over- and under-achievement relative to I.Q. was associated with high and low scores respectively on all three of the value orientations *except for* the one grammar school in the study, in which only the active-passive orientation related to over- and under-achievement. This is in line with the findings of Banks and Finlayson,[66] who found little relationship between value-orientations and achievement in two grammar schools and in the 'academic' streams in a comprehensive school. It may be, therefore, that the questionnaire is too crude an instrument to pick up the differences between boys who all have relatively high levels of achievement values.

More recently Craft[67] has made use of the same framework in interviews with a sample of mainly Catholic working-class parents in Dublin, in which mothers and fathers were interviewed separately. Of two groups of adolescents, matched for social class, religion, ability, family size, sex and age, those staying on at school beyond the minimum school leaving age were found to have parents who had significantly higher achievement values on the activity, time and relational dimensions of the Kluckholn/Strodtbeck schema. Of the three dimensions, the orientation to time appeared to be the most important. Moreover mothers appeared to be more important than fathers.

One aspect of the achievement syndrome which has not yet been discussed is achievement motivation, sometimes called the need for achievement. This is a psychological concept developed by McClelland and his associates but one which has an obvious affinity with the concept of achievement values. In order to measure achievement motivation projective tests have been devised in which the subject is presented with a set of rather ambiguous pictures and asked to make up a story about them. These stories are then scored for evidence of achievement motivation using an elaborate scoring system.

Further work on achievement motivation has revealed that its relationship to actual achievement is not altogether clear. While some studies have found a relationship between high achievement motivation scores and achievement measures, including school grades, other studies have failed to find any such relationship.[68] This may be due to deficiencies in the measure itself, since it does not have high test reliability. On the other hand the need for achievement is conceived by McClelland as a very generalized drive and there is no reason to suppose that it will necessarily be directed towards either educational achievement or occupational success. Rosen therefore has suggested that achievement motivation and achievement values represent 'genuinely different components of the achievement syndrome'.[69] Conceivably then, high achievement values coupled with low achievement motivation will not lead to high achievement; nor will high achievement motivation lead to success at school if the achievement values or goals are centred elsewhere. It is for this reason that Strodtbeck suggests that 'the joint use of these measures would provide a more efficient predictor of over-achievement'.[70]

Although, therefore, much work clearly remains to be done before the concept of the achievement syndrome can be said to have been adequately explored, there is enough agreement among researchers to indicate that it has a part to play in the understanding of school achievement. What is perhaps less clear is the way in which value-orientations and achievement motivation form part of a wider set of cultural values or life-style, and the relationship between a particular style of life and systems of social stratification or social class.

4 Social class and family life

The attempt to explain how it is that working-class families hold different values from middle-class families depends essentially upon the development of a theory to explain how their different life chances and life experiences predispose them towards different views of the world around them and of their place in it. This problem has always interested sociologists, and there is no space here to review all the work, both theoretical and empirical, which has been done in this sphere. All that will be attempted is to draw attention to those aspects of it which appear to be particularly relevant to the problem of achievement. In general, attention has been focused upon three different aspects of working-class life, all of them to some degree interrelated. They may be briefly summarized as material life chances, working conditions, and opportunities for status.

Traditionally, those in working-class or manual jobs have earned less than those in middle-class or non-manual occupations. Moreover this is still largely true, in spite of a rise in the standard of living of the working classes, and some overlap between certain highly-paid workers and certain types of non-manual employment. Working-class employment has also been characteristically insecure. Not only has it been more liable to unemployment during periods of depression, but also few manual workers are employed on more than a weekly basis. This contrasts with the typical monthly, quarterly or even permanent tenure of most non-manual jobs. Manual workers also have less chance of advancement in their jobs.

Within the work situation itself there are also important differences which may have implications for working-class attitudes. Manual work is frequently carried out in unpleasant working conditions. It may be dangerous, dirty, or physically strenuous. Frequently it involves long hours, or shift work. Often it is less intrinsically rewarding, and perceived as such, even when it is highly paid. It is also less likely to involve authority, responsibility or power. Finally, many studies have shown that manual work is low in the prestige or status hierarchy of all modern societies.[71]

It is reasonable to expect that these radically different life and work experiences will be reflected in the attitudes of the working classes both to work itself and to other aspects of their lives, and there have been many attempts to show that this does indeed occur. It has been argued, for example, that the working class will value different attributes in their working situation, prizing such qualities as security more than other aspects of the job, and there are a number of studies which show that this is the case. In a widely-based international comparison using national sources, Inkeles has shown that those in higher-status occupations report more job satisfaction and are more likely to want a job which is interesting and stimulating. They are also less likely to want security or certainty in a job and are more willing to take risks to get promotion.[72]

The lack of security, combined with lack of opportunity, are also likely to influence the expectations of the manual worker. He may well lower his aspirations to what seems meaningful or reasonable in his circumstances, and this may influence his hopes not only for himself but also for his child.

The deprivation of the manual worker, both in his working situation and in his material standard of living, is also seen as profoundly influencing his view both of himself and of the world around him. Squibb, for example, has recently argued that working-class values 'have been forged and are still being forged by socially external and objective forces'[73] and argues that much of the thinking on working-class values fails 'to see the connections between the sub-value system, the stratification system, and the social system'.

The manual worker is also less likely to share in the middle-class achieving orientation described by Kluckholn. His own lack of power to alter his situation, his uncertainty about the future, his sense of insecurity, will, it is suggested, lead him to see the world as dominated by luck or chance,[74] rather than under his control. He is not likely to spend time planning for a future which is not only unpredictable but largely out of his hands. He will naturally gravitate towards the getting-by attitude described by Kahl, and he will do this because of his own experiences in coming to terms with his own environment. Neither is he likely to share in the individualistic approach of the middle classes. 'Getting ahead' for the manual worker 'must rest in the progressive increase of the rewards which they gain *from their present economic role*'. [75] For this reason he is likely to emphasize collective or group mobility through trade-union representation and trade-union power.

The low status ascribed to manual work, and especially to unskilled work, may also influence the worker's own self-esteem. He may accept the opinion of others as to his lack of ability and may transfer this to his children. High ambition in such circumstances may appear as inappropriate or even absurd. Parents with such an attitude may not only fail to encourage their children to achieve; they may not even recognize the achievement of their children unless it is drawn to their attention.[76] Recent work on the child's self-concept of ability has suggested not only that it is related to achievement but that parents are an important source of the child's self-image.[77]

So far in this discussion we have treated social class as if it were a homogeneous category. In fact, this is very far from the case, and studies in the differences within social classes show them to be both complex and heterogeneous. This serves to emphasize the importance of research into intra-class differences. Although much fewer in number than those concerned with comparison between classes, the researches carried out in this field are sufficient at least to indicate certain important areas to which further attention should be paid.

One of the main ways in which to differentiate between working-class jobs is in terms of skill, and it has been shown that, even when ability is held constant, the children of skilled workers perform better at school and are more likely to go on to higher education than are the children of the unskilled. Skilled and semi-skilled workers also have higher aspirations for their children than unskilled workers. Some studies have also suggested that foremen as a group stand in an intermediate position between the middle and the working classes.[78]

There is, therefore, clear evidence of differences both within the working classes and the middle classes, corresponding to the level of skill demanded on the job. In the absence of sufficient evidence we. can unfortunately only speculate as to why these differences occur. The more favourable position of the skilled worker or foreman relative to the unskilled worker, in terms of the status of the job, its chances of promotion and, usually, its material rewards, offers several possible reasons for the working-class differences that have been found. The lower-class family may well have fewer expectations for the future and so lower aspirations for themselves and their children. They may have less self-esteem and be less self-confident. They are also less likely to have acquired achieving values as a consequence of their particular life experiences, either during their own childhood or later. Within the middle classes those in lower-middle-class occupations will be differentiated from the upper-middle classes by their earnings, their status and their educational level. This may well reflect upon the horizons they set for their children.

On the other hand, we cannot overlook the possibility that the cause of the difference is of a much more complex and subtle kind, arising not as a consequence of their class position but as one of its causes. The foremen and skilled workers are likely to include far more upwardly mobile individuals than the unskilled workers, and so are those in the upper-middle rather than the lower-middle occupations group. It is at least possible that the personality and value orientations which helped the upwardly mobile families to succeed will also be passed to their children. Smelser, for example, in a study of upwardly mobile, stationary, and downwardly mobile families concluded that 'achievement at the level of the family was influential in the development of such personality factors as strength, power, self-direction and distance from others'.[79]

On the other hand, other workers have emphasized downward mobility, and especially maternal downward mobility as an important factor in school achievement and parental ambition. Cohen, for example, found that mothers who had married downward from a white-collar background had a higher probability of having a son planning to go to college than mothers who came from a manual-worker background. This was also true of mothers holding white-collar rather than manual jobs. Fathers' downward mobility was however unrelated to the sons' plans for entering college.[80] Floud, Halsey and Martin also found that mothers whose occupation before marriage was superior to that of their husbands were more likely to have children who were successful in the 11 + than other mothers.[81] Kohn, in his study of parental values towards the upbringing of children, found that working-class mothers holding white-collar jobs were closer to the middle class than other working-class mothers, and so were those with relatively high educational attainment.[82] Such mothers therefore are not only likely to be motivated by a strong desire to regain status; their close association with the middle classes through their social origin, their job or their educational background, has provided them with the necessary knowledge, and quite possibly values, which will ensure for their children a successful school career. Cohen, for example, concludes that 'we can speculate that the influence of the parents on the probability of mobility takes place at a very early stage when basic attitudes towards school work are being formed. The crucial role of the parents may be to send the child to school with a receptive attitude toward the values and norms advocated by the school personnel.[83]

In discussing fathers, emphasis is more often placed upon blocked mobility, or mobility pessimism. Swift, for example, found that 'with the middle class, the father's dissatisfaction with his job and its prospects related significantly to the likelihood of his child's success in the 11 + .[84] Cohen found for her sample that working-class fathers who were similarly dissatisfied were more likely than other fathers to have sons planning to go to college.[85] Kahl found that his 'getting ahead' fathers were unhappy and dissatisfied with their occupational status.[86] This would appear, indeed, to be a factor of some considerable importance, but we still need to know whether it operates simply as a determinant of parental ambition vicariously expressed through the child, or whether, as Kahl's argument would suggest, it operates at a deeper level. The 'mobility pessimism' itself, that is to say, may be the result of strong achievement values or an achievement drive which has for some reason been blocked.

At the same time Harrington has suggested that when blocked mobility leads to frustration, and pressure on the child to succeed *in place of* the parent, the result is likely to be unfavourable for the child's mobility. 'The family in which educational success is too much the price of parental approval to be enjoyed for its own sake,' she argues, 'is unlikely to throw up creative ability, and where the child is treated as an extension of the parental self-image, self-direction cannot be expected.'[87]

Many of the findings with respect to social class differences in family life are also applicable to differences between Negro and white families in the United States, since Negro fathers are more likely to be employed in unskilled manual work, and less likely to be employed in occupations involving authority and responsibility. In addition they suffer the 'discriminatory social caste-class system in America with its historic origins in the institution of slavery'.[88] The social class gradations are also less marked for Negroes, 'because Negro life in a caste society is considerably more homogeneous than is life for the majority group'.[89] Research on the specific problems of Negro self-identity is however relatively sparse, since race and class are often confounded; such research as there is, is concerned almost exclusively with lower-class family life, and findings are often contradictory.[90] There is however evidence that Negro students have aspirations as high or even higher than white students.[91]

This review of family life serves therefore to underline the general conclusions already drawn, that our only hope to understand more about class differences in achievement is by a greater understanding of the general socialization process. We need to know how the child acquires not only the values and skills of his group but, even more significantly in a society where education is a major key to social mobility, the ability and the motivation to learn new skills and new values. This requires, it is hardly necessary to add, more than the sociological approach alone. It is an interdisciplinary concept and requires interdisciplinary methods, and in particular an emphasis on the relationships between personality and social structure. If however sociology is to make its full contribution it is vitally necessary that it should go beyond the descriptive studies of social-class differences with which it has frequently been content in the past, and consider, as it is indeed beginning to do, the actual process of socialization itself. Before moving on to this topic, however, it is necessary to look briefly at what evidence we have on the special case of the achievement syndrome and its relationship to the education of girls.

5 Women: a special case

We have already noticed that the pattern of sex differences in school achievement are quite different from those associated with social class. Girls tend to do better than boys right through the primary school and it is only in the later stages of secondary education that they begin to fall behind. On the other hand their achievement seems to be even more strongly dependent on social class background than the achievement of boys. There are also very marked differences between countries in the extent to which girls stay on at school and go on into higher education. Yet, although these sexual disparities in educational achievement have long been known, they have attracted much less interest than the inequalities in educational opportunity between social classes or racial and ethnic groups. This is now changing rapidly, and although the evidence is still meagre, a sociology of sexual differentiation is on its way.

One of the reasons for the lack of interest in sex differences in educational achievement is that they have been accepted as unproblematic or 'natural', relating as they do to the sharp differences in the social and occupational roles of men and women which characterize all societies to some extent, although there are of course major differences both in comparative and in historical terms. To a large extent women in contemporary industrial societies are not seen as fully involved in the occupational structure at all, other than in terms of their husband's job, and studies of social mobility customarily calculate the movement of a woman in terms of the difference between her father's occupation and that of her husband, rather than her own. It is significant, too, that Turner, in his study of the correlates of ambition, measured the ambition of girls in terms of the job they wanted for their husband, arguing that 'it can be safely assumed that the husband's occupation is the key status for most women in American society'.[92]

Under these circumstances education will have a different meaning for girls and their parents. Although its functional or vocational element may not be entirely unimportant, particularly as women work not only before marriage, but increasingly, return to work afterwards, the subordinate part played by the wife's occupational role will undoubtedly set limits to her own ambition. At the same time education may come to have an important symbolic function, particularly for the middle classes,[93] even when it is not seen as preparation for a career. Clignet, for example, has drawn attention to the fact that 'the relatively easy access of French women to institutions of higher learning is not perceived as incompatible with the perpetuation of the traditional role imposed upon them'.[94] The very high proportion of middle-class girls going on to college in the United States has also gone hand-in-hand with a strong orientation towards marriage and a family rather than a career.[95]

It is against this background that we must set the lower educational aspirations of both girls and their parents. The Wisconsin study, for example, found that parents were not only less likely to encourage high educational aspirations for their daughter, but when funds were short were more likely to spend them on their son's education.[96] The Robbins Report also drew attention to the 'lack of parental enthusiasm for their daughters' higher education'.[97] This may express itself in a variety of ways. Douglas, for example, claimed that when middle-class parents send their daughters to fee-paying schools they seek social rather than academic advantages.[98]

On the other hand there is some evidence that this is changing. There is a new militancy on the part of academic women and there have been attempts, particularly in the United States, to end discrimination not only in higher education but in academic and other employment.[99] If this mood continues it seems likely to have far-reaching effects on the attitude of women towards their career. A recent study of women from a New England university graduating in 1967, 1968, 1969, and 1970 found that the commitment to work was increasing all the time.[100] The striking finding by Lueptow that achievement values were higher for females than for males in a recent study of high-school seniors may also be interpreted as a sign of change, although there is no strictly comparable material for an earlier period.[101]

It should perhaps be added that these recent changes may be to the benefit of middle-class rather than working-class women. The increase in the proportion of women graduate students in the United States and women undergraduates in this country may very well mean that only middle-class girls are approaching the pattern of entry into higher education already set by middle-class boys. If this is so, then without a corresponding change in aspirations on the part of working-class girls and their parents the gap in the educational achievement of working-class and middle-class women could well widen. Moreover, under conditions of heavy competition for university places middle-class women could even come to displace working-class men. Hutchison and McPherson in a survey of entrants to Scottish universities over a ten-year period between 1962 and 1972 have demonstrated that this was indeed the case, particularly in the over-subscribed non-science areas.[102] This is further evidence of the complex interrelationship between sex and social class in educational achievement, since it makes it clear that sexual inequalities exist within the much wider framework of social class differences in achievement. On the other hand the key to an understanding of both sexual and social class inequalities has seemed to many to lie in differences in the pattern of socialization, and particularly to that part of the socialization process which takes place within the family. It is to this area of the sociology of education that we must now turn.

5 The family, the socialization process and achievement

1 Social class, child-rearing studies and the achievement syndrome

It is perhaps useful to begin this chapter by looking briefly at what we know of social class differences in child-rearing behaviour since these are fairly widely documented, at least in the United States, and present us with a fairly consistent pattern of findings over a wide range of behaviour. Bronfenbrenner, for example, in a widely quoted summary of a large number of studies concluded that 'though more tolerant of expressed impulses and desires the middle-class parent has higher expectations for the child'. Moreover, in matters of discipline, working-class parents are more likely to employ physical punishment, while middle-class families rely more on reasoning, isolation, appeals to guilt, etc. At the same time, studies report the middle classes as 'more acceptant and equalitarian while those in the working class are orientated toward maintaining order and obedience'.[1]

Kohn has attempted to relate working-class techniques of child-rearing to working-class values. He argues that 'the conditions under which middle- and working-class parents punish their pre-adolescent children physically, or refrain from doing so, appear to be quite different. Working-class parents are more likely to respond in terms of the immediate consequences of the child's actions, middle-class parents in terms of their interpretation of the child's intent in acting as he does. This reflects differences in parental values. Working-class parents value for their children qualities that ensure respectability; desirable behaviour consists essentially of not violating prescriptions. Middle-class parents value the child's development of internalized standards of conduct; desirable behaviour consists essentially of acting according to the dictates of one's own principles.'[2] Kohn specifically relates parent-child relationships to

differences in the conditions of life, and particularly the occupational conditions of the different social classes. It is, he suggests, the
greater degree of self-direction present in middle-class occupations
which leads them to value self-direction in their children and so
encourage such qualities as curiosity and self-control. Working-
class parents, on the other hand, stress such qualities as honesty,
obedience, and neatness, because in their working lives what is
mainly required of them is that they should follow explicit rules laid
down by someone in authority.[3] Along rather different lines
McKinley has argued that 'the greater punitiveness and the more
common rejection of the child by parents in the urban lower classes
is a consequence of the parent's greater frustration and stronger
feelings of threat'.[4]

In a later paper with Carroll, Kohn considered class differences in
the allocation of parental responsibilities. He found that middle-
class mothers tended to emphasize the father's obligation to be as
supportive as the mother herself, whereas working-class mothers
saw the father's responsibilities as lying more in the imposition of
constraints. Middle-class fathers tended to agree with the mothers'
conception of their role, especially as it applied to sons, but
working-class fathers seemed to see child-rearing as their wives'
responsibility and rejected not only the supportive but also the
constraining or disciplinary role.[5]

The research described so far has been entirely American, and it is
interesting to speculate how far national differences in child-rearing
affect this picture. Cross-national studies made at the Department of
Child Development and Family Relationships at Cornell University have found, for example, considerable differences in child-
rearing methods between England, Germany and the United States,
including such aspects as parental warmth, parental control, and
parent-child contact. On the whole, parents in the United States are
higher in parental warmth and parental contact and lower in parental
control than are English parents.[6]

It seems likely, however, that within countries class differences
will elsewhere follow similar patterns to those reported for the
United States. In England, for example, the study by the Newsons of
social-class differences in infant care suggested that working-class
families used more physical punishment. Working-class fathers
were also less likely to participate in the care of the child.[7]

There have been several attempts to develop typologies of child-rearing which would differentiate between the middle and working classes. Kerckhoff, for example, has suggested a three-fold typology of parent-child relationships. This includes the basic permissive-restrictive differentiation noted by Bronfenbrenner; a distinction between love-orientated and power-assertive forms of the parent-child relationship; and a third dichotomy based on the significance of explanation in parental discipline. He distinguishes between parental responses that are simply expressive and those that are explanatory; that is to say, when there is an attempt to make the values explicit.[8]

Finally we may look at Bernstein's distinction between positional and person-orientated families. In the positional family, power, or the right to command, is in terms of formal status, such as age or sex. There is a clear separation of roles, both as between husband and wife and parents and children. In the person-orientated family status ascription by age and sex is much reduced, and behaviour is subject to discussion with parents.[9] Bernstein suggests that the positional family is characteristic of the traditional working class which is embedded in the community, whereas the person-orientated family is characteristic of the middle-class family.

Bernstein's typology clearly owes a great deal to previous work into child-rearing patterns, but he has also carried out an intensive study of a group of middle- and working-class mothers in which they were questioned extensively on their behaviour towards their children.[10] On the basis of these interviews Bernstein and his associates have constructed an index of maternal communication and control. High scores on this index are obtained by mothers who, for example, do not avoid or evade difficult questions, rely on explanation rather than coercive or threatening forms of control, and value highly the educational use of toys. They found a relationship between high scores on their index of communication and control, and high scores on a measure of educational orientation. Mothers who scored highly on this measure read to their children frequently, were favourably disposed towards the teachers, and took positive steps to prepare their child for the start of school. Bernstein and his associates also found that middle-class mothers were more likely to achieve high scores on his index of communication and control, although it must be remembered that these findings are based on the mothers' own reports rather than on a series of observations.

On the other hand a study by Wootton, although on a small scale, provides striking confirmation of class differences in parent-child interaction even when more direct methods are used. Recordings were made in the homes of 20 four-year-old children with no researcher present, and the talk of parents and child subsequently analyzed. The pattern of control that emerged is closely comparable to that described both by Bernstein and by the Newsons in Nottingham. There was also much more interaction between middle-class parents and their children. For example, longer discussions took place in middle-class homes, and middle-class parents were more involved with their children in games requiring a high degree of adult participation. At the same time, in working-class homes, the television was switched on for longer periods of time, and working-class children tended to play more outside the home. Wootton, as do the Newsons and Bernstein, stressed the more constructive use made by middle-class parents of the child's fantasy. As a result of these differences, Wootton argues, the working-class child is left more in charge of his own construction of reality.[11]

An interesting paper by Ford, Young and Box, although not making explicit reference to Bernstein's theory, describes the working-class family in terms which are strikingly similar to his position-orientated family. They argue that the particular childhood experiences of the working classes limits the development of role-playing abilities; they 'are able only to play but not to play at roles'.[12]

The discovery of class-linked patterns of child-rearing does not in itself explain social class differences in school achievement, although it may provide us with useful cues for further research. Nor must the differences which have emerged be taken too far. In the first place it is not easy to discover a simple yet effective technique for studying parental behaviour as distinct from attitude. Observational techniques can be devised, but they tend to be impracticable for use with large samples. At the same time child upbringing is an extremely complex phenomenon that cannot be contained within a simple formula. The Newsons, for example, have argued that 'it is the *values* behind child-rearing techniques that are important, rather than the techniques themselves', and 'those values need to be seen in the context of the whole situation in which the family lives'.[13]

Moreover, even though there is a consistent pattern running through these research findings which cannot be overlooked, critics have not been slow to point out that the differences to be found, even if significant in a statistical sense, are often quite small in magnitude. This point has recently been made in a re-examination and updating of Bronfenbrenner's analysis of the use of corporal punishment,[14] and the same criticism can be made, for example, of Kohn's highly influential study. Differences *within* classes therefore become of crucial importance. Bernstein, for example, locates his positional family in the 'traditional' working class and suggests that it is its close links with the community that gives it its special characteristics. He suggests that changes in England since the war which have tended to differentiate the working-class family from its community may be creating the conditions for more individualized relationships.[15]

Toomey has described what he calls 'home-centred' working-class parents, who show a high level of expenditure on the home. He suggests, tentatively, that 'one of the key features in the emergence of this new home-centred pattern is the withdrawal of the husband from strong involvement with his independent group of male friends'. Toomey found that home-centred working-class families in his study showed a greater degree of interest and participation in the children's education, and higher educational attainment on the part of their sons even when the income of the family was held constant. He does not, however, provide any information on patterns of child-rearing.[16]

An alternative approach is to examine in a more direct way the relationship between child-rearing patterns and measures either of the achievement syndrome or achievement itself, and although such studies are not always strictly comparable, nor even altogether consistent in their findings, they are worth examining in some detail.

Rosen has carried out an interesting observational study of parent-child relationships in an experimental situation. Although only 40 boys and their parents were studied they were carefully selected and I.Q. was held constant. The boys were given five tasks involving both mental and intellectual skills, and an attempt was made to involve the parents in their sons' performance. Rosen concluded that the parents of boys with high achievement motivation tended to have higher aspirations for them to do well at the tasks. 'They set up standards of excellence for the boy even when none is given, or if a standard is given will expect him to do better than average. As he progresses they tend to react to his performance with warmth and approval or, in the case of the mother especially, with disapproval if he performs poorly.' The mothers of boys with high achievement motivation tended to become emotionally involved in the boys' performance, whereas the fathers were willing to take a back seat. Rejecting dominating fathers were associated with low achievement motivation in their sons.[17]

A further study by Rosen compared socialization patterns and achievement motivation using samples of boys from the United States and from Brazil. There were considerable differences in the scores for achievement imagery, the mean score for the American boys in the sample being more than twice as large as the Brazilian score. At the same time Brazilian mothers were less likely to train their sons in self-reliance, autonomy and achievement. This is associated with a characteristic family structure in which authoritarian fathers were combined with protective and indulgent mothers.[18]

Studies of school achievement have also emphasized the same features of parental control. For example, a study of high scorers in reading amongst Grade One children described this same mixture of 'emotionally positive interaction' and 'controlling, preventing and prohibiting disciplinary techniques'. Low scorers, on the other hand, 'seem to be liberally treated to direct physical punishment'. The study concludes that the high scorers 'perceive their parents as having a controlling and limiting role', but that 'this circumstance is counterbalanced by concrete evidence that these controlling persons love them'.[19] A more recent study by Drews and Teahan investigated the attitudes of mothers of over- and under-achievers, of both high and average intelligence. The two groups were matched with respect to father's occupational status. The authors found that the mothers of high achievers were more authoritarian and more restrictive than the mothers of low achievers.[20]

On the other hand, the findings of other studies are to some extent contradictory. Morrow and Wilson, for example, studied the family relations of bright over-achieving and under-achieving high-school boys as they were perceived by the boys themselves. The groups studied were relatively homogeneous in intelligence and socio-economic status. The authors found that over-achievers were more likely to describe their families as sharing recreation, ideas and confidences, and 'as approving and trusting, affectionate, encouraging (but not pressuring) with regard to achievement, and relatively non-restrictive and non-severe'.[21] It is not clear, however, how far the contrast in the two sets of findings is due to the differences in method between the two studies. Morrow and Wilson studied the boys' reports of their families, whereas Drews and Teahan studied the responses of the mothers to a questionnaire. This difference may be quite an important one in that several studies have suggested that the successful high-school student is conforming, orderly, docile and conventional.[22] If this is so, then it is possible that such conforming and docile boys do not perceive their parents as controlling even when they are making considerable demands upon them.

Another important difference between the two studies is that, whereas Drews and Teahan were concerned only with mothers, Morrow and Wilson asked the boys about their parents. Yet the work by Rosen and others on the achievement motive has indicated that the roles of mother and father may be very different in the development of a high need for achievement. Indeed, in the study of *boys* it is the mothers who play the dominant role in 'achievement training', and the fathers must be prepared to stand aside. Authoritarian fathers are associated with low achievement motivation. Studies which mix boys and girls and which ask simply about parental attitudes and behaviour may therefore be misleading.

The other aspect of the achievement syndrome is achievement value, and there are some, although not many, studies which attempt to relate child-rearing methods to level of achievement values. Douvan, for example, investigated the occupational aspirations of 1,000 high-school boys from white-collar and skilled-manual families. On the basis of these aspirations she separated those whose aspirations were above those of their fathers' occupations, that is those whose aspirations were upward, from those whose aspirations were downward. Using the boys' own perception of their parents, she found that the upward-aspiring boys reported their parents as likely to employ 'mild and essentially verbal discipline and use physical punishment infrequently'. At the same time these boys reported a congenial relationship with their parents. They shared leisure activities, and projective measures revealed little covert hostility towards parental figures.[23] This study has a number of weaknesses. The boys' own perceptions were the basis rather than the parents' attitudes and behaviour, and no attempt was made to differentiate between mothers and fathers. Nevertheless it points up two features which have received considerable attention in child-development studies, the emotional involvement of parents and child and the use of verbal rather than physical methods of discipline.

A number of writers have drawn attention to the significance of love-orientated techniques of discipline, which focus on using the love relationship with the child to shape his behaviour. These techniques 'are more likely to be correlated with internalized reactions to transgressions (feelings of guilt, self-responsibility, confession) and with non-aggressive or co-operative social relations. On the other hand, power-asserting techniques in controlling the child are more likely to correlate with externalized reactions to transgression (fear of punishment, projected hostility) and with non-co-operative, aggressive behaviour.'[24] Reasoning along similar lines, Rosen has suggested that the employment of love-orientated methods of control are likely to lead to the internalization of parental values. Using questionnaires based on Kluckholn's value orientations he compared 122 mother-son pairs, the boys varying in age from 8 to 14. Mothers whose values were similar to those of their sons were found to resort to love-orientated techniques, such as displays of affection, reasoning and appeals to standards, rather more frequently than mothers whose sons tended not to share their values. They were also more likely to resort to early independence training measured by Winterbottom's questionnaire items. On the other hand, mothers with a strong achievement orientation were no more likely to have a son sharing their values than mothers with low achievement values.[25]

An interesting attempt both theoretically and methodologically to investigate the relationship between child-rearing techniques and value orientation is undoubtedly Strodtbeck's study of family power, need for achievement and achievement values.[26] Family power was measured in terms of the amount of participation in family discussion by family members, using Bales' interaction process categories to analyse a tape-recording of the discussion. Strodtbeck found a very complex relationship in which the crucial factor appeared to be the balance of power between the father and mother in relation to the power of the son. Where the mother's power was high, so were her achievement value scores, and those of her son. Strodtbeck suggests as a possible interpretation of these findings that low decision-making power in the family results in a generalization of this inadequacy to matters outside the family. However, as Strodtbeck himself points out, it is 'unwise to generalize too much on the basis of one specially selected set of families', and he offers his hypothesis as 'highly tentative until confirmed by further research'.

More recently, Katkovsky, Crandall and Good have found a relationship between children's beliefs in their own control and responsibility for events and parental behaviour. Using both interviews with parents and questionnaires, they found that where parents were rated as protective, nurturant, approving and non-rejecting, children were more likely to believe that they, rather than someone or something else, were responsible for their intellectual achievement.[27] Elder, in another recent study, has laid emphasis on the frequency of parental explanation.[28]

Banks and Finlayson in the study described earlier[29] also examined patterns of child-rearing in relationship to school achievement. The child-rearing measures were based upon lengthy interviews with both parents, who were then rated in terms of warmth and approval, and methods of discipline and control. It was found that successful parents were more likely to have affectionate and above all approving relationships with their children. They were also more likely to use reasoning and explanation, and avoid the more coercive forms of discipline. Further analysis revealed a relationship between social class background, patterns of child-rearing and a high level of need for achievement. At the same time, these same differences in patterns of child-rearing also differentiated between successful and unsuccessful boys *within* the working class. This was particularly striking since the parents of successful working-class boys did not seem to be significantly better off either in material standards or in educational background than parents of unsuccessful working-class boys.

Interestingly, a recent study using black children from working-class families in Harlem came to very similar conclusions. An experienced social worker rated the families on a number of dimensions of parental behaviour and attitudes. High-achieving children in comparison with low achievers were found to come from homes where there was a high level of parental interest, an orderly home environment, the use of rational discipline and an awareness of the child as an individual. In this study, however, high achievers seemed to come from somewhat better socio-economic circumstances within the working class.[30]

As Anderson has pointed out, 'perhaps reports from parents about how they rear their children reflect as much as they explain the school attainment of these children'.[31] There is certainly some evidence in the Banks and Finlayson study that 'the warm, loving and highly approving parents of these successful boys were responding, in part at least, to the behaviour of their sons, who seemed, from the interviews, to be ready to conform to adult expectations to an unusually high degree'.[32] On the other hand, from the evidence available in this study and elsewhere, it does not seem possible to understand the discipline techniques used by parents simply as a response to the behaviour of their children. Rather we have to come to terms with a complex pattern of interaction in which many different kinds of relationship are involved.

Research into the socialization of girls and its relationship to achievement has recently been examined in some detail by Boocock.[33] One of the most important sources is Maccoby's review of studies of early sex role differentiation and training[34] which demonstrate the way in which parents influence and strengthen the very different interests and attitudes expressed by boys and girls from a very early age. The 'feminine' personality characteristics encouraged in girls, such as obedience, friendliness, and affection, are helpful to school achievement, particularly in the early years, and may indeed, as Sexton has argued, lead to many boys, and particularly the more 'masculine' boys, becoming misfits at school. She found that 'the more masculine the boy the lower his academic average'.[35]

At a later stage, and particularly in college or university, the picture changes. As Boocock sums it up, 'to the extent that girls are socialized not to be competitive, they tend to inhibit intellectual activities that might be defined as unfeminine. They may still want to get good grades, where this reflects obedience and the desire to please people, but not to perform at such a high level as to appear aggressive'. The high-achieving girl is therefore more 'masculine' than other girls. Kagan and Moss, for example, found that girls who were bold and daring from the ages 10 to 14 became the most intellectual women as adults.[36]

There is also some evidence that, whereas warm, supportive mothers and democratic rather than authoritarian fathers are important in the production of high-achieving boys, the reverse is true for girls. As Boocock puts it, what 'girls benefited from was *freedom* from maternal restrictions, plus supportive behaviour from their *fathers*'.[37] This is also borne out interestingly enough by accounts of

107

the relationship between nineteenth-century feminists and their fathers.

2 Language and learning

So far in this chapter no reference has been made to the work undertaken by Bernstein and his colleagues on language. Yet clearly the acquisition of language is not only a highly important aspect of socialization but would seem to have implications of a crucial kind for all human learning, and not only the learning that goes on in schools. Lawton, in pointing to the origins of much recent work in the writings of Russian psychologists like Luria and Vygotsky, has emphasized that 'language is the uniquely human attribute which enables us to learn, think creatively and change socially'. Indeed language, he goes on to point out, 'not only helps us to understand *why* things are as they are, but it also enables us to see what *might* be'.[38]

Bernstein's major contribution has been, again in Lawton's words, 'to illustrate a connection between social structure, language use, and educability'.[39] He has tried, that is to say, to relate social class differences in school achievement, or educability, to class differences in language use or linguistic codes.

In his early work in particular[40] Bernstein was chiefly concerned with mapping two linguistic codes characteristic of the middle classes on the one hand, and the working classes, particularly the lower working classes on the other. At this stage social class is loosely defined but is mainly seen in terms of such attributes as level of education and economic function. At first he called these linguistic codes public and formal language, but as his theory develops these are replaced by the terms restricted and elaborated codes.

Although the differences between the two codes can be expressed in terms of their grammatical differences it is an understanding of their function in communication which is at the heart of Bernstein's theories. Fundamentally,[41] the restricted code is a language of *implicit* rather than *explicit* meaning. It is characterized by both simplification and rigidity. The vocabulary is drawn from a narrow range. The speaker's intentions are relatively unelaborated verbally, and there is an emphasis on concrete descriptive, tangible and visible symbolism. The elaborated code on the other hand encourages the speaker to focus upon the experience of others as different from his own. Speakers are forced to elaborate their meanings and make them both explicit and specific.

The restricted code, Bernstein argued, 'orients its speaker to a less complex conceptual hierarchy and so to a lower order of casuality. What is made available for learning through elaborated and restricted códes is radically different'. In this way he links the linguistic codes to the concept of educability.[42]

The restricted and elaborated codes are linked by Bernstein to the typology of family control which was described in the previous section. In the positional family judgments and decision-making is a function of *status*. A child who challenges that authority is told 'Because I tell you', or 'Because I'm your father'. Such a system of communication, Bernstein argues, does not encourage the verbal exploration of individual intentions and motives, or the verbal elaboration of individual differences and judgments. It is in this kind of family system that we find the restricted code.

In the person-orientated family, in contrast, the role system actively promotes an orientation towards the motives and dispositions of others, since there is less separation of roles, and rules and behaviour are subject to discussion. In consequence social control will be based upon 'linguistically elaborated meanings' with power used only as a last resort. Special forms of arbitration, reconciliation and explanation will develop, which will necessitate an early promotion of language development.

In his later writings the family control system is the link between the linguistic code and social class. If the elaborated code is more likely to be found in middle-class families it is only because such families are more likely to use person-orientated systems of control. Moreover, as the last section indicated, the research of Bernstein and his associates in the late sixties was concerned to demonstrate class differences in mothers' communication and control.

Although his typology of family control, therefore, assumes an increasingly important aspect in his general theory, it is also necessary for Bernstein to demonstrate that there are in fact differences in children's speech, of the kind that he describes. Bernstein himself first demonstrated social class differences in children's speech, and shortly afterwards his findings were confirmed by Lawton in a study of both spoken and written language.[43] A number of significant papers have recently been published which take these early studies very much further. Perhaps the most interesting is the report of the study by Hawkins[44] in which two groups of five-year-old children, one working-class and one middle-class, were given a series of picture cards and asked to tell a story. When the stories were analyzed striking differences were found. Because the middle-class children tended to be more explicit, and context-independent, they were able to communicate far more information than the context-dependent working-class children.

The research reported so far has all been by Bernstein and his team, but his general orientation has been supported by a number of studies chiefly in the United States. Perhaps the best known is that by Hess and Shipman who observed the behaviour of Negro mothers and their four-year-old children in experimental teaching sessions.[45] Much earlier, Schatzman and Strauss, analyzing the speech of adults, found a tendency on the part of lower-class respondents to describe events as seen through their own eyes, and less ability to take the listeners' role.[46] The Institute for Developmental Studies at the New York Medical College, under the direction of Martin Deutsch, has conducted investigations into the language patterns of deprived children and discovered a deficiency in the 'abstract and categorical use of language'.[47]

More recently Ward has used Bernstein's distinction between positional and person-orientated families in a study of language learning by rural black children in Louisiana. She found differences in the manner in which the mothers of these children and middle-class mothers perceived their role as teacher; a difference which sometimes had subtle linguistic consequences.[48]

An interesting study from Hungary has looked at social class differences in speech using material from the Bernstein Research Unit. Like Hawkins they found social class differences in the level of context-dependency of children's speech. Moreover working-class children living in a high status area showed less context-dependence in their speech than those living in a low status area.[49]

The evidence from these sources is, of course, inadequate as a full test of Bernstein's theory, which is not only complicated and subtle but extremely general and comprehensive. Moreover, not unnaturally, some of the widespread attention given to his work has been of a highly critical kind. Indeed, since some of these criticisms have been answered by Bernstein himself and by others, there is now a widespread literature on the controversy, and it is only possible to provide a very brief summary here.[50]

Most of Bernstein's critics derive their position from the work of the American linguist Labov, who is critical of the methodology of much of the work that has been done on children's speech. Labov argues[51] that an adult must enter into the right social relations with a child if he wants to find out what he can do. To substantiate this point Labov has compared relatively formal interviews with interviewers talking very informally with black children. The amount and complexity of talk produced was very much greater in the informal situation. Moreover studies made by Labov in the ghetto area revealed a community in which the competitive exhibition of verbal skills in various games and contests, for example ritual insults, was a source of peer-group status.

The failure of these highly-articulate black boys to do well at school is explained by Labov in terms of the low value attached by the peer group to academic success. Reading in particular is rarely if ever used outside school. Although Labov concedes that middle-class speech is different, he argues that it is not necessarily more useful. The elaborated *code* indeed, he suggests, may be no more than an elaborated *style*.

Much of the debate between Bernstein and his critics has centred upon the extent to which the restricted code is an inferior form of speech. Bernstein has consistently denied that he intended to convey any judgment of this kind, but Grimshaw for example has pointed out that by using terms like descriptive rather than analytic, and concrete rather than abstract, his account carries implications of inferiority even if they were unintended. Consequently the argument that the restricted code is different rather than inferior does not really help us a great deal, because what is really at issue is the relationship, if there is one, between language and educability. Halliday, in an interesting foreword to Vol. II of *Class, Codes and Control,* has argued that educational failure cannot be reduced to linguistic failure in the sense of underlying logic or language form. Nevertheless he accepts that there *is* a relationship between language and school success or failure, and that it lies, as Bernstein suggests, in the *social* functions of language in different groups, and its effect on the child's social learning and his response to education. The development of Bernstein's theories, therefore, lies in what he himself has described as a discontinuity between school and home, and it is for this reason that much of his recent theoretical work has been on the school. It will be necessary therefore to return to Bernstein's theories in a later chapter.

3 The concept of cultural deprivation

The concept of cultural deprivation came to prominence in the 1960s in the United States, in an attempt to explain the educational problems of children from Negro and white lower-class families. By placing the emphasis on differences in culture, rather than on material circumstances, the concept had obvious associations both with the work on value orientations described in the previous chapter, and on the linguistic theories of Deutsch and Hess and Shipman in the United States, and of Bernstein in England. Moreover, since low income, poor housing and other aspects of material poverty can be seen as a form of deprivation, so it was natural to refer similarly to cultural deprivation for those whose cultural background was seen as a source of under-achievement at school.

In fact, however, as critics were not slow to point out,[52] the term is a misleading one, since it seems to imply that the groups in question have no culture of their own, just as the concept of linguistic deprivation is sometimes taken to imply that the groups in question have no language, or are non-verbal. While it is doubtful whether those who coined the term had this in mind, it is true that the concept easily lends itself to what Williams has described as a deficit theory of educational under-achievement, and the view that what is needed is a kind of cultural injection as an antidote. This approach has been particularly influential in the development of pre-school enrichment programmes in the United States, and is well exemplified in the approach of Bereiter and Englemann, Deutsch and other structured programmes of intervention. It also lies behind such large-scale pre-school programmes as the well-known Head Start.[53]

Although programmes like Head Start and the earlier Great Cities Schools Improvement Programme started off with great enthusiasm, later attempts at evaluating their success were rarely able to demonstrate any substantial and lasting improvement. In consequence the mood changed to one of profound pessimism and it became widely accepted that compensatory education in the United States had failed. It seems likely however that this is a premature conclusion since not only many of the schemes themselves but also the methods of evaluation can be shown to be inadequate.[54] Moreover there *are* examples of successful ventures including the work of Bereiter and Engelmann already mentioned, and the Early Training Project at Peabody College. It is in general the more structured and the more intensive programmes which have succeeded, and, as Hunt has pointed out, the 'traditional play school has little to offer to children of the poor'.[55] In this country, too, there have been pre-school programmes which appear to have had some success.[56] On the whole however the evidence indicates that to make compensatory education work will be neither easy nor cheap.

At a more radical level compensatory education has been criticized for its almost exclusive attention to what are seen as the deficiencies of the individual child and his family. Bernstein, for example, has claimed that the concept 'serves to direct attention away from the internal organization and the educational content of the school'.[57] Keddie in similar vein has suggested that 'schools could become flexible in their willingness to recognize and value the life experience that every child brings to school'.[58] This line of thinking has sparked off much useful research into schools and the part they play in fostering under-achievement. It will be considered in subsequent chapters.

Yet another attack on compensatory education has come from those who argue that the problem of under-achievement is one of poverty and discrimination, and that these must be solved outside the school.[59] Morton and Watson go further and see compensatory education as part and parcel of a liberal ideology which 'advocates social change in piecemeal fashion within the existing framework of social institutions'.[60] From this point of view compensatory education programmes may even be seen 'as a diversion from the pusuit of genuine egalitarian policy'.[61]

The idea of the community school appears to be one way out of this dilemma. Many compensatory education programmes have, it is true, experimented with closer ties between the parents and the school but most of these have taken the view that they were training the parents to prepare their children for school. The community school in contrast is an attempt to regenerate the community through the school. In Halsey's words, 'the school must set out to equip their children to meet the grim reality of the social environment in which they live and to reform it in all its aspects'.[62] The aim is to turn the community into a school and the school into a community'.[63]

Although Halsey's report on the Educational Priority Areas is enthusiastic about the community school many problems still remain. The most obvious danger, as Halsey himself recognizes, is that of creating a curricula restricted to local horizons, rather than in C. Arnold Anderson's words, a 'bridge between cultures. Unless we reject the emerging world culture, curricula must be broader than the patterns for living to be found in the homes of pupils.'[64]

At a more fundamental level in the argument, however, is what Goody and Watt have called the conflict between oral and literate culture. Writing, they argue, 'establishes a different kind of relationship between the world and its referent, a relationship that is more general and more abstract'. The consequences of literacy, in their view, are wide-reaching and can be seen for example in the idea of logic as 'an immutable and impersonal mode of discourse' and in the distinction between myth and history.[65] Although Goody and Watt are writing primarily of the transition from non-literate to literate societies there is a very real sense in which working-class culture as described by both Bernstein *and* Labov still retains, to a much greater extent than the middle classes, the characteristics of an oral culture. From this point of view, therefore, the school must be seen as bridging a wider gap than that between the parochial and the national or even the international. Moreover it is an issue which cannot be solved by arguments about the relative values of working-class or middle-class culture, or even by a kind of cultural relativism which argues that cultures are different but equal. Clearly these are complex issues which ultimately take us outside the sociology of education into the world of political and moral choice. Nevertheless the discussion provides a useful link between socialization in the family on the one hand, and the politics of education on the other, as well as pointing towards the sociology of the school.

6 The politics of education

1 *The structure of power relationships*

Sociologists have until recently shown little interest in the political dimensions of the educational system and much of the work on educational decision-making has been undertaken by related disciplines. Past editions of this book have drawn extensively from comparative education, from political science, and from educational administration for the contents of this chapter. While the necessity to draw on other disciplines still remains, the growing discontent with the structural functional approach has led some sociologists to examine the process of education not as reflecting the needs of society but as expressing the dominance of one group over another. Bourdieu for example defines the sociology of education specifically in terms of its role in understanding 'the contribution made by the educational system to the reproduction of the structure of power relationships and symbolic relationships between classes'.[1] He sees education as 'one of the most effective means of perpetuating the existing social pattern'[2] and therefore as a profoundly conservative force in society. This arises largely because what the education system both hands on and demands is an aristocratic culture and above all an aristocratic relationship with it.[3] By treating socially conditioned aptitudes as unequal 'gifts', he argues, the school legitimates the transmission of the cultural heritage. Bourdieu's analysis leads him directly into the study of the school curriculum, and into methods of pedagogy and assessment, and will therefore be treated in detail in subsequent chapters.

In the writings of Althusser the educational system is seen in Cosin's words, 'as a site of the class struggle'.[4] In the school the child is provided 'with the ideology which suits the role it has to fulfil in a class society'.[5] In fact, Althusser argues, the school has largely replaced the Church as the dominant Ideological State

Apparatus. It is by an 'apprenticeship in a variety of know-how wrapped up in a massive inculcation of the ideology of the ruling class that the relations of production in a capitalist social formation, i.e. the relations of exploited to exploiters and exploiters to exploited, are largely reproduced.'[6]

One important consequence of looking at educational systems in this way is a revision of the liberal view of educational history, and in particular the faith in schools as levers of social change and reform. For example Richard Johnson, in an examination of educational policy in early Victorian England, has argued that it is best understood as a concern about authority and social control which was 'expressed in an enormously ambitious attempt to determine, through the capture of educational means, the patterns of thought, sentiment and behaviour of the working class.'[7]

In the United States, where the faith in the educational process was greater, the move to demythologize the history of schools has been taken up enthusiastically.[8] Katz for example used the sub-title 'the illusion of educational change in America' in his study of developments in American education. He argues that industrialization and bureaucratization, hand-in-hand, have moulded the American school in the light of values consonant with 'city life and large-scale manufacture'.[9] They have emphasized the values of punctuality, of standardization and system, and of professionalization. 'Newly industrialized people', he suggests, 'must learn to reward a man for what he can do rather than for what he is'.[10]

An interesting outcome of this new approach in the history of American education is a reappraisal of progressive education. Katz, for example, argues that despite the rhetoric of its sponsors, 'progressivism was profoundly conservative, for it sprang from a search for social order.'[11] A similar theme is evident in the work of Spring, who sees the stress on group work, social adjustment and cooperation as a preparation for employment in the modern factory system.[12] This approach is of particular interest because it attempts to relate the educational system to the economy not directly through a functionalistic theory of social needs, but indirectly through the activities of dominant groups in society. Nevertheless, as in structural functionalism, there is the danger of over-simplification. As Lucas has pointed out in a review of Spring's book, 'the plot depends heavily upon imputing the worst of motives to the entire cast of characters'.[13]

A somewhat different analysis of progressive education in the United States is provided by David Swift who argues that the ideology of progressive education helped solve the social problems facing the schools, as a result of their attempt to provide a system of secondary education on a far greater scale than had ever been attempted. Their task was complicated both by the massive immigration which occurred during this period and by the heavy commitment to equality which produced the largely unstreamed comprehensive school. The progressive ideology, he suggests, with its emphasis on cooperation rather than competition, and its stress on expressive activities, helped to legitimize the non-academic curriculum taught by a largely non-academic teaching staff.[14] In this kind of analysis however we are back in a largely structural functional framework.

Margaret Scotford-Archer and Michalina Vaughan have explicitly rejected both the structural functionalistic explanation in terms of social needs, and the Marxist explanation in terms of the class struggle in favour of a model of educational change drawn from Weber's studies of bureaucracy, religion and status. They attempt to develop a general theory of the means by which groups exercise control of educational resources and the ways in which a rival group may challenge this control. Significant factors in this process are the distribution of resources and ideological debate.[15]

An alternative to structural functionalism derived largely from the writings of Weber is also suggested by Collins, who puts forward what he calls a conflict theory of stratification. He suggests that the basic units of society are status groups, who struggle for advantages of wealth, power and prestige. Control over the educational system is important because of the part played by schools in the teaching of particular status cultures.[16]

Smith also sees education in the context of a structure of competing groups, rather than social classes, and may, therefore, be seen as closer to a Weberian than a Marxist analysis, although he does not specifically ally himself with any particular approach. His discussion of the sources of power as resting either on a direct appeal to authority, or the ability to manipulate strategic resources, also seems to owe more to Weber than to Marx.[17]

A more traditional approach to the study of power relationships is through the process of decision-making itself. This method has the advantage of avoiding the dangers of an overly simplistic conspiracy theory, but overlooks the important area of what Bachrach and Baratz have called 'non-decisions'. The process of non-decision making is significant because it allows only relatively minor disputes to become the subject of political conflict.[18] Consequently studies of decision-making in education, or elsewhere, should take into account not only the overt conflicts over policy decisions but also what Etzioni has called the 'community of assumptions' which go unchallenged.

This is well illustrated by Rodney Barker's recent analysis of the part played by the Labour Party in educational policy-making between 1900 and 1951.[19] During this period the Labour Party was in conflict with the Conservative Party on a number of educational issues, of which perhaps the most striking was its long campaign for free secondary education for all. After the Second World War, when the 1944 Education Act had made some form of secondary education a reality for all children, the Labour Party turned increasingly towards the idea of the common or comprehensive secondary school. During this period, too, it gradually formulated its policy towards the public school. It is easy therefore to see the Labour Party as strongly egalitarian in its ideology, in continuous opposition to the elitist policies of Conservative governments, and as promoting during its years of office, egalitarian educational reforms.

In fact, as Barker's study illustrates, the reality is more complex. There was, during the whole of this period, an element of elitism in the Labour Party, although it was strongly meritocratic rather than aristocratic in its implications. The issues which aroused Labour M.P.s during the years after the First World War were 'those which seemed to involve a threat to free, fair and competitive access to the secondary school'.[20] Even after the Party became associated with the idea of the comprehensive school the grammar school 'still held its place in their hearts as the paradigm of educational excellence'.[21] At the time of the 1944 Education Act and for some years afterwards only a radical wing of the Party firmly supported the comprehensive school and this allowed the establishment in most areas of a dual system of grammar and modern schools, even when the Labour Party was in power, at both the national and local level.[22]

An analysis of the comprehensive school movement in France between 1918 and 1940 also shows the reformers confused, between egalitarianism and meritocracy, and equality of opportunity and equality. As in the Labour Party in England the main thrust of the movement was in broadening the social basis of recruitment to the existing educational system.[23]

2 Patterns of administrative control

The structure of administrative control in education is usually conceived by sociologists and others in terms of centralization or decentralization of State control. Hopper for example includes as one of the main discussions of his typology of educational systems, the degree of centralization and standardization. He argues that this is high, for example, in France, Sweden and the U.S.S.R., low in the U.S.A. and Canada, and medium in West Germany, Australia and England.[24] In France for example, schools are tightly controlled even down to the details of the daily curriculum. The U.S.S.R. is another very highly centralized system where details not only of school policy but of day-to-day administration are laid down by the State.

The United States, in contrast, has a very decentralized system. Any interference on the part of the Federal Government has been jealously guarded against. For this reason the State is the administrative unit concerned with educational control. Even at the State level however there is relatively little central control and local school districts, governed by elected school boards, have had considerable autonomy. England, like the United States, has a tradition of decentralization which has deeply influenced the development of education in this country. Not until 1944 did the minister in charge of education have the power to compel backward local authorities to raise their standards, and the initiation of educational plans still remains the prerogative of the local authority, and the control of the curriculum and of activities within the school are still very largely under the control of the school itself. There is however, less local autonomy than in the United States, and the unit of administration at the local level is the local authority rather than the school board. For this reason it is customary to describe the English system as a partnership between central control and local initiative.[25]

More recently, however, there are clear signs that in both England and the United States there has been a growing tendency for power to be concentrated in larger units at the local level, largely in order to secure the resulting economies of scale. At the same time there has been an increase in the power of the central government. In England for example, the Ministry of Education, later the Department of Education and Science, has since 1944 steadily increased its power over such diverse areas as school buildings, the supply of teachers and the curriculum.[26] Even more radically, perhaps, there has been an increase in the power of the central authority over developments in higher education, not excepting the formerly largely autonomous universities.[27] In the United States there is a similar tendency to increase the power of both the State and the Federal Government.

Crozier has suggested that styles of administrative control tend to be characteristic of the entire social structure. They are 'determined by basic cultural traits, and, at the same time, feed back on them'.[28] In France there is a marked social distance between those at different hierarchical levels, such as students and teachers, teachers and administrators, workers and managers. An absence of face-to-face relationships between subordinates also leads, in his argument, to an inability to cooperate for constructive proposals, whether in organizing effective unions or stable political majorities. In decentralized societies, in contrast, there is not only greater contact between superiors and subordinates, but individuals 'do not try to avoid face-to-face relationships'.[29]

Discussions of centralized and decentralized systems of education frequently assume the greater efficiency of centralized forms of control. Small districts in particular may be unable to meet the needs of their own students for qualified teachers or specialized equipment, particularly if they are expected, as they often are in the United States, to finance themselves from their own resources. This produces problems in both small rural areas and city slums. A decentralized system also allows very great differences between areas in educational provision, and indeed centralization has often appealed as a means of producing greater equality in the allocation of resources. In the United States in particular centralization has been seen as the most appropriate method for ending the educational exploitation of black students.

A decentralized system, however, is more likely to be in touch with the wishes and needs of the local community, since a high degree of centralization tends to give greater power to teachers and administrators. The French system, it is suggested, 'may limit the significance of inequities but alienate individuals and induce them to believe they have little control over their own fate'.[30] There is a tendency for local aspirations to be 'channelled toward the centre of the political system through appropriate networks'.[31] It is interesting to note that the development of a more centralized system in the United States has led to demands for a measure of *de-centralization* to provide community control of neighbourhood schools. In the dispute between the New York City Board of Education and the Ocean Hill Brownsville Community, for example, the parents, mainly black, banded together for the right to have control over their own budget, the right to hire and fire the staff, and to engage in contracts and subcontracts.[32]

A centralized system may also become rigid and stereotyped, and one of the advantages of a measure of decentralization is that it makes possible a high degree of innovation and experiment. In Britain for example, it is possible for schools of all kinds to explore a variety of types of organization, of curriculum and of teaching methods on the initiative of local educational authorities or of individual schools.

This dichotomy between centralized and decentralized systems of control although useful up to a point does not however do justice to the very numerous administrative patterns that prevail. Smith[33] for example, has suggested that educational systems may vary along three quite distinct dimensions, lateral autonomy which refers to the number of autonomous agencies within the system, vertical integration which refers to the extent to which an agency is subject to regulation by a superior agency, and centralization which refers to the extent to which delegation occurs within administrative hierarchies. He suggests that although France is high on all three dimensions, and the United States low, thus corresponding to the traditional concepts of centralized and decentralized systems, the case of England is more complex. In the past, for example, England had a high degree of lateral autonomy as many agencies were concerned, quite independently, with the educational process. At present lateral autonomy is intermediate between that of France and the United States, as is the degree of centralization, but in the dimension of vertical integration England is closer to France than to the United States. When there is a high degree of lateral autonomy there may well be differences between agencies in the degree of vertical integration and centralization. In both the United States and in England for example, institutions within the private sector may well have much greater individual autonomy than those inside the administrative structure of the States. Similarly, the control of higher education may follow a very different pattern from that of the control of schools. Within higher education too, there may, as in England, be differences in the system of administrative control as between universities and other types of higher education. The universities, for example have enjoyed much greater autonomy than either the colleges of education or the new polytechnics both of which are in the control of the local education authorities.

The relationship between financial support and administrative control is also a very complex one which permits of no easy generalization. It is true that the granting of public funds will usually be accompanied by some degree of public control, so that private institutions usually have more autonomy than similar bodies receiving public funds. This is true, for example, of public and private secondary schools both in the United States and Britain. On the other hand, as Mushkin has pointed out, there are many ways in which school systems can be given aid from national funds, while still preserving a high degree of local autonomy. 'Grants-in-aid and even tax-sharing schemes are highly flexible tools of inter-governmental finance. They can be shaped in small or large sizes; they can be designed to cover all the costs or only a negligible share. They can be used to equalize variations in local tax resources or make more equal the local tax burdens required for new programme expenditures. They can be used to shape the direction of certain educational programmes, for example for more or fewer vocational schools. Supporting grants have been given to finance all or part of educational programmes, and in addition grants have been offered to encourage demonstrations and experiments.'[34]

Similarly the 1907 Free Place Regulations in England were a deliberate attempt to open up secondary schools to able working-class children, and grant-aid was given only on condition that at least 25 per cent of free places were made available to children from the public elementary schools. It is interesting to notice that these grants were conceived, not only as a spur to local authorities, but also to the, then numerous, endowed grammar schools.

Much of the Federal aid available to schools in the United States also comes into this category. There are, for example, national grants available to develop new high-school textbooks in chemistry and mathematics, to retrain high-school teachers, and to provide summer schools for gifted high-school students interested in science and mathematics.[35] The National Defense Education Act of 1958 also provided a new national system of student aid. All of these examples of financial aid involve no attempt to take control of the actual administration of the schools. A high level of financial assistance is therefore quite compatible with considerable local and institutional autonomy, even if the two are by no means always found together. Mushkin has also shown that there is no need for the decentralized system to forego the advantages of government support. The extent to which government grants can be used to initiate experiments or benefit particularly disadvantaged areas has already been noted. Other government agencies have the task of giving information and advice when it is needed. In Britain, for example, the H.M.I.s have long played a significant part in both primary and secondary education.[36]

One particularly interesting feature of the system in the United States is what Kirst has called the 'crucial role of the judiciary'. The 1954 Supreme Court decision on the illegality of segregated education is an outstanding example, but Kirst claims that 'very large extensions of federal influence have emanated from judicial rulings'.[37] More recently, laws making it illegal to discriminate in admissions or employment on grounds of race, creed, colour, sex or national origin have led to further losses in the autonomy of individual colleges.[38]

The implications of different patterns of control may also vary as a result of differences in historical development and cultural styles. Blondel, for example, has argued that in terms of formal patterns of control, the 'State possesses a whip hand' over the continental universities, and Britain 'is the only European country where there is a legal break between the universities and the State'.[39] Yet the situation in practice is not so different, and in France for example, in spite of the apparent governmental control over matters of curriculum and the appointment of staff, the real decisions are taken by academics just as they are in Britain. Conversely, Blondel argues, the absence of formal control does not of itself ensure independence. He cites the example of the private universities in the United States, which, although independent of the State, are controlled by lay boards who have been known to interfere radically in academic affairs.

One of the main reasons for the academic freedom enjoyed by university teachers in Western Europe, including Britain, is the persistence of aristocratic values which give a superior status to intellectuals. This clashes not only with authoritarian governments, but with the egalitarian values of modern societies. In the United States, the low value placed on the intellectual explains the lack of respect for academic freedom in both State-controlled and private colleges and universities. States, for example, often demand that certain courses be required, or they may prohibit certain subjects. They may order certain kinds of research to be undertaken and reject others. They can and do exert considerable control over the admissions of students, and less frequently over the appointment and dismissal of academic and other staff.[40]

Smith's distinction to which reference has already been made, between power based on authority and power based on the ability to manipulate strategic resources, is obviously very relevant here. So is his distinction between three types of authority, legal authority, professional authority, and the authority which derives from membership in a particular status group.[41]

3 The school and the local community

So far in this chapter we have been concerned at a macro or societal level of analysis. In fact, however, and particularly, although by no means exclusively, in a decentralized system, many educational decisions are taken at the level of the local community. It is, moreover, at this level that decisions made nationally must be implemented, and where they may run counter to local interests and goals.[42] Fortunately, American sociologists are deeply interested in educational decision-making in the local community and the number of such studies in Britain is also now rising. In spite, therefore, of significant gaps in our knowledge, the empirical ground for a study of the politics of education at the community level is under way.

In the United States the school board is the most powerful agency through which community needs and community wishes are represented. For this reason it is useful to begin with an examination of the role of the school board in the American system. The system of elected school boards responsible for the educational needs of the local community, as distinct from all-purpose local authorities which cover a wide variety of functions, has persisted in the United States from the earliest days of public education. This is in contrast to England where school boards were replaced by all-purpose local authorities as long ago as 1902. Moreover the American school boards are normally responsible for much smaller districts than are the English local authorities, so that it is possible to consider them as community agencies in a way that is no longer possible in England. Nevertheless, it is still possible for the school boards to have little real relationship with community affairs and little actual influence on the schools. Consequently we have to ask both how and under what circumstances the school boards actually represent the community, and also to what extent the school boards are able to exert control over the school system. These two questions are, as we shall see, interrelated, but it is convenient to begin by treating them separately. It is also necessary to consider the extent to which a community may impinge upon the school system by other means.

Studies of school board members indicate that they tend to come from the upper or upper middle classes, with a high proportion in professional occupations.[43] According to Crain,[44] involvement in prestigious civic activities, activity in political party work, and activity in some special interest group, such as an ethnic group or organized labour, can all lead to school board membership, and so can the possession of personal wealth and educational expertise. School board membership can be seen as a civic or a political activity and some school board members see it as a route to political advancement. The effect of this kind of background on the policies of school boards is less clear and the evidence that we have suggests that school board members are less conservative than their social status would suggest. Brookover and Erickson[45] conclude that 'perhaps the occupation of the school board member is less important than his intended audience'.

Bidwell has summarized a large number of studies which seem to indicate that the school board is most likely to represent community values when 'the school itself is a community institution, that is the extent to which the schools of a community symbolize its identity and values and provide a focus for the integration of community life.'[46] In such areas there is considerable and active interest in the school and its affairs. The teacher and the principal are likely to be well known in the community, and the school building may be a centre for community activities. Under such circumstances the board is likely to speak for the community rather than the school.

Although school systems as community institutions, in this sense, are more likely to be found in rural areas and small towns where school districts are still small, Bidwell argues that the degree of urbanization alone does not seem to be a critical variable. 'The crucial factors would appear to be the pluralism and segmental quality of community life typical of but not always present in large urban centres.' For example Seeley, Sim and Loosley, in their study of Crestwood Heights, show that a suburban community, even in a highly urban area, can make the school system the centre of community interest if the population is sufficiently homogeneous and child-centred. In Crestwood Heights community control was indirect but nonetheless strong. For example, the board of education used adherence to community values as an important criterion in their choice of director of education.

Where the community is heterogeneous or divided there is no longer sufficient social solidarity to maintain community control of the schools. A study by Vidich and Bensman of a small rural community in New York State shows clearly how this can happen even in a small community which continues to take considerable interest in the affairs of its schools. For historical reasons the majority of members of the school board represent rural interests, and the 'rural members have traditionally been "respectable" prosperous farmers who have been residents of the township for all or most of their lives',[48] but the rural interest is by no means the dominant one in the town, which includes professionals, industrial workers, traditional farmers, shack people and the marginal middle class. Moreover rural dominance has had important consequences for the school. Although farmers represent only one-third of the population, great emphasis in the school curriculum is placed on home economics and agricultural training. Between 1945 and 1951, 21 out of a total of 57 male graduates took the agricultural course, yet only four of the 21 were engaged in farming in 1951. Although the major opportunities for the school graduates lie in industry, business or college, courses preparing them for their career remain at an elementary level. Nor are these the only ways in which rural interest predominate. Jobs in the school bus service, which provides the major political plums that the board has to offer, tend to go to farmers, and teachers from a rural background are favoured in making appointments. Local business interests challenge the school board when school policy affects local business, and these occasions are a major source of controversy over school board affairs, but other interests in the town are represented only through the Parent-Teacher Association.

Much interesting light is thrown on the politics of education at the community level by studies of the process of desegregation. Since the Supreme Court pronounced segregation illegal in 1954,[49] desegregation has proceeded gradually, although often slowly and not by any means always peacefully. Moreover, the existence of widespread residential segregation has made the integration of schools, especially in large urban areas, impossible without the creation of special programmes to transfer children from one area to another, or an extensive rezoning of schools. In fact, in certain large northern cities 'de facto' segregation, as it is called, has actually increased since 1954.

Crain, in a major study of school desegregation,[50] found that school boards which were receptive to civil rights groups and their demands had a high degree of group cohesion. Individually the members were of *high* socio-economic status with *liberal* rather than conservative attitudes. Perhaps the most interesting point he makes is that the school boards which responded most readily to the civil rights movement were in cities which were still largely run by the old civic elite.[51]

Other studies have found that a large negro population is a distinct barrier to desegregation, possibly because it stimulates white resistance. In the North, desegregation was most likely in urban areas in which the educational level of the population was relatively high. In the South a large white sub-population appeared to be the chief hindrance to desegregation.[52]

A great deal of light on some of these issues is thrown by Lilian Rubin's case-study of a 'bussing' controversy in California. At the outset the school board was captured by a group of upper-middle-class liberal integrationists who attempted to use 'bussing' to integrate the schools. They were quickly opposed by a group of anti-integrationist conservative opponents, and in four years the liberals were out of office, and the integration plans abandoned. The conservative opposition was largely from the lower-middle and working classes. They differed from the integrationists not only in having less education but in their educational goals. Whereas the liberals stressed spontaneity and initiative, the conservatives stressed discipline and the three Rs. Rubin however is at great pains to argue that the conservatism and authoritarianism of the anti-integrationist is to be found in 'the objective conditions of their lives', and in 'their hopes, dreams, and fears'.[53]

A similar point is made by Swanson in a study of a school integration controversy in New York City. Opposition, as in the Rubin's study, was found particularly in families at the margins of lower- and middle-class existence. These families had been upwardly mobile from ethnic ghettos, and were hoping to enjoy such middle-class amenities as home ownership, uncrowded and good schools, and safer living conditions.[54]

Both Rubin and Dye stress that weak and vacillating leadership was an important aspect of the situation. The same point is made by David Rogers, who has examined the failure of desegregation in New York, in spite of early support from the board. Another factor which emerges from his study is the part played by a powerful bureaucracy which was opposed to innovation. The unplanned alliance of some school officials, white parents and real estate interests created a strong and effective opposition.[55]

One of the most important sources of community pressure on both the school boards and the school system itself is the parents, either as individuals or organized through Parent-Teacher Associations. The school superintendents studies by Gross[56] mentioned the P.T.A. as a major promoter of public education more frequently than anything else, and both the school superintendents and the school board members mentioned parents as a source of pressure. Indeed 92 per cent of school superintendents and 74 per cent of school board members cited parents and the P.T.A. in their answers to this question.

On the other hand, Bidwell has argued that the P.T.A. is primarily a school-dominated organization since it is 'a means of channelling parent pressures in organizationally acceptable ways, while maintaining parents' involvement and adequate school-parent communication'.[57] Vidich and Bensman show how the high-school principal in a small town can use the P.T.A. for the purpose of gaining acceptance for his educational programmes, 'without, however, making this obvious to the community. For, through the process of committees and agendas, it appears publicly that P.T.A. members themselves, when making their reports, have originated the ideas which have been given them by the principal. Through the complexities of this procedure, the P.T.A. voices the policies of the principal and, in turn, the principal uses the P.T.A. as an informal political instrument against those interests in the village and town which oppose his programme. While doing this, however, he is careful to restrain the P.T.A. if it gets over-ambitious.'[58]

Gans, in his study of Levittowners, has illuminated the highly complex relationship between parents and school systems in a new suburb catering predominantly for lower-middle-class residents. The school superintendent not only took the initiative in founding the P.T.A. but 'personally recruited the actual P.T.A. founders from people he knew and trusted'.[59] His aim was to prevent dissatisfied parents from creating pressure groups which would challenge his policy. Nevertheless he was soon embroiled in the struggles he had hoped to avoid. The first group to cause trouble was the minority of highly-educated, upper-middle-class parents who formed themselves into a Citizens' Committee for Public Schools, and waged several campaigns, some of them successfully, for better educational provision. Later on, a more serious threat came from Levittowners 'who demanded less expensive schools devoted to little more than basic teaching functions'.[60] At one angry meeting, called to protest at the size of the proposed school budget, there was violent criticism of the superintendent's salary and at a newly suggested administrative post for curriculum planning. Other objections raised included teachers' salaries, which some Levittowners thought too high. Much of this opposition came from Catholics who resented having to pay for schools their children did not attend, while having to fund the parochial school as well, but in addition some of the working class in the town opposed educational 'frills' they did not want for their own children. Minar[61] has also presented data suggesting that political conflict over local schools occurs mainly in working-class school districts.

Other local community influences which are likely to exert pressure either on school board members, or on school superintendents, or on both, include local business and commercial organizations, tax-paying associations, the press, churches and political pressure-groups. At the same time Gross's study indicates the extent to which individuals bring pressure to bear for purely personal reasons. Once again we have far too few studies which analyse these pressures and assess their influence. Vidich and Bensman, however, describe the way in which local businessmen unsuccessfully attempted to coerce the school into supporting local shops rather than patronizing lower-priced firms elsewhere.

In spite of the informal pressures of community interests, formal control of the school system lies, of course, with the elected representatives. Kerr, however, in a recent study has presented a picture of the school board members as relatively helpless when confronted with the expertise of the administrator. He argues that under some conditions, which may not be uncommon, school boards chiefly perform the function of legitimating the policies of the school system to the community. This is particularly likely where the electorate fails to watch the representative after his election.[62]

A major study by McCarty and Ramsey suggests, on the other hand, that there are a number of structures of power, of which the inert board, completely dominated by the superintendent, is only one. Their findings indicate however that this type of board is most likely to be found in areas where there is a feeling of resignation. The factional board, in contrast, is dominated by representatives of bitterly opposed factional groups, and the superintendent, far from dominating the board, has to be an alert political strategist to survive. This kind of power structure, they suggest, is characteristic of big cities. The third type of board, which they call pluralist, is also representative of different interests in the community, but there are no permanent factions, and a constant process of realignment. With this kind of board the superintendent becomes a professional adviser, and as such, of course, may have considerable *influence*. Finally there is the community dominated by one particular power group, as in a one-company town. In this case both the board and the superintendent have little independence of action.[63]

The influential study of Massachusetts school superintendents by Gross, Mason, and McEachern suggests that school superintendents and school board members perceive their roles differently, with each group tending to assign greater responsibility to its own position. The professional ideology of superintendents is one that restricts the role of the school board to a mainly fiscal responsibility whereas the school board members tend to see themselves as having wider powers.[64] At the same time there is evidence that the better-educated board members are themselves more likely to adhere to the professional view of their role. Moreover better-educated board members and better-trained superintendents are more likely to be found in the larger school systems.[65] It is in this kind of situation, it would seem, that we find McCarty and Ramsey's pluralistic board and professional superintendent.

The findings of Gross and his colleagues also suggest that the involvement of the school board in decision-making will vary according to the issue under discussion. This may explain Crain's finding that in all but one of the school systems he studied it was the school board that made the decision and not the superintendent.[66] It should always be remembered however that it is the administrator and his staff, not the school board, who have to implement the decision once it is made. Rogers' study of the New York City School Board and its attempt to desegregate the city schools argues that the opposition of the administrative bureaucracy was an important element in its failure.[67]

Baron and Tropp[68] have drawn a very strong contrast between the power of the local community in the United States and in England. 'Whereas in England it is the teacher who represents to the community in which he works "nationally" accepted values, in America it is the community that interprets to the teacher the task he is to perform.' This fundamental difference flows in large part from differences in the administrative structure. In England, as we have seen, the educational system is, in contrast to the United States, highly centralized, and the Department of Education and Science exercises a fairly close supervision over many aspects of school policy. At the local level, moreover, education is in the hands, not of locally elected school boards, but of general-purpose local authorities elected very largely upon national party lines and pursuing national rather than local policies. The effect, Baron and Tropp argue, is to insulate the schools from popular pressure at local level.

Nor is the English parent as likely to exert pressure on the school. Parent-Teacher Associations are not only less common but, when they do exist, appear to have more limited functions. Moreover they are often strongly opposed by head teachers, who fear they will lead to interference by parents in the working of the school. A recent study of West Ham, for example, concluded 'that the hostility of the head teachers towards Parent-Teacher Associations is the decisive factor in their virtual absence from the local sphere of influence'.[69] In Reading, too, Parents' Associations are severely limited to fund raising and social activities. 'In the main when there is interest in the school, heads try to channel it into fields other than the actual courses given in the school. The nearest approach to pressure arose when the Parents' Association of one school which was to have new buildings went to the M.P. when the school was repeatedly expunged from the

131

building programme. This is not to say that there have not been attempts to found more ambitious types of associations, but they have been very definitely discouraged.[70]

Moreover the National Federation of Parent-Teacher Associations does not see itself as a pressure group. Its policy is to work with the head teacher and it accepts that a P.T.A. cannot be formed if the head teacher and staff do not want it. The Confederation for the Advancement of State Education, on the other hand, arose out of a protest group of parents in Cambridge in 1960, and is a much more militant organization. Its aims also include a greater say for parents in the educational process. The launching of the Home and School Council as a campaigning organization for the further development of parent-teacher associations and similar organizations is also evidence of a more militant approach to the involvement of parents in the educational process. As yet, however, the amount of parental support for such a policy is small and appears to be largely middle-class in origin.[71]

It is arguable, however, that political parties exert considerably more influence at the local level in England, because of their important role in local elections. In a case study of 'Townley' for example, Saran showed that each time political control of the council changed the Chief Education Officer was required to prepare new policy outlines. In 1946, for example, a Labour controlled council started to experiment with comprehensive schools, in spite of some opposition both within the Labour Party itself, and from the grammar schools. In 1949 the Conservative Party came into power and the plan was reversed, although three experimental comprehensive schools were allowed to stay.[72] This is by no means an isolated instance.[73] Boaden's study of county boroughs found, for example, that Labour councils spent more on education than Conservative councils. Indeed Labour councils spent more whatever the context of need in which they found themselves, suggesting a more favourable orientation on their part both to public spending and to education.[74]

Byrne and Williamson have argued that local education authorities tend to concentrate their resources on 'elite' secondary school expenditure to the detriment of other sectors of the school system.[75] Their point is strongly reinforced by Eileen Byrne's[76] study of resource allocation in the three contrasted areas of Lincoln, Nottingham, and Northumberland. She found an assumption in all three areas that the more able children need more resources, not only in terms of longer at school, but also in terms of staff, equipment and books. This view was shared by Chief Education Officers and Education Committees alike, including, at least during the 1940s and early 1950s, members of the Labour Party. A challenge to this view in Lincoln in 1956, however, was linked to a takeover by a new Labour group. The new Chairman of the Education Committee initiated transfer to grammar school from secondary modern school at 15, in spite of opposition by the Chief Education Officer.

The ambivalence within the Labour Party, which has already been discussed in connection with central government, is also reflected in the study by Batley, O'Brien and Parris, on Darlington and Gateshead.[77] In Darlington, many of the older members of the Labour group were anti-comprehensive, and in Gateshead too the Labour Party was less than enthusiastic. Consequently plans for comprehensive reorganization were delayed for long periods, even when the Labour Party was in office. In Darlington the first move came from within the Labour Party in 1955, but the issue was not finally resolved until 1967. Gateshead, although a Labour stronghold, did not introduce a comprehensive policy until 1964.

Although these studies clearly indicate that party politics are a factor in educational policy at the local level, there is little doubt that the most powerful influence at this level in England is the Chief Education Officer. J. M. Lee, for example, in his study of Cheshire, has strongly emphasized the importance of the permanent officials in the administration of local government at the county level, which he suggests, is a direct consequence of the scope and complexity of the tasks facing a local authority.[78]

The case-studies of Darlington and Gateshead already referred to[79] also bring out the crucial role of the Chief Education Officer. At Darlington, for example, it was not until he himself was converted to the idea of comprehensive schools that the Labour group were able to proceed with their plans. At Gateshead, too, the introduction of a comprehensive policy in 1964 coincided with the appointment of a new Director. Eileen Byrne's study also brings out the importance, and even the personal idiosyncrasies, of individual Chief Education Officers.[80]

Peschek, in his study of West Ham, also draws attention to the power of the officials, and in particular the Chief Education Officer. The education committee as such has little power and it is the members of certain key sub-committees such as the Schools Sub-

Committee who share power with the officials. In Reading the Director of Education has been a particularly powerful figure. 'Percy Taylor, who died suddenly in 1962, was looked up to as one of the best Education Officers Reading had ever known. He was an efficient administrator and had a great gift for getting people to like him and accept his way of looking at things. During his period of office there were few things on which the Education Committee did not take his advice. The whole of the Development Plan was his . . . No question came up without leadership from Taylor. No building programme would be proposed but by Taylor. When some pressure group wanted something it was to Taylor that they came and the Committee would largely take Taylor's judgement on whether or not to grant their request.'[81]

This is not to suggest, of course, that the local councillors have a negligible role. As Kogan and Van der Eyken have pointed out, they 'select their fields of battle on criteria of political importance', and these issues then get into the committee, political group network. On the other hand the 'day-by-day or year-by-year creation of policies'[82] is in the hands of permanent officials. An interesting example of how this operates in practice is provided by Saran. When a decline in pupil numbers made 'Townley' less dependent on direct grant and independent schools, the officers attempted for a number of reasons to cut the number of local education authority places at these schools. When this policy was defeated in committee, the lay-out of the form issued to parents was altered by the officers to draw less attention to places in the direct grant and independent schools and more to grammar school places. This 'control over administrative detail', Saran argues, 'gives the officers opportunities for playing a subtle role in achieving their own ends.'[83]

If, however, the Chief Education Officer appears as a powerful figure in English education, it must be noted that there are some ways in which he has less influence than his American counterpart. Not only is there a greater degree of State control in England, but the power of the administrator over the schools in his care is very strictly defined so as not to usurp the authority of the head of the school. Traditionally the headmaster or headmistress of an English school is expected to function as a leader rather than as a part of an administrative bureaucracy. All the teaching methods and procedures, all matters relating to curricula, the relationships with parents and the control of teachers and their duties are recognized as matters for the head to decide and education committees will rarely try to interfere. Moreover this view of the head is supported and encouraged by the central government and by the H.M.I.s, so that it is not easy for a local authority to take control, even if it wished to do so. This is in sharp contrast to the position of the American school principal. 'By and large, the American school superintendent is responsible to his school board for all aspects of the education given in the schools of a city or district; school principals are his subordinates and he is expected to give leadership, whether autocratic or democratic in nature, in purely educational topics, such as curriculum-building and the evolution of appropriate teaching methods.[84]

The closure by the Greater London Council of Risinghill Comprehensive School is an interesting example of the problems that arise when a local authority is at odds with one of its head teachers. The headmaster, Michael Duane, an ardent advocate of progressive education, appears to have aroused the antagonism of traditionally oriented teachers in his school as well as the G.L.C. Inspectorate. The ostensible reason for closing the school was the fall in the applications for entry, rather than Mr Duane's progressive views, although the head's administration of the school was blamed for the falling entry.[85] Certainly Mr Duane throughout his career appears to have been extraordinarily naive in his attitude to authority[86] and this, coupled with the G.L.C.'s sensitivity to the comprehensive school issue, was undoubtedly a factor in the situation. Nevertheless the incident illustrates very well both the scope and the limitations of a headmaster's authority.

The balance of power between the 'politicians' and the 'bureaucrats' must also be taken into account at the State as well as the local level, but on the whole the weight of the evidence would appear to favour the civil service.[87] This is illustrated above all by the career of the great Permanent Secretary, Robert Morant, whose influence, although it has been much misunderstood,[88] was nevertheless of far greater importance that that of any of the politicians under whom he served.[89] Although of course power ultimately lies with the political head of the department, and the influence of party decisions can be discerned within educational policy, there is no doubt that the general impression is one of continuity, and that changes, when they occur, are usually gradual rather than abrupt. The 20 years after 1944, for example, showed few variations in government educational policy according to either individual ministers or the party in power, even on such controversial party issues as comprehensive reorganization or the reform of the independent schools. In fact, of course, this is due to the superior expertise of the permanent civil servant, but it is undoubtedly exacerbated by the frequent changes in political appointments in many government departments. An interesting account of the balance of power between the minister and his department is provided by the revealing interviews with Edward Boyle and Anthony Crosland, both men who might be expected to be strong rather than weak in their dealings with their permanent officials. In fact, although of course the minister always has the power of veto, it is the civil servants who emerge as the major policy-makers.[90]

It is very clear therefore that to locate the area of formal authority, whether it is at the local level as in the United States, a 'partnership' as in England, or a central authority as in France or the u.s.s.r., is only the beginning of the search for the real *seat* of power. Although a welcome start has been made we need more research into the decision-making process in education at all levels, from that of the central government down to the school itself.

4 The political functions of educational systems

In so far as schools are an aspect of what Durkheim called moral education, they are involved inevitably in the process of political socialization; that is the transmission of values, norms and social attitudes. In some societies this may mean transmitting a relatively unchanging culture and traditional attitudes to the new generation. At other times it may be seen as more important for the schools to serve as agencies of change. In post-revolutionary Russia, for example, the schools were given the task of destroying the old bourgeois values and creating new values appropriate to a socialist society.[91] Education may also be required to smooth the path of innovation by breaking down traditional attitudes and so lessening the resistance to change.

There will also be differences between societies in the extent to which schools are used openly for the inculcation of values, and those in which the process of political and moral socialization is carried out primarily at the latent rather than the manifest level. Zeigler and Peak have suggested that this will vary according to the degree to which societal integration has been achieved.[92] Another factor of some importance to which they also draw attention is the extent to which a society will permit the expression of demands which depart from the existing consensus. Tolerance of nonconformity, they point out, is itself a social norm, and it is the educational system which bears much of the responsibility for its continuation.

Another important agency of moral education is the Church, and it is no accident that there has always been a close link between education and religion, or that the Church or churches have been reluctant to hand the responsibility for schools over to the State. Conflict between Church and State is, however, only one aspect of the relationship, and the development of educational systems has often been deeply influenced by the conflict between rival churches.

Scotford Archer and Vaughan, for example, in their study of educational change in England and France between 1781 and 1848, use as one of their main themes the ideological debate between Anglicans and Nonconformists and the attempts of each group to gain control of the developing educational system.[93]

Debates between Anglicans and Nonconformists continued to play a significant role in educational development in this country throughout the nineteenth century, although the intervention of the State in the provision of schools, and its growing importance in the 1800s and 1870s, changed the nature of the debate. Rivalry between the churches however still dominated the controversies over the 1902 Education Act. Cannon,[94] in a comparison of the influence of religious groups in the 1902 and the 1944 Education Acts, has concluded that differences between rival groups were much less important in 1944 than in 1902. In 1944, faced with what they perceived as the growth of a secular society, internal divisions seemed less important than maintaining some sort of hold on the schools. Evidence of the significant part still played by religious leaders in 1944, and their determination that religious teaching of some kind should continue in the schools, is provided by R. A. Butler's memoirs which describe in vivid detail the events leading up to the Act.[95]

Overtly totalitarian regimes openly use their schools to inculcate conformity, submissiveness and uncritical loyalty to the State. In Japan, for example, before the war the schools were expected to encourage submissive acceptance of the existing order. The principal instrument for the inculcation of these principles was the teaching of morals. 'A minimum of one hour per week of morals was mandatory in all schools, from elementary through the secondary schools. But apart from the formal morals course, the ideas were worked into the curriculum and into school life in any way the ingenuity of the educators could devise.'[96] Moreover inside the classroom, 'self-expression was discouraged and disagreement with teachers and elders severely frowned on'.[97]

In Russia, too, emphasis in the schools has been on the indoctrination of the pupil in conformity and obedience as well as in love for the Soviet system. In the school itself, 'the atmosphere was pervaded by a spirit of discipline and hierarchy', and teachers were warned 'not to coax students but rather to demand obedience, for only in this way would students develop the desired moral qualities'.[98]

There is every indication that the educational system of the U.S.S.R. has not only transformed a largely illiterate and traditionally oriented population into both a literate and industrialized work force, but it has also managed to produce a generation who are in the main ideologically committed to the social order. At the same time, observers have noted some signs that the process of indoctrination is by no means complete. There is evidence of a small number of young people who are disenchanted with the system, and a much larger number who are not only politically apathetic but to some extent opportunist as well.[99] Students in particular have been accused of a dislike of manual labour, of elitist attitudes, and of putting their own career before service to the State. The 1958 school reforms, with their introduction of the concept of 'polytechnical education', were designed to teach the dignity of labour and to prevent the development of a new upper class. Khrushchev, for example, spoke bitterly of the distinction that still exists in the Soviet Union between mental and manual work. 'This is fundamentally wrong and runs counter to our teaching and aspirations. As a rule, boys and girls in secondary school consider that the only acceptable path in life for them is to continue their education at higher schools. Some of them even consider [work] beneath their dignity. This scornful and lordly attitude is to be found in some families. If a boy or girl does not study well and fails to get into college, the parents frighten him by saying that if he does not study well and fails to get into college he will have to work in a factory as a common labourer.'[100]

Moreover, it should not be overlooked that the schools, as such, have only been expected to play a small part in the total process of indoctrination. Indeed, the aim of a totalitarian system is to ensure that every agency of socialization is involved in the process. Directly and indirectly, Grant points out, 'the communist viewpoint is put over at every stage of schooling, and reinforced by other media of communication outside the schools, such as the theatre, films, radio, television and the Press, while the youth organizations act as a link between the school and the world outside.'[101] This is in striking contrast to most democratic systems where the various media of socialization are only loosely controlled.

One of the reasons for the partial failure of the Soviet system's indoctrination programme may be their relative lack of interest in early childhood socialization, and their somewhat aloof attitude to the family as a child-rearing unit.[102] Possibly even more significant, however, are the contradictions which have clearly arisen between the official ideology and the actual experiences and observations in everyday life. The existence of a privileged elite group, and income and status differences between manual and non-manual workers, are likely to serve as serious handicaps to the full acceptance of the official doctrine of the equality of all forms of service to the State.

This is not to suggest that democratic as well as totalitarian societies do not attempt to indoctrinate their children in the religious, moral and political values dominant in the society. The process, however, is normally less conscious, partly because there is less emphasis on the production of new values, and partly because of the greater tolerance of nonconformity. There are however differences between democratic societies, and the United States, for example, with its problem of integrating large numbers of immigrant children, is more concerned with the inculcation of patriotism than England.

There is some evidence from the United States that the school is more important than the family in political socialization, and that the family is chiefly important in the transmission of preference for a particular political party.[103] On the other hand, compliance to rules and authority is the major focus of civic education in both the elementary and the secondary school. Hess and Torney[104] found that the elementary school 'under-emphasized the rights and obligations of a citizen to participate in government'. Moreover, 'teachers tend not to deal with partisanship or to discuss the role and importance of conflict in the operation of the system'. Zeigler and Peak make the same points with respect to high schools, which they suggest 'might be doing a better job than Russia of grinding out loyal, compliant citizens'.[105] High school textbooks in civics, for example, not only avoid controversial positions but ignore all unpleasant aspects of American life.

These findings appear to contradict the relationship which has been shown to occur between level of education and democratic attitudes. Lipset, for example, has argued that 'data gathered by public opinion research agencies which have questioned people in different countries about their beliefs on tolerance for the opposition, their attitudes towards ethnic or racial minorities, and their feelings for multi-party as against one-party systems have shown that the most important single factor differentiating those giving democratic responses from the others has been education'.[106] Particularly impressive in this connection is Lipset's evidence that the working classes and the less-educated tend to be more authoritarian in their attitudes, and to be more likely to favour extremist political and religious groups. In addition we have already noted, in this chapter, the tendency for opposition to racial integration in schools to come from the working and lower-middle classes. There is also some evidence that the higher the educational level of a country the more likely it is to be a democracy.

Lipset's picture of the working class as authoritarian has however been criticized as over-drawn. It has been pointed out, for example, that another characteristic of the working-class respondents is the tendency to give uncertain or no opinion responses, and that in fact the proportion holding extremist or anti-democratic views in the working classes is probably fairly low.[107] Nor is a tendency towards authoritarian views found only amongst the working classes. As Lipset himself has pointed out, 'data from numbers of countries demonstrate that classic Fascism is a movement of the propertied middle classes'.[108] At the same time there is no necessary connection at the national level between education and democracy, and both Germany and Japan are examples of countries which have in the past combined a high educational level with a totalitarian form of government.

The effect of college on students in the United States has however now been well established. In a recent major review of research in this field, Feldman and Newcomb show that *in general* the impact of college on students is in the direction of a decline in authoritarianism and conservatism, in a commitment to religion, and a growth in sensitivity to aesthetic experiences and in intellectual interests.[109] There is also evidence that certain colleges, and more especially the small residential four-year college, have more effect on students than other types of college or university. Within some colleges at least there are also differences between faculties. The Selvin and Hagstrom study, for example, found that men studying the social sciences and the humanities were considerably more libertarian than those studying engineering, education or business.[110] Only a part of this difference, however, was an effect of college itself. As Selvin and Hagstrom point out, there is a great deal of difference in the kind of students attracted by different subjects or faculties, just as colleges and universities vary in the receptivity and interests of the kind of students they select. It has been found, for example, that the highly productive colleges in terms of future scholars and scientists 'attract highly motivated students who are more inter-directed, socially independent, receptive to learning, non-authoritarian, theoretical, aesthetic, unconventional and creative'.[111]

The best-known account of the impact of college on values is Newcomb's classic study of Bennington.[112] The students concerned, who came in the main from upper-middle-class conservative families, became more radical in their attitudes as a result of their stay at Bennington. According to Newcomb's analysis, the teachers' interest in and attitude to social and political issues appears to have been the crucial factor. Because the student leaders were strongly influenced by their teachers, liberal opinions enjoyed popularity and prestige, and incoming students were consequently exposed to such opinions not only from the teachers but as part of the student culture. Significantly, it was the students who were most involved in peer-group activities who were the least conservative.

A follow-up study of the Bennington alumni 25 years after showed that the attitudes developed at Bennington had tended to persist. The majority of them described themselves as liberal rather than conservative in politics. They were also less conservative than sisters and sisters-in-law who had not graduated at Bennington. Moreover, although students at Bennington in the 1960s were more involved in aesthetic pursuits than in the political sphere, students were still expected to show a tolerance for unconventional attitudes and behaviour on the part of others, and failure to comply with these standards met with criticism and isolation.[113]

All of these studies have been concerned with the United States.

Clignet[114] however has argued that the relationship between education and political attitudes varies cross-culturally. In particular he suggests that it will depend on the conceptions that different cultures hold of 'both political processes and the role that intellectuals may play in such processes'. The effects of education, therefore, are different as between the United States with the largely decentralized nature of its institutions, and the largely centralized France.

Further knowledge of the impact of education on political values would seem to depend, as Zeigler and Peak suggest, on an examination of the techniques of instruction, the structure under which schools are governed and the patterns of occupational recruitment and socialization of teachers. There is also the possibility that changes in political attitudes are the result of exposure to pupil or student subcultures. All of these issues will be taken further in subsequent chapters.

5 The deschooling movement

Although the ideas of the deschoolers span, in one way or another, almost all the topics discussed in this book, it seems most appropriate to include them in a chapter on the politics of education, because of the overtly political context to their argument. On the other hand, some of the issues they raise have been discussed in earlier chapters, and others will be considered subsequently. The main purpose of what must be only a brief account is to set the movement itself, if it can be called such, in a sociological frame of reference.

On the other hand it is not easy to decide on who the deschoolers are, or even on what the now widely accepted term 'deschooling' means. As Lister has pointed out, there have been school-critics as long as there have been schools',[115] but none of them, with the possible exception of Rousseau, have been deschoolers. He traces the origins of the deschooling movement to Paul Goodman, who as early as 1947 was raising questions about the relationship of man to the modern urban industrial environment. The most significant of the deschoolers is however Ivan Illich, and his book, *Deschooling Society*, is now the classic work on the subject.[116]

Hargreaves has made a useful distinction between the deschoolers like Illich and Reimer, and what he calls the New Romantics. The deschoolers, he suggests offer 'a fundamental critique of our current educational system and of contemporary society, and propose a radical, alternative structure',[117] whereas the New Romantics, of whom there are many varieties, propose reformist alternatives. Their dominant concern, he suggests, is with the content of the curriculum and the nature of pedagogy, rather than the basic institutional structure of schooling. It is with the deschoolers that we are concerned at present, although the ideas of the New Romantics will be discussed in subsequent chapters.

Fundamentally, what Illich and Reimer are arguing is that the functions of schools have little to do with education, and more to do with indoctrination into what are essentially myths or false values. Schools are also divisive, since not only do attempts to achieve equality within the system fail, but more public money is spent on the rich than on the poor. Schools also contribute to the continuation of underprivilege between nations, because of their cost. Only rich nations can afford the amount of schooling that the United States provides. Furthermore, deschoolers set the educational crisis firmly at the centre and as the source of a world crisis which faces modern man with annihilation.

The solution is the setting up of a deschooled society. Compulsory education, schools and teachers must be abolished, and the command of educational resources must be put in the hands of the learners, who learn what they want, how they want it, and at what age they want it. This would be achieved by the provision of various 'networks', which include such ideas as direct access to resources for learning such as museums and libraries, and the establishment of 'skill exchanges' and other devices which would bring together both learners and those who possess the skills they need to acquire. At the same time there would be an end to formal qualifications, and occupational selection would be based only on ability to do the job.

The deschoolers are very insistent that the changes they propose are intended to have a radical outcome, although it is not always clear how the abolition of schools will at the same time revolutionize the world. It seems however that what they have in mind is essentially a change of consciousness, and a change in values. No longer indoctrinated by a bureaucratic educational system, itself the servant of the economy, men and women will be free to choose an alternative way of life.

A critique of the deschoolers can be mounted on a number of

different levels and only a brief review of some of the main weaknesses in their position can be attempted here. Lister, for example, draws attention to a fundamental evasion of all questions of political power, an evasion which springs from their ties with the liberal anarchist rather than the Marxist radical tradition. Lister describes their vision as apocalyptic and millenarian,[118] and Margaret Fay, in a review of Illich's *Deschooling Society,* has drawn attention to the strong charismatic appeal of the deschoolers to a generation of American educators who have lost faith in themselves.[119]

There are also many criticisms that can be made about the lack of an empirical grounding in the deschoolers' descriptions of schools, and there are frequent and serious ambiguities and inconsistencies in their general analysis. Illich, for example, as Fay points out, dismisses science and technology on the one hand, and on the other assumes that the deschooled future will be based on a highly automated technology.

It is perhaps the alternatives to schooling which have received most criticism, even from those who are otherwise highly sympathetic to the deschooling approach. Huberman,[120] for example, is highly critical of the networks, suggesting that they are possibly laying the foundations for a new bureaucracy. Moreover he suggests that far from equalizing opportunities, it may be the already disadvantaged who might gain less from the new arrangements. This is because the already privileged will be better able to use this system, as they have used others, to their own advantage. Similarly Lister has drawn attention to the dangers of giving greater power to the family.

Hargreaves has concluded that Illich and other deschoolers are rather impractical visionaries. Nevertheless he believes that they are important for the sociology of education because they have challenged some of the traditional wisdom embodied in the field. More especially, of course, they are important because they have challenged the assumption, accepted by sociologists of education, along with teachers and educators, that more schooling for more people is inherently a good thing. They have also challenged the accepted view of the teacher as educator, and emphasized all the other roles that teachers play. Whatever the final verdict on the deschooling movement, it is highly possible that the dialogue they have started will prove to have been a fruitful one.

7 The teaching profession

1 Development of the profession

In any attempt to construct a sociology of the school, a study of the teacher must at all times have a central place. The crucial position of the teacher in the educational process has indeed been widely recognized, and studies of teachers as a group have been fairly widespread, so that we now have a fair amount of knowledge of the characteristics of teachers in Britain and, to some extent, elsewhere. First, however, it is necessary to look briefly at the structure of teaching as an occupation, since, although it is customary nowadays to think of teaching as a unified profession, in reality teachers form a very diversified group. As Brookover and Gottlieb have pointed out, 'The range of teachers is very great. They teach in everything from kindergarten to graduate school; in schools supported by churches, by private corporations, by foundations, by taxpayers; on assignments ranging all the way from the entire first eight grades in one to private sessions with a student in need of individual attention.'[1] Moreover these different types of teacher not only perform different roles: there are also frequently differences in remuneration, status, qualifications, sex, social-class background and many other characteristics.

One of the most usual ways to categorize teachers is in terms of the age-range of the pupils. Those teaching younger pupils in primary or elementary schools are distinguished in this way from those who teach in secondary schools, while those working in higher education form another and quite distinct category. An alternative system of classification is in terms of the subjects taught. The broad differentiation here is between academic and practical subjects. When this is combined with the age-level of the pupils, it gives us important subdivisions between teachers in different types of secondary school, or between various kinds of higher education. Yet a further distinction which has been of great importance historically is made in terms of the social origin of the pupils. This is particularly important where middle- or upper-class children are educated in separate schools. In addition, wherever State education has been provided, mainly for the children of the poor, there may be important distinctions between teachers in State and independent schools.

Tropp has described the development in Britain during the nineteenth century of the new profession of elementary school teacher. Faced with the need to give the rudiments of education to the children of the poor, the demand was for a whole new army of teachers who could be provided at little cost. As Tropp puts it, 'in the 1830s and 1840s the great question was whether education could mitigate the dangers inherent in an ignorant industrial population or whether it would, by teaching the poor to read and write, make them a still greater danger to society. An important but secondary question was – who was to provide the education and what should be its nature? Once it was conceded that education should be extended to the poor through the medium of voluntary religious societies and that this education should be suffused with morality and religion, it became obvious that the main need was for a supply of efficient, religious and humble teachers.'[2]

The answer was found in the pupil-teacher system, a method of teacher training already practised on the continent. Under the pupil-teacher system the most intelligent and moral pupils of the elementary schools were apprenticed as pupil-teachers to the headmaster at the age of 13. During their five years' apprenticeship they received one and a half hours' a day teaching from the headmaster and for the rest of their time acted as a teacher in the school. After five years of satisfactory service, those who were successful in a competitive examination were given scholarships for a further period of education in a Training College. A teacher's certificate, which carried the right to an augmented salary and a pension, was granted either on the successful completion of the Training College course or to those passing an external examination for practising teachers. The certificated teachers were, however, the elite of the profession. In 1855, for example, almost all certificated teachers had headships, and even at the end of the century a shortage of Training College places, especially for women, meant that not only were many teachers uncertified, but that many of the certificated teachers were untrained.

The effect of the pupil-teacher system was to produce several generations of teachers who had been educated within an almost completely closed system. Only the period at Training College was, for those who achieved it, a break from the elementary school, and even this was an enclosed world within the elementary tradition. As befitted their social origin and limited educational background, teachers were expected to be humble, to show gratitude for the 'charity' to which they owed their education and training, and to refrain from any excessive ambition to improve their lot.[3] Indeed, during the middle years of the century in particular teachers were constantly under fire for their conceit and ambition.

At the other extreme from the elementary school teachers were the masters at the major public schools. 'The task of a master in a public school was to teach the classics to the sons of the upper class and to those who were being educated with them. He had to be acceptable both to the parents and to the headmaster on academic and personal grounds, and his background was a matter of some importance.'[4] Not only was an Oxford or Cambridge degree almost essential but there was a tendency on the part of public schools to recruit from amongst their own boys, which reached an extreme form at Eton. According to Bamford, 74 per cent of those appointed to Eton between 1801 and 1862 were old Eton boys. In the main the masters at the major public schools were of middle-class professional origin, and the headmasters often came from eminent families.

The high status of the public school master was maintained not only by means of his educational background but also by his connection with the Church. Until the second half of the nineteenth century it was customary for the masters as well as the head to be clergymen. 'The first significant number of lay appointments for Eton, Harrow and Rugby occurred in the 1850s but not till 1870 for Shrewsbury.'[5]

The position of the headmaster was particularly important. Not only was he in complete control of his school and its staff, but he enjoyed great prestige outside the school. Moreover, even after the introduction of laymen as masters, the headmaster remained a clergyman. Frequently, too, the headship of a major public school was only a 'stepping stone to higher things'.[6] Promotions to deaneries and bishoprics were common, and even an archbishopric was by no means out of the question.

It was customary too for the headship to command a high income even where the assistant masters were poorly paid. Indeed, in spite of their qualifications, assistant masters in all but the top public schools were frequently not only very badly paid but had little hope of promotion. In such schools the turnover of staff was often high. Moreover, below the ranks of the public schools, in the endowed grammar schools and preparatory schools, salaries were so poor that frequently the master looked jealously at 'the rapid improvements which were being made in the training and education of the masters of schools of a lower grade'.[7] Nevertheless, even if poorly paid, the grammar school teachers shared in the public school rather than the elementary school tradition and enjoyed a higher status than elementary school teachers.

The completely separate elementary tradition did not, however, outlast the nineteenth century. Modifications to the system had started in the 1880s with the development of pupil-teacher centres in the large towns, where pupil-teachers were taught in central classes. At the same time attempts were made to improve the teaching in the Training Colleges and to bring them into closer contact with the universities. With the reorganization of secondary education that followed the 1902 Act normal entrance to the elementary teaching profession was only through the secondary school.

Even in the long term, however, the ending of the pupil-teacher system did not remove the cleavage within the profession. In practice the elementary school teacher continued to be recruited from the training colleges and the secondary school teacher from the universities. 'Until the 1940s,' asserts Tropp, 'only unemployment could drive the graduate into the elementary school.'[8] The abolition of the elementary system in 1944 was a further and indeed a major step in the unification of the profession, but the elementary tradition was still perpetuated, partly by the distinctions operating within secondary education, and partly by the continuation of the college training.

Some recent trends have, however, brought teacher training into a closer relationship with the universities. The first major step in this direction was the lengthening of the college course in the early 1960s from two to three years. Subsequently, the establishment of the four-year B.Ed. degree in the colleges opened the way for much closer links with university departments. Current moves following the James Report have brought further changes to the colleges.

Some have moved even closer to the universities, while others have been brought into the orbit of the polytechnics. To a large extent, therefore, the dual system of teacher education is coming to an end.

The development of teacher training in Britain has been described at length because it is paralleled in general terms, if not in detail, in all the European countries and in other parts of the world. The education of the poor, that is to say, has developed separately from the education of the elite. Whereas secondary education has always had close ties with the universities in its outlook and its subject-matter and has had as its function the transmission of 'culture', elementary education in its origin at least was simply intended to 'gentle the masses'. Consequently whereas the teacher in the secondary school needed to be educated in the full sense of the word, the elementary school teacher had only to be trained. Primarily, it was the limited conception of the education of the masses which entailed the narrowness of the education and training of their teachers, and only as the standards expected of elementary education have risen do we find any major changes in the pattern of teacher training. Thus the normal schools of continental Europe were designed as institutions parallel to the academic secondary school, giving some limited general education and some practical training for teaching. For example, in the normal schools set up in France by a decree of 1833, the sons of small farmers and manual labourers were trained as elementary teachers. 'They received a moral and religious education, lessons in reading, grammar and practical geometry. They were given some notions of the everyday applications of science, of French history and geography. They were shown how to draw up certificates of birth, deaths and marriages, and how to graft and prune trees. They were initiated into teaching method by attending the primary schools attached to the *Ecoles Normales*.'[9]

Most countries in both Eastern and Western Europe still have teacher-training colleges which lie below the universities, not only in social esteem, but also in admission qualifications. Fiszman, for example, shows that in Poland there are three levels of prestige in teacher training: the universities, the higher schools of pedagogy, and the schools of teacher education. The last prepare teachers for the elementary schools. As in England, however, there have been attempts to raise the status of this level of teacher training. In 1966-7 the two-year course was lengthened, and the schools themselves are eventually destined to disappear.[10]

In France, too, there have been major changes in the status of the normal schools. Since 1973 they have been part of the system of higher education although not on a par either academically or socially with the universities. The same is true of Germany, where, in spite of considerable changes in recent years, teacher education has a marginal status within higher education.

In the United States the progress towards a unified system of teacher-training has gone further than anywhere in Europe, even though standards initially were just as low, and improvements during the nineteenth century were no faster than in Britain. Normal schools were founded from the 1830s onwards, but the growth in their numbers was very slow. Moreover, like their European counterparts, entry requirements were so low that one of their main functions was to complete the pupils' secondary education. Many went straight into teaching on leaving school. Improvements in teacher-training in the United States have occurred chiefly in the present century, and it is in this period too that the system has moved away from the European pattern. In 1910 two-year normal schools were common, following after two years or less at a high school. By 1930 the normal schools were being supplanted by teachers' colleges organized to provide a three- or four-year programme and asking for four years of high-school preparation. Today a bachelor's degree representing four years of preparation beyond high school is almost universally required, and the teachers' colleges are themselves undergoing transformation into multi-purpose institutions.[11] An even more important development is that elementary and secondary teachers are frequently trained in the same institutions, although secondary school teachers are usually expected to have higher qualifications.

In attempting to understand the reasons for the direction taken by teachers' education in the United States, the absence of a distinctive elementary and secondary tradition must take pride of place. The early appearance of the comprehensive high school, and its dominance in the field of secondary education, has meant that all prospective teachers pass together through the high school. At the same time the meaning of secondary education has been altered. It is no longer a selective education, preparing a minority for elite status, but must cater for the needs of all children. Moreover, the frequent absence of streaming and setting in the schools, and the existence of many small schools, means that the specialist subject-teacher is rare in the

American context. Consequently, not only has much greater attention been paid to teaching methods in the training of secondary school teachers, but their education is much less subject-centred than is customary in Europe. Bachelors' degrees held by both elementary and secondary teachers are normally degrees in education. Indeed critics of the American teacher-training system frequently argue that American teachers are inadequately prepared for academic teaching.[12]

The scope and flexibility of American higher education also makes it easier to integrate it with teachers' education than is likely to be possible in most of Europe, where university teachers often show resistance to a closer relationship with teacher-training institutions. This is partly because of the greater willingness in the United States to accept practical and vocational subjects as part of higher education. At the same time, the existence of what Riesman calls the academic procession allows an aspiring teachers' college to turn itself into a multi-purpose college or university. Consequently, even if the education of teachers frequently has less prestige than other kinds of higher education, this is not a distinction which creates a rigid barrier within the profession.

Teachers in universities in Britain share with the public school teachers the same origin in the Church. Formerly university teaching was carried out largely by clergymen, often as a temporary occupation while waiting for a living, and it was only late in the nineteenth century that university teaching emerged as a full-time career. Rothblatt,[13] in his study of nineteenth-century Cambridge, has provided us with a fascinating picture of the process. The new group of dons who emerged, he argues, 'were distinguished by their professional interest in scholarship, by their intention to make university teaching a career, and by their desire to revive the unique features of a collegiate university, the close relation between fellows and students'.

In Germany the pattern of development was somewhat different. The growth of the universities was closely connected with the evolution of the German bureaucracy, and their great influence and esteem sprang from their 'active participation in the system of state examinations and privileges and from their traditional role as guardians of learning.'[14] Scotland, on the other hand, provides us with yet a different tradition. As Davie[15] has shown, the Scottish universities escaped both the aristocratic and the classical emphasis of

Oxbridge. They were also much more democratic, in the sense that they were open to a much wider sector of the population than universities in either England or Germany. McPherson, for example, has described them as organized on principles of contest rather than sponsored mobility.[16]

Light, in an attempt to provide some guidelines for the study of the academic profession, has drawn on all three traditions to provide three different models of academic man: the first, the Oxbridge model, is the intellectual and moral teacher of the ruling class; the second, the Scottish model, is the teacher who provides useful knowledge to anyone qualified to hear; and the third, the German model, which has had most influence in the United States, is the man who establishes new frontiers of knowledge. The existence of these three different traditions explains some of the contradictions within the profession and particularly the uneasy compromise within it of teaching and research. As Light puts it, 'ostensibly a professor is hired to teach', but 'the basic nature of his career depends on the professional activities which he does in his time off'.[17]

The study by Halsey and Trow of British academics also showed considerable variations in academic orientation both as between the concept of the role, and the conception of the university. When these are combined, they distinguish between the elitist researcher who is largely meritocratic in his orientation, and the elitist teacher who in fact is probably the most common and who, in consequence, shapes 'thousands of unpublished decisions made in colleges and committees'.[18] At the other extreme are the expansionist researchers who see the university as a 'spearhead for economic growth', and the expansionist teachers who are strongly represented in social science faculties. Somewhat surprisingly the Colleges of Advanced Technology, now part of the university sector, were dominated 'not just by teachers but by elitist teachers'.[19]

Studies have also revealed the extreme differentiation of the American system. Not only are there whole sectors of the system where the teaching function is dominant, largely to the exclusion of research, but even within the leading universities there are a group of men and women, but disproportionately women, who are not oriented primarily or exclusively to research.[20]

At the same time there have been quite rigid distinctions between teachers in universities and teachers in other forms of higher education in terms of qualification and pattern of recruitment. The teaching staff in colleges of education, for example, have been recruited principally from the ranks of practising teachers,[21] and have for this reason tended to represent the higher reaches of the teaching profession, rather than to link up with the university teachers either in interests and attitudes or in their sense of identity. The technical college teacher has also been quite sharply differentiated, in part by the tradition of part-time teachers, in part by the emphasis on industrial experience.[22] There is however some evidence that the rise in status of some technical colleges has influenced their recruitment. Newer teachers in the polytechnics are less likely to have come from industry, and are better qualified in academic terms than their seniors.[23] In this respect the polytechnics appear to be following in the footsteps of the former c.a.t.s. A study at the point of transition from c.a.t.s to universities showed that the youngest age-group were more like the universities both in social-class background and in class of degree.[24]

In the United States, in contrast, the structure of higher education does not allow for differentiation of quite this kind, although, as we have seen, there is a distinct tendency for status distinctions to occur between departments and also between institutions, according to their position in what Riesman has called the academic procession. Nevertheless, teachers of higher education can be and are viewed as a single group in a way that is at present impossible in Britain.

However, the pattern of recruitment to college teaching in the United States still has much in common with the more elitist European tradition from which it sprang, and entry to the profession is still governed entirely by academic qualifications. This emphasis is supported by the pattern of doctorate training which is now the major pathway for entry into the profession, for very few ph.d. programmes include any provision for teacher training and they can be viewed essentially as apprenticeships in research.[25] At the same time the main promotion opportunities arise as a result of publication and research.[26] Indeed, because of the influence of the German tradition, it could be argued that there is even less emphasis on the teaching function in the United States than in Britain. The effect of this is not only to differentiate college teachers from school teachers, but to emphasize loyalty to the discipline rather than to the profession as such, with implications that will be discussed in a later section.

At the same time the very rapid development of college education in the United States since 1900 has meant an enormously rapid expansion in the number of college teachers, so that they now represent a vast and historically unique professional class in American society.[27] The consequences of this enormous expansion are likely to be very far-reaching both for the standards of the profession and for its status in the community. Some of these implications will be taken up later in the chapter.

2 The social-class background of teachers

The social origin of the teaching profession is closely related to the method of recruitment, and the availability of training. As we have seen already the pupil-teacher system in nineteenth-century England was an important avenue of social mobility for the clever and ambitious working-class child. At the same time the lowly social origins of the elementary school teachers was a factor in the low status given to the teaching profession. Consequently it is of interest to examine the few studies which give us accurate information on the social origin of teachers. Fortunately, the study by Floud and Scott[28] based on a sample survey of teachers in England and Wales in 1955 provides us with a very detailed picture of the social origins of the profession, which confirms the impression received from earlier and smaller studies. Their results show clearly that although teachers are recruited from all levels of the status hierarchy they come predominantly from the lower middle and the skilled working classes. These overall figures however are less interesting than the differences which the study shows to exist within the profession. The following table,[29] sets out these differences as they occur not only between various types of school, but between men and women teachers.

It will be noticed that women teachers in all types of school, but particularly in grammar schools, have a higher social origin than men teachers. This undoubtedly reflects the greater alternatives open to men, and particularly to male graduates. Teaching still offers more opportunities to the educated girl than most other careers open to her. The other important distinction is between those schools inheriting the elementary tradition and those still influenced by the secondary tradition. The social origin of the teachers is quite considerably higher in the grammar schools than in either the primary or secondary modern schools. The difference

Table Eight

Social origin of teachers in grant-earning schools, England and Wales, 1955

(A) MEN

Father's occupation when teacher left school			*Type of School*	
	Primary	Modern	Maintained grammar	Direct-grant grammar
	%	%	%	%
Professional and administrative	6.0	7.5	12.5	19.8
Intermediate	48.3	45.9	55.1	61.9
Manual, skilled	32.5	36.5	25.3	14.6
Manual, semi- and unskilled	13.2	10.1	7.1	4.0
All	100.0	100.0	100.0	100.0
(N)	1,251	1,178	1,209	544

(B) WOMEN

	Primary	Modern	Maintained grammar	Direct-grant grammar
Professional and administrative	8.8	11.4	17.8	30.4
Intermediate	52.2	54.8	63.1	57.4
Manual, skilled	29.6	28.1	16.4	10.4
Manual, semi- and unskilled	9.3	5.7	2.7	1.8
All	100.0	100.0	100.0	100.0
(N)	1,449	1,083	1,100	733

between the maintained grammar and direct-grant grammar is an interesting reflection of the relationships generally found between the social class of the pupils and of their teachers. Nevertheless, although teachers of working-class origin are rare in the direct-grant grammar schools, it is true for these schools, as for the rest, that the largest group of teachers are from the lower middle classes.

Floud and Scott have also tried to trace changes in the recruitment of teachers by means of a comparison between cohorts of teachers entering the profession at different periods. Such a comparison shows remarkably little change in the proportion of elementary school teachers from working-class families entering the profession before 1920 and of those entering since 1945. On the other hand, there has been a fairly steady decline in the social-class origin of grammar school teachers. In the case of men teachers this has mainly taken the form of a decline in those entering from the professional and administrative classes, but for women teachers there has been in addition an increase in those entering from manual-worker families.

Other more recent studies of the social background of teachers generally confirm the findings of Floud and Scott that teachers tend to be drawn from non-manual backgrounds, and those from manual worker families are mostly from the upper working class.[30] A study by Kelly of lay teachers in Dublin city schools, however, found a higher proportion of teachers from non-manual families, particularly amongst women teachers. Indeed as many as 34 per cent of women had fathers in professional and managerial employment, which is only comparable, in the Floud and Scott study, with women teachers in direct-grant schools. Very few of the Dublin teachers, either men or women, came from manual worker families.[31]

Bernbaum, in a study of headmasters, found that their social origins generally reflected differences in the teaching profession as a whole. There were also differences in the educational background of headmasters of grammar schools and the headmasters of comprehensive and secondary modern schools. Headmasters of grammar schools, for example, were much more likely to have been educated at direct-grant and independent schools, to have been to Oxbridge, and to have achieved a first-class degree. They were also more likely to have graduated in an arts rather than a science subject.[32]

The studies available to us suggest that the social background of teachers in the United States does not differ profoundly from that of Britain. A recent study by the National Education Association found that in 1971 34.1 per cent of teachers had a manual worker background, and 56.5 per cent a background in the middle classes, including 5.5 per cent from clerical or sales occupations.[33] A study by Betz and Garland suggests, however, that when age-groups are compared the proportion of men from working-class or 'blue collar' occupations has increased over time at both elementary and secondary level.[34]

On the other hand, although secondary school teachers are frequently expected to have higher qualifications than elementary school teachers, there is no evidence that they are of a higher social origin. Indeed a study by Carlson[35] suggests that the reverse is true. He found that female elementary school teachers had the highest social origins, and male secondary school teachers the lowest. As many as 48 per cent of male secondary teachers, according to his study, are from the working or lower classes as compared with 23 per cent of female elementary school teachers. While these findings may not be typical of the United States as a whole, and while they may conceal important differences within secondary education, they do lend support to the impression that the United States system has avoided the stigma of the elementary tradition.

This is not to assert, of course, that differentiation is absent from the American teaching profession, any more than it is absent from the American school system. Rather it is less institutionalized than in Europe which has had sponsored mobility and the selective secondary school. It may well be, for example, that there are differences in social origin within schools between teachers trained in different ways or teaching different subjects. There also seems to be differentiation between schools of the same type according to the social characteristics of the pupils. There is some evidence, for example, of 'a tendency for Negro teachers to be placed in schools where there are strong concentrations of Negro youth',[36] and it may well be that teachers of working-class origin are to be found predominantly in working-class schools. Becker, for example, in his study of the Chicago public school teacher found that one major career pattern consists in moving from the lower-class school, in which teaching begins, to a school with a higher proportion of middle-class pupils.[37]

Becker's findings are reinforced to some extent by the recent study by Herriott and St John. They report that teachers in schools where the pupils are in the lowest socio-economic status come from a background 'which can be characterized as more urban, more "blue collar", with less formal education and lower incomes than those of the teachers from schools of highest socio-economic status'.[38] Of these differences, however, only those relating to the type of community and father's occupation were statistically significant. Moreover, nowhere are the differences extreme. In the case of the father's occupation, for example, 30 per cent of teachers in schools of high socio-economic status, and 43 per cent of teachers in schools of low socio-economic status had fathers in 'blue collar' occupations. Thus, even in schools where the majority of pupils were from low-status families, the majority of teachers had come from 'white collar' homes.

The social origin of college and university teachers is to some extent governed by the social background of the college and university student and, as we have seen, this is likely to be predominantly middle-class in character even in countries like the United States. There is, however, some evidence that American college teachers are of lower social origin than other comparable professional groupings.[39] There is also evidence that social class origin is related to success in the academic profession. Using samples of university professors and of recent recipients of doctorates. Crane[40] found that respondents of lower class social origin were less likely to be employed in top-ranking universities. Moreover, this finding applied even to those with ph.d's from major universities.

In Britain too Halsey has shown that university teachers are less middle-class in social class origin than the administrative class of the Civil Service, although both groups recruit from the same university undergraduate population. He found that 79 per cent of direct entrants to the administrative Civil Service were born in social classes I and II compared with 60 per cent of university teachers. The social origin of the scientific Civil Service on the other hand closely resembles that of the university teachers. The administrative class also have a more exclusive educational background than either the university teachers or the scientific Civil Service. They were, that is to say, more likely to have been educated in the private sector of secondary education and at Oxford or Cambridge. A further point of some interest is that university teachers fairly precisely reflect the educational and social composition of the undergraduate body generally.[41]

There are however differences within university teachers which suggest that the recent expansion of the universities has led them to widen the social basis of their recruitment. The younger university teachers are much more likely to be from the working classes, and this is particularly true of those under 30. There are also differences within subjects, with those of middle-class origin markedly over-represented in medicine, and under-represented in the social sciences. Vice-chancellors and principals, however, continue to be recruited pre-eminently from Oxford and Cambridge.[42]

3 The status of the teacher

The social origin of any occupational group both reflects and is a reflection of the status of the group; and the social origin of teachers is a reflection above all of the ambiguity of their status, which needs to contain the two traditions: the teacher of the rich and the teacher of the poor. Undoubtedly the status of the grammar school teacher, in Britain as in Europe generally, is higher than that of the elementary school teacher, yet in judging the profession as a whole it is the influence of the elementary tradition which seems to be the stronger. The Registrar General, for example, places school teachers in Class II, the Intermediate class, and not in the category of higher administrative or professional employees in Class I. Similarly, the London School of Economics, in its study of social mobility, found that the elementary school teacher was ranked by members of the general public alongside the news reporter, the commercial traveller and the jobbing master builder, but below a Nonconformist minister, and certainly below the traditional professions.[43]

In the United States, too, the status of the teacher is an intermediate one. In 1947, in a study of the status of various occupations, the National Opinion Research Centre found that the school teacher was ranked in public opinion surveys only slightly above the average. Indeed, Lieberman in a critical survey of the teaching profession in the United States concludes that 'teachers are finding it more difficult than ever before to maintain their present intermediate status, let alone raise it to the level of such occupational groups as doctors and lawyers'.[44] Moreover, even though teacher-training is now carried out more and more frequently in multi-purpose institutions, Conant, amongst others, has pointed to the low esteem in which degrees in education are generally held.[45] It is therefore worth looking closely at some of the factors influencing the present status of teaching as an occupation.

One of the major problems facing the teaching profession is its very rapid rate of expansion. At first this affected only the elementary school teacher, and we have already examined some of the effects of this expansion on recruitment and training. During the twentieth century, however, secondary and, later, higher education have experienced rapid development and, although the United States was affected earlier and more profoundly, since the last war there have been rapid increases in both secondary and further education in most European countries. Both the scale and the rapidity of the expansion have meant that there has been an almost continuous shortage of qualified personnel to staff the schools, and at all times, but particularly during periods of rapid expansion, the profession has included large numbers of unqualified teachers. In the nineteenth century the proportion of unqualified women teachers was as high or higher than those who were qualified, and even in 1900 as many as 40 per cent of teachers in elementary schools were not qualified.[46] During the twentieth century, however, standards in elementary school teaching have risen considerably, and a survey in 1962 by the National Union of Teachers found that only six per cent of teachers in primary schools were unqualified. On the other hand teaching, even secondary school teaching, is a long way from being a graduate profession. Although the majority of teachers in grammar schools are graduates, this is true of only a minority in the secondary modern schools, who are still recruited in large part from the training colleges. The N.U.T. survey found 20.2 per cent of graduates amongst men teachers in secondary modern schools and 13.0 per cent of graduates amongst the women. In maintained grammar schools they were 81.5 per cent and 72.7 per cent, respectively. Primary schools are staffed almost entirely by non-graduates.[47]

Recent developments in the colleges, to which reference has already been made, may however be changing this pattern of recruitment by bringing nearer the all-graduate teaching profession. At the same time the rapid growth of comprehensive schools is breaking down the distinction within secondary education and bringing university- and college-trained teacher together in a single school. We are also moving from a long period of teacher shortage into the possibility of an over-supply of some kinds of teachers, although to what extent this is a temporary phenomenon, produced by financial problems, and to what extent it represents a real change in the long-term pattern of teacher demand has yet to be seen. Its effect in the short run however is likely to raise the qualifications of teachers, particularly when it is combined, as it is, with a fall in demand for teachers in higher education.

In the United States the teacher shortage has been more serious and the problem of unqualified staff more acute. We have already noticed the low level of education of elementary school teachers, which lasted into the early years of the present century. Even as late as 1908 a study of 735 high-school graduates in the State of New

York showed 117 of them directly entering teaching, as compared with 122 going to the normal schools.[48] The very rapid increase in the number of high schools at the end of the nineteenth century also produced a similar problem in the secondary schools. Indeed it has been estimated that the development of high schools had outrun the available supply of college-trained teachers as early as the 1870s and 80s, and the situation was to worsen later. Moreover, there were substantial variations even among neighbouring states.[49]

From the 1920s the level of education of school teachers gradually improved, but so did the standards expected of the profession, so that the number of unqualified teachers continued to be high. Moreover, since the 1940s there has been a serious shortage of teachers, which has accentuated the problem. Consequently although the great majority of teachers in elementary as well as secondary schools by the 1950s had a bachelor's or higher degree, in 1955 'there was not a single state in which every elementary teacher possessed at least four years of college training'.[50] Moreover, in 1960 about one fourth of all teachers still had had less than four years at college.[51]

Consequently, as Lieberman points out, although the higher requirements now expected of teachers may eventually help to raise the status of education as a profession, the present status of education as a profession is based chiefly upon the much lower requirements in force during the past four decades'.[52] As in Britain, however, a period of financial stringency, combined with a fairly drastic and probably long-term decline in the expansion of higher education is likely to raise the level of entrants to the profession.

Another problem for the teachers is that although their educational level is rising, so is that, not only of other professional occupations, but of the population in general. Consequently the improvements in the last 50 years have enabled teachers to maintain their status but not necessarily to improve it. This is particularly true in the United States, where the meaning of a bachelor's degree has changed radically, due to the rapid expansion in higher education. In Britain, however, as in Europe generally, expansion in higher education has been at a much slower rate, and it seems likely that the improvements in the educational background of school teachers has done more to improve their status than have the even greater improvements in teacher education in the United States.

A further characteristic of the teaching profession which is closely related to its status is the balance within it of male and female teachers. The proportions of women in elementary school teaching in the United States is so high that it can be reasonably described as a woman's occupation. A survey made by the National Education Association in 1956 found only 14 per cent of elementary school teachers to be men. Teachers in secondary education are, however, evenly balanced.[53] This preponderance of women has characterized the profession since the end of the nineteenth century, although the proportion of men teachers is now steadily rising.[54] Men, however, predominate in educational administration, including the post of school principal.

The proportion of women in education in the United States is probably greater than anywhere else in the world. In Britain, for example, although the proportion of women teachers is higher than in many European countries including France and Germany,[55] it is less than in the United States. About three-quarters of teachers in primary schools are women and roughly half of those in secondary schools. This is another reason to believe that the status of teachers in Britain and in Europe generally, is higher than in the United States.

One of the main reasons why teaching can still attract women into the profession when it is hard to recruit men lies in the lack of alternatives open to the educated woman, even when there are many such alternatives available for a man with similar qualifications. Not only is the salary scale favourable in comparison with what she could earn elsewhere, but working conditions, hours and holidays are often not only reasonable in themselves but fit in well with the responsibilities of a family. The profession is, therefore, particularly attractive to the girl who is looking for a job she can return to after she is married.[56]

The fact that many women in the profession see it as a temporary job rather than as a permanent career also has a profound effect on their expectations. The initial salary, the length of training, the possibility of rejoining the profession after a break of several years: all of these considerations are of more importance than ultimate salary or promotion possibilities. Consequently, the aspects of jobs which deter potential male recruits may not appear as disadvantages at all to many of the women entering the profession.

At the same time, the very appeal of the profession to women may diminish its attractiveness to men; for once any occupation becomes accepted as a woman's job, the idea grows that it is unsuitable for a man. According to Brookover and Gottlieb, 'teaching is associated with motherhood, with the training and socialization of the young, and with the protection of the needy. So firmly entrenched is this popular image in our society that it becomes difficult for a man who wants to enter the field to withstand the social pressures against doing so. The authors have talked with numerous college girls who are majoring in elementary education and find that few of them would be willing to consider as a husband a man who makes teaching his life's work.[57]

The size of the teaching profession is also an important factor in the status it is awarded and, particularly, in the extent to which it can expect high rewards for its services. The cost of maintaining a well-qualified and highly-paid teaching profession in the context of mass secondary education and an expanding system of higher education requires the backing of a community which is not only wealthy, but highly committed to education and willing to spend generously on the public services. The United States, with its tradition of private affluence and public squalor, is not likely to be willing to reward the large number of school teachers on the same level as the doctors. Lieberman has calculated that in the year 1954–5 equalizing teachers' salaries with the incomes of doctors would have required a sum larger than the total amount spent upon public education in that school year.

At the same time there is no evidence that teachers in the United States are at present falling behind other groups in terms of real income gains, although progress in this respect has been uneven. The years between 1920 and 1930 were favourable for the teachers, and they made large gains in comparison with other groups, but subsequently they lost ground, particularly between 1940 and 1950. Since 1950 the growth rate for teachers' salaries has been comparable to the growth rate for all professions. On the other hand the earnings of men teachers, although higher than those for women teachers, are nevertheless well below that of other professional men. Non-white teachers also earn less than white teachers and there are substantial regional differences. This probably explains the high level of 'moonlighting' by American teachers. One study of teachers in Georgia, for example, found that as many as one in four held second jobs for added income. They found that moonlighters were more likely to be male, white, young, with large families and a non-working wife.[59]

In Britain there is also evidence of considerable fluctuation in the teachers' financial position over time. After the First World War the real salaries of teachers improved greatly, and in subsequent years the teachers' union had considerable success in fighting salary cuts during a period of falling prices. Between 1938 and 1956, however, teachers' salaries did not rise sufficiently even to maintain their 1938 standard of living, although this relative decline in earnings was shared by other salaried workers and was part of the general improvement in the position of the working classes during this period. Since 1956, however, the teachers, along with salaried workers in general, have maintained and even improved their position. Within the profession, on the other hand, there have been important sectional differences. In the first decade after the war differentials narrowed, but the improvement since 1956 has included a widening of differentials both between primary and secondary school teachers, and grammar and secondary modern school teachers.[60]

A recent study of teachers in Poland has drawn attention to their very low salaries, particularly at the lower levels of the profession. Although teaching itself still has a high status in the community, the elementary school teacher, in particular, as well as those at the secondary level who have not graduated from the more prestigious forms of higher education feel themselves to be professional failures. The result has been a feminization of the profession, the prevalence of 'moonlighting' and a high turnover out of teaching altogether.[61]

On the other hand, the teaching profession also suffers, as Bryan Wilson[62] has pointed out, from the high level of diffuseness of the teaching role. The roles of the doctor or the lawyer, for example, are easier to define; there is a definable expertise involving an objective body of knowledge which is almost completely lacking in the case of teaching. It is true that teachers sometimes attempt to claim such a body of knowledge, and in the United States in particular there has been a widespread development of courses in 'education', but such courses have not yet met with general acceptance as either desirable or even necessary for the intending teacher. Conant,[63] for example, points out that 'many academic professors believe that the courses given by professors of education are worthless'. In Britain, teachers in grammar schools frequently have had no training for teaching at all. Consequently there is a tendency for teachers to fall back on the subjects they are qualified to teach, and where this is a highly esoteric body of knowledge in its own right, teachers can often command high prestige. Yet such a ranking system, by confusing the difficulty of a subject with the difficulty of teaching it, does less than justice to the role of the primary school teachers and, indeed, to the whole primary stage of the education process as well as to the education of the less able child.

One of the important strategies by means of which a professional group maintains both its status and its financial position is the control over entry. This enables it to regulate the supply of its services to the market not only by restricting training to prevent an over-supply but also, and perhaps even more importantly, by precluding the use of unqualified personnel in times of shortage. This aspect of professional status has however always eluded the teachers who, both in this country and in the United States, have had neither the formal status of civil servants, as they have in France for example, nor the self-government of autonomous professionals. One of the main reasons for their failure to attain a greater degree of professional status has been the opposition of the State, which has always jealously guarded its control over teacher supply. As Noel and Jose Parry have pointed out, the State gained control over education before the teachers had had time to build up a strong professional organization, so that, unlike the doctors in 1911 and 1948, they were unable to bargain from strength. At the same time the divisions in the profession, both between elementary and secondary education and between men and women teachers, enabled the State to divide and rule.[64]

The status of the college teacher, although it would appear to be invariably higher than that of the school teacher,[65] is also subject to considerable ambiguities, of which the most important is the discrepancy between the economic rewards of the profession and its educational level. This seems to be particularly acute in the United States, where academic salaries, especially at the lower end of the professional hierarchy, are not only strikingly low but have declined in relative terms since the pre-war period. Thus 'by 1957, physicians had gained 93 per cent over their 1939 real incomes—and over 400 per cent in dollar income; dentists had gained 54 per cent; lawyers about 45 per cent. During the same period the real income of the academic man actually *declined* 8.5 per cent - from an income already inadequate in 1939.'[66]

Because their earnings are so much less than others of similar educational background, it has been argued that 'there is a strong tendency for academics to withdraw from the general middle-class population and establish a distinctive and relatively isolated sub-culture'.[67] There is also evidence that some college teachers, at least in the United States, experience a high level of status anxiety. For example, Lazarsfeld and Thielens in a study of social-science professors found that a large proportion of their sample felt themselves held in low esteem by other occupational groups and particularly by businessmen.[68]

We can only speculate on the reasons for the relatively low socio-economic status of college teaching in the United States. It is likely, however, that the rate of expansion has reduced the elite nature of the profession, especially when it has meant the inclusion under the general higher-education umbrella of colleges offering courses and subjects at different academic levels. To this we may add the low prestige of intellectuals in the United States.

In Britain there has not been the discrepancy between economic reward and educational qualifications that there has been in the United States.[69] No doubt this is due to the small size of the profession in Britain and also the clear and unambiguous distinctions within higher education, which have maintained status and income differential between university teachers and those in colleges of education and technical colleges. It is likely too that the Oxbridge don still dominates the popular image of the university teacher. More recently, however, the expansion of the universities and developments within the binary sector, which have blurred the distinctions between the different parts of the higher education system, have challenged the pre-eminence of the university teacher in terms of both status and income. In this, as in other ways, Britain's educational system is moving albeit slowly in the direction of the pattern set by the United States.

4 The teacher organizations

No account of the teaching profession would be complete without some consideration of the part played in its development by the various teachers' organizations, and it is useful for this purpose to make a comparison between the professional teachers' organizations in Britain and their counterparts in the United States, and to attempt to assess their contributions to the professional status of the teachers in the two countries.

The largest organization of educators in the United States is the National Education Association, founded in 1857 when the presidents of 10 State educational associations issued a call to the teachers of the country to form a national organization. This organization, then the National Teachers' Association, joined in 1870 with the National Association of School Superintendents and the American Normal School Association to form the N.E.A. Membership of this Association is open to anyone actively engaged in the profession of teacher or other education work.[70] This means that not only teachers, but principals, superintendents and other professional workers are all members, leading to the charge on the part of many teachers that the N.E.A. is dominated by administrators.

The main achievement of the N.E.A. has been in meeting the needs of its members for specialist information. The Research Division, which was created in 1922, provides members with information and consultative services on a very wide scale. The other main professional activity is the National Commission on Teacher Education and Professional Standards, which was established in 1946 with the declared aim of the advancement of professional standards, including standards for institutions which prepare teachers.

On the whole, however, the N.E.A. in spite of its size and importance, has not been a particularly militant organization, largely because of its limited view of its function. Indeed, Lieberman points out that for many years it took the view that as a professional association it was not concerned with things like teachers' salaries. Consequently, its predominance has been seriously challenged by the teachers' unions, the overwhelming majority of which are affiliated with the American Federation of Teachers. This is essentially a trade union of teachers, and superintendents are excluded. The A.F.T. is itself affiliated with the trade-union movement as a whole in the form of the Combined American Federation of Labour and the Congress of Industrial Organizations. Although the first teachers' unions date from the beginning of the century, the spread of the movement was handicapped by the general opposition to trade-union activity in the United States, which led to severe opposition from local school boards including the dismissal of teachers who were union members. Since the 1940s, however, when the general opposition to trade unionism began to decline, membership of the A.F.T. has increased rapidly, although the total membership is well below that of the N.E.A. It also tends to be concentrated in large cities.

167

The A.F.T. has been concerned in the main with salaries and conditions of service rather than with the wider issues of professionalism. Consequently, although active in the field of teachers' civil and professional rights, including such issues as racial discrimination, it has tended to neglect those professional functions which have been the main concern of the N.E.A. There is also some evidence that this difference in emphasis is reflected in the membership. A recent study by Lowe of one school district found that both sex and teaching level were associated with membership, elementary school teachers being more likely to join the N.E.A. than secondary teachers, and men less likely to join than women. The most significant of the findings, however, was that dissatisfied teachers were more likely to join the A.F.T. than to join the N.E.A.[71] A more widely-based study by Rosenthal also found sex important. Men were not only more likely to join a teachers' union but schools with large proportions of men on their staffs appeared to facilitate union membership.[72]

During the 1960s both the N.E.A. and A.F.T. have become considerably more militant. The N.E.A., for example, called one of the biggest teachers' strike in the history of American education in the state of Florida. The one-day strike by the A.F.T. in New York in 1962 was also a turning-point in its history, and established the union as a permanent part of the educational power in New York. Even more significant in the history of teacher unions was the series of strikes by the New York branch of the A.F.T. in 1968. Both prolonged and bitter, these strikes were fought primarily over the issue of decentralization and community control which the A.F.T. saw as a threat to the tenure and other rights they had gained for themselves in their relationship with the professional administrators at City Hall.[73] The year 1968 also saw the founding of the National Association of Afro-American Educators with the aim of increasing not only community and parental control over the school but also the introduction of curricula and instructional material with a strong black orientation.

Consequently, although in the past teachers' organizations have been weak and have had little influence in shaping policy or even in preventing interference in educational matters by other groups, there is evidence that this is now changing. Rosenthal, for example, concludes from his study of teacher organizations in New York, Boston and San Francisco that, at least in the cities, 'the transformation of teacher organizations has been startling'. On the other hand, their impact so far has been confined largely to salaries and related matters, and in comparison with teacher organizations in some other countries they have had little say on educational policies generally.[74]

There have been several attempts to explain the increasing militancy of American teachers. A study by Cole of New York teachers pointed out dissatisfactions with pay scales, and the problems, including discipline, faced by teachers in certain types of school. Factors which led dissatisfied teachers towards militancy included the changed attitude towards civil disobedience, including strikes. Moreover the very success of the minor militant innovations pushed the leaders towards greater militancy. Changes in the type of teachers entering the profession, and particularly the increase in the number of men in secondary schools, may also have led to a greater sympathy for trade union activity generally. He found that in general young teachers were more militant than older teachers, and men more militant than women. Family background was also important, as was political affiliation.[75] A study by Chaney compared school districts which have experienced teacher strikes with those that have not. He found that the districts where strikes occurred were larger, provided a high level of support for the A.F.T. as distinct from the N.E.A., and had achieved a higher degree of formalized collective bargaining. The teaching force in these districts was more likely to be young, better-educated, and male.[76] The explanation of teacher militancy, therefore, must be sought at the level of changes in the characteristics of teachers, in dissatisfaction arising from changes in the job itself and in rates of pay, in the growing size of administrative districts, and in a growing acceptance of strike action and militancy as appropriate forms of political action.

The National Union of Teachers, the largest and most important of the English teacher organizations, was founded in 1870, largely, as Tropp has related, in response to the Education Act of that year.[77] Although originally formed to protect the interests of the elementary school teacher, it now includes in its membership teachers from both primary and secondary schools. Like the American Federation of Teachers, the N.U.T. does not include administrators who have their own associations.

Apart from the N.U.T. there are also four secondary associations, mainly representing teachers in the grammar schools. Headmasters, headmistresses, assistant masters and assistant mistresses each have their own association. To some extent the N.U.T. and the Joint 4, as the secondary associations are often called, are and always have been in opposition over fundamental issues of policy. Even in the 1890s, for example, the controversy over the future of the higher grade schools found the N.U.T. representing the elementary school teachers, and the secondary association representing the grammar schools, on opposite sides of the fence.[78] Another period of opposition followed the attempts after the 1944 Education Act to unify the teaching profession, and reduce differentials between graduate and non-graduate teachers.[79]

The greatest rival of the N.U.T. is however the National Association of Schoolmasters. Founded as a breakaway organization, its members were originally brought together by their opposition to equal pay. When they failed in this campaign, the organization turned its attention to the career prospects of those, particularly among the non-graduates, who were, unlike many of the women teachers, likely to spend their lifetimes in the school. They have focused consequently on the problems of the male teacher, and in recent years have had a good measure of success.

Although the N.U.T. is not, strictly speaking, a trade union, it has from the start concerned itself with issues arising out of the conditions of employment of teachers. Foremost of these is teachers' salaries which, since the end of the First World War, have been settled by negotiations between representatives of the main teachers' associations and the local authorities, subject to government approval. Apart from salaries, superannuation, security of tenure, and the freedom of the teacher from outside interference have all been issues of central importance. In this respect the N.U.T. resembles the A.F.T. rather than the N.E.A. At the same time the N.U.T. has always been deeply concerned with the professional status of teaching, and has worked constantly to raise the level of recruitment to the profession. Although unsuccessful in their attempts to gain control of entry to the profession, their efforts to resist dilution have often succeeded. For example, they were able to block suggestions made in the mid-1950s for either a general lowering of the standard of entry or some kind of apprenticeship scheme. They have also been successful in resisting the large-scale recruitment of teachers' assistants.

The success of the N.U.T. as a professional organization can be attributed in part to the early development of a sense of professional awareness, clearly defined objectives and a militant and able leadership, but above all it has made itself into a powerful and influential pressure group at both the local and the national level. From the very early days of the N.U.T. every effort was made to influence the local School Boards, the Department of Education, and Parliament itself, and this tradition has continued to the present day. Moreover, as early as 1877, the N.U.T. began to plan the election of a teacher M.P., and in 1893 the first two sponsored candidates were elected.

Tropp has drawn attention to the considerable influence of the N.U.T. not only on such matters as salaries, pensions, and tenure, but also upon many issues of national policy. It was, for example, in the forefront of the opposition to the system of 'payment by results', and was one of the early supporters of the doctrine of secondary education for all.[80] In terms of political affiliation, too, the sponsored M.PS nearly all belong to the Labour Party. Manzer however has argued that the N.U.T. 'must now be regarded as a powerful conservative influence in the politics of English education'.[81] This conservatism is expressed chiefly in the refusal to sacrifice certain long-standing educational ideals, as, for example, a unified teaching profession, and the employment of teachers' aides, both of which, in Manzer's view, stand in the way of the solution of problems of teacher supply.

It is however at the local level that we can perhaps see the influence of the teachers' associations most strongly. Peschek, in his study of secondary education in West Ham, has illustrated how teachers' organizations can operate as a powerful local pressure group. Indeed, in a survey of the influence of the West Ham Teachers' Associations over a number of years, he concludes that no major changes in local education authority policy have taken place in West Ham without consultation with the Teachers' Association.[82]

Studies at the local level, however, show that the issue of teachers' influence on policy-making cannot be defined simply in progressive or conservative terms. To begin with, there are political differences between the rank and file membership and the leadership. Although, as we have seen, the M.P.s sponsored by the N.U.T. are predominantly members of the Labour Party, this does not seem true of teachers generally. A recent survey, for example, disclosed that three-quarters of primary school teachers vote against the Labour Party, and so do almost as many of those teaching in secondary schools.[83]

At the same time, attitudes to issues like comprehensive school re-organization do not appear to be related very closely to political party affiliation. Teachers who oppose a plan for comprehensive schooling may do so because it threatens their security of tenure or promotion prospects, just as teachers may approve a plan because it seems to offer them a chance to do their work more effectively.[84] It is for this reason that local secondary school associations will often oppose such a move, and the N.U.T. approve it.

From time to time in its history the N.U.T. has also undertaken more direct action. In 1907 teachers were withdrawn from schools in West Ham, and in 1914 the N.U.T. forced the closure of schools in Herefordshire, as part of its aim of a national salary structure. More recently the N.U.T. has entered another militant phase and in 1956, as part of its fight against the Superannuation Bill, called on its members to cease collecting school savings.[85] In 1958 the N.U.T. Conference for the first time rejected a provisional agreement on salaries recommended by the N.U.T. Executive. Since then, token strikes, the refusal to supervise school meals and to work with unqualified teachers, have been employed as part of the fight for changes in working conditions and salary scales.[86]

To some extent this militancy on the part of the N.U.T. has been a reaction to the growth of the more militant N.A.S., but this growth is itself symptomatic of increasing dissatisfaction in the teaching profession. Much of the appeal of the N.A.S. is to non-graduate men teaching in secondary schools, and it is this group, Manzer[87] has argued, who have also been an important source of discontent inside the N.U.T. itself. Grace,[88] in his study of teachers, also found that perception of role conflict was greatest for men teachers in secondary modern schools, particularly in working-class areas. Similarly a study by Deem[89] of militant and non-militant teachers found that the militants in her sample were almost all male, few were graduates, and they came predominantly from comprehensive or secondary modern schools. Deem draws particular attention to the crucial role played by the graduate/non-graduate division in teaching in this country. Her research, although only on a small scale, clearly indicates that militancy occurs in the non-graduate group of teachers, who are at the greatest relative disadvantage in the occupation as a whole with regard to salaries, conditions, and status.

It is interesting in this connection to note that in France, where teachers are also divided by background and training, the teachers' organizations also represent divided interests and loyalties. The secondary teachers tend to identify with the higher civil service. On salaries they favour the maintenance of a hierarchy of differentials, whereas the primary teachers prefer across-the-board increases. The secondary teachers are also more traditional and elitist with respect to educational policy.[90]

On the other hand status within the teaching profession is not necessarily a bar to militancy. In the United States, associations of college teachers and university professors have 'adopted bargaining and sanction processes formerly employed only by unions'.[91] In Britain, the Association of University Teachers has called its first strike. It is not clear however whether this reflects a change in the recruitment of university teachers, a dissatisfaction with salaries and conditions, or a change in attitude towards militancy as a suitable strategy for protest. Indeed it is probable that all three are involved.

To study teachers as a professional group is however to consider only one aspect of the influence of teachers on education. They operate most significantly at the level of the school, and within the school at the level of the classroom. Not only are many policy decisions made at this level, but even those which originate at higher levels of the power structure have to be implemented in the school. Further chapters therefore will be concerned with the teacher in both the organization of the school and in relationships within the school. First, however, it is necessary to look at some of the new developments in what can best be called the sociology of educational knowledge.

8 The sociology of educational knowledge

1 *The definition of the field*

The content of education has by no means been neglected in the sociology of education, and previous editions of this textbook have explored in some detail the relationship between the economy, the division of labour, and scientific and technical education in secondary schools and universities. The new interest in the curriculum is however concerned with the content of education at a different and more fundamental level. By starting from a position *within* the sociology of knowledge, the new thinking, as Michael F. D. Young has described,[1] explores the implications of treating knowledge as socially constructed, and the curriculum as socially organized knowledge. In consequence, not only do new problems arise, but old problems go through a significant change of emphasis. The question at issue for example changes from 'Why do some children fail?' to 'How do rates of educational success and failure come to be produced?' Similarly schools are seen as knowledge-processing as well as people-processing organizations. Stratification is still a major theme but it is now the stratification of *knowledge* which is of central concern. At the same time, culture, rather than structure becomes the chief organizing principle and Bourdieu, for example, is concerned with education as a system of thought, and the educational process as the transmission of culture.[2]

Bernstein has provided us with a useful map of the new approach to the study of educational knowledge. He distinguishes firstly the curriculum itself, which defines what counts as valid knowledge. Secondly there is pedagogy, or the way in which the curriculum is transmitted, and this defines what counts as a valid transmission of knowledge. Thirdly there is evaluation, and this defines what counts as a valid realization of this knowledge on the part of the taught.

174

Through these three 'message systems' as he calls them, formal educational knowledge is realized.[3]

All three of these message systems are of central importance in the sociology of educational knowledge, and may be said, between them, to form the core of the subject. Moreover they are areas which, in terms of research, are now developing quite rapidly, and which are likely to prove to be important growth points in the future. For this reason it seemed appropriate to bring them together into a completely new chapter.

2 *The curriculum*

Although, as we have seen, the central government in Britain now plays an important part in educational decision-making, developments in the content of education, Young argues, are largely decided outside Westminster.[4] To some extent this is a consequence of the traditional autonomy in these matters granted to the headmaster or headmistress and which does in fact allow a considerable degree of freedom to the individual school. Against this however must be set the constraints of the system of external examinations which, in secondary schools at least, allows the universities a considerable amount of influence on the content of the curriculum.

Considerable light on this process is shed by a recent study of the attitudes of a sample of sixth-form teachers from both maintained, direct grant, and independent schools, and which also included an examination of the role of university selection procedures. It was found that the universities, through their individual departments, exerted pressure not only for high A level passes but also for particular and often restrictive combinations of subjects. Interestingly enough, teachers themselves were not aware of this as a constraint because of the shared attitudes of teachers and university staffs. The authors show that only in comprehensive schools, which are trying to cater to the needs of a new kind of student, is there any sense of conflict.[5] Sixth-Form Colleges, the authors suggest, may also offer a challenge to these traditional attitudes. The study offers a particularly interesting example of the way in which attitudes persist over time, since specialization is not only a value shared by both teachers and universities, but is linked into the daily life of schools and the career structure of teachers.[6]

The traditional pattern of decision-making on the curriculum in Britain has recently been challenged by the setting up of the Schools Council in 1964. It was originally conceived at the Ministry of Education[7] as a response to developments in knowledge, particularly in science, and the increasing number of pupils in full-time education. At this stage it was simply a study unit staffed jointly by inspectors and administrators. This apparent interference by central government into an area where there had previously been autonomy was received coldly by teachers and local education authorities alike and the Schools Council which eventually took the place of the original study unit was designed as a partnership of central and local authorities and the teaching profession.

Young has suggested that the Schools Council is a particularly significant area for the politics of educational knowledge. He argues that the predominance of the universities and the academic expert leads to an acceptance of the basic structure of academic subjects. Similarly there is little challenge to traditional ideas of what constitutes good teaching.[8] Consequently the limits of educational change, and what counts as innovation are closely defined.

Hoyle[9] has attempted to set out the main bodies involved in the diffusion of curriculum innovations. The Schools Council heads the list but it also includes such diverse bodies as publishers, professional organizations, the H.M.I.s, teacher training institutions at various levels, examining bodies and teachers' unions. Little research has however been conducted in any of these agencies, or into the relationships between them.

One very important aspect of the stratification of knowledge which has been of much concern in the new approach to the sociology of education, but which also links it to the old, is the way in which a differential social evaluation of knowledge is linked to a differential access to knowledge. The distinction between elementary and secondary education has of course traditionally implied a difference in the content of education as the name elementary itself implies.[10] Even when the subjects were the same, the standard aimed at was different, and there were many subjects, of which perhaps Latin is the best example, which were exclusively part of the secondary tradition.

The development of tripartite and bipartite systems of secondary education has also been linked with differing curricula, appropriate in the words of the Norwood Committee, to different types of mind. Moreover, although to some of its advocates the comprehensive school has implied a common curriculum, most of the early experiments in comprehensive education favoured segregation by ability. Specialization on academic and non-academic lines has also been a feature of comprehensive schools including many of the common secondary schools in the United States.

One of the main criticisms of the Schools Council is that it accepts and perpetuates the idea that children of different abilities need a different curriculum. Shipman, for example, has pointed out that innovation tends to be concentrated in courses for the less able pupils, leaving the traditional subject framework intact for the pupils of above average ability. The consequence may be to 'divide education into two systems in the 1970s as effectively as selection has done in the past'.[11]

Differential access to knowledge is also linked with the distribution of resources. Eileen Byrne[12] has shown graphically, for example, how assumptions about the nature of the education required by different children influenced resource allocation to the consistent advantage of the more able children. It was believed not only that they needed longer in school, but also that they needed more highly paid staff and more money for books. Curricular distinctions were also widespread, and these often led to transfer difficulties. For instance, general science rather than the three separate sciences was considered appropriate for the secondary modern school. At the same time teachers got higher status and higher rewards for teaching the ablest rather than the less able children.

Eileen Byrne also produces evidence of discrimination by sex, both in the allocation of resources and in terms of curricular choice. Even in mixed schools heads tended to channel girls to biology and boys to physics.[13] Work is also now in progress on the effect of the curriculum on sex role stereotyping in schools in the United States.[14] Sexton has argued, on rather different lines, that the verbal emphasis in schools, and the neglect of technical and practical subjects, gives girls an advantage, and goes a good way to explain their superior performance in the American school system.[15]

The French sociologist Bourdieu is also interested in the differentiating function of education. He argues that the educational system demands a cultural competence that it does not itself provide, and which, because it is part of what Bourdieu calls the 'cultural unconscious',[16] can only be acquired through the family. The educational system, therefore, gives an advantage to those who come from educated families, or, as Bourdieu phrases it, are the possessors of 'cultural capital', and consequently reproduces the existing structure of distribution of cultural capital between classes. There is, therefore, a close analogy between cultural capital and economic capital, and indeed possession of one often implies possession of the other.[17]

Teachers, Bourdieu argues, 'are the products of a system whose aim is to transmit an aristocratic culture'.[18] This aristocratic culture values style and taste, and talent and precocity are regarded highly. Subjects which depend on these virtues and therefore offer the best investment for cultural capital tend to attract pupils from a higher social level than those subjects which demand the less highly valued habits of dedication and industry.[19]

The comparative studies carried out by Ben-David however suggest that this is not necessarily so in all societies. Although secondary and higher education in Europe has placed considerable emphasis on the acquisition of items of the traditional culture of the upper-middle classes, this has not been particularly true of the United States. Here, as Ben-David points out, the 'much wider scope of studies creates a more flexible standard of achievement and, as a result, a greater variety of attitudes and motivations can be satisfied within the educational system. That is why secondary and higher education in the United States can cater to a wider range of class differences and to people with a somewhat wider range of motivation and intelligence test scores than elsewhere.'[20]

Bernstein, in his writings on the curriculum,[21] has approached it from a somewhat different angle. He has been chiefly concerned to develop a framework within which different types of curricula can be classified, and has made use, as in his other work, of a series of dichotomies from which ideal types can be derived. Within this framework he distinguishes two main types of curricula: the *collection* type, where the contents are insulated from one another, and the *integrated* type, where the various contents do not go their separate ways. He uses the term *classification* to refer to the strength of the boundaries between contents, or, in Parsonian phraseology, the degree of boundary maintenance. The collection code, by definition, implies strong classification; the integrated code, the opposite. Traditionally, European education has been based on strong classification but Bernstein discerns a movement, albeit weak at present, towards the integrated curriculum. There are however two different types of integration, with rather different implications. As in English infant schools, the child may continue to have one teacher, but the differences between subjects may become blurred, or, on the other hand, the subjects may remain, but the barriers between teachers may be broken down, as in some types of team-teaching. Alternatively, of course, although this is a much more radical change, barriers between subjects *and* between teachers may weaken or disappear.

When classification is strong, the training of teachers involves socialization into subject loyalties, and knowledge comes to be seen as private property. Children, as Bernstein, phrases it, are 'encouraged to work as isolated individuals with their arms around their work'. As classification weakens, the old oligarchic subject hierarchies break down, to be replaced by horizontal relationships. Teacher autonomy is reduced but the discretion of pupils is increased as the emphasis upon states of knowledge is replaced by an emphasis upon ways of teaching. On the other hand, although boundaries are weak or blurred at the surface level, the integrated curriculum may at bottom rest upon closed explicit ideologies. This is because of the need for greater homogeneity in the transmission and assessment of knowledge, so that where the ideologies are not shared, 'the consequences will become visible and threaten the whole at every point'.

Smith,[22] in a recent commentary on Bernstein's paper, has drawn an analogy between the concept of collection in Bernstein, and sponsorship in Turner. Although Bernstein is concerned with patterns of authority and identity at the micro level, and Turner is concerned with patterns of stratification at the macro level, there are many points of similarity between them. Smith points out, for example, that each acknowledges a Durkheimian inspiration; that each is concerned with boundary maintenance, although Bernstein is interested in areas of knowledge, and Turner in categories of students; and that Turner shares Bernstein's interest in the effects on personality of experiencing different kinds of educational socialization.

The change from a collection to an integrated curriculum is likely, Bernstein has argued, to provide resistance because it disturbs subject identities and concepts of property. Shipman, in a detailed study of a curriculum project[23] has challenged this assumption. In the schools he studied, mostly secondary modern schools, resistance of this kind was rarely found. Indeed, although the original intention was to develop integrated studies along the lines of team-teaching, with subject specialists working on common themes, most schools went for integration at what Bernstein calls *teacher* rather than *teachers* level. It is perhaps significant that this form of integration, although it requires teachers to become generalist rather than specialist in orientation, requires less co-operation than team-teaching, and so does not entail the same level of ideological consensus.

It may also have been significant that the schools involved were secondary modern rather than grammar schools, since the college-trained teacher is less likely to have been socialized into strong subject loyalties than the university graduate. This too, as Bernstein has pointed out, may be why this form of integration curriculum has developed furthest in the infant school. It is interesting in this connection to notice that Anderson found that teachers with little professional training and prior teaching experience were more willing to try new techniques and more interested in new developments in the curriculum than highly trained and experienced teachers.[24]

In describing the transition, as he sees it, from one kind of curriculum to another, Bernstein does not attempt to develop a theory of curriculum change. In a short passage at the end of his paper he does, however, suggest very briefly, that changes in the division of labour, and a crisis in the structure of power and principles of control are both involved. Although Bernstein sees the movement for the integrated curriculum as an attempt to alter the power structure, he does not relate the power struggle, if such it is, to any particular groups in society and he is indeed closer to Durkheim than to either Weber or Marx in his interpretation of the integrated curriculum as 'symptoms of a moral crisis'.

Young, on the other hand, followed Weber in laying stress on the differential social evaluation of knowledge in terms of the dominant group's ideas of the educated man. In his study of the Chinese literati,[25] for example, Weber paints a vivid picture of the narrow, bookish character of their education and its reliance on classical texts. Knowledge of these texts not only defined the educated man but controlled entry into the administrative elite. Wilkinson, too, has argued a similar thesis about the classical curriculum of the nineteenth-century public school: 'In both Imperial China and Victorian England,' he argues, 'the gentleman ideal was promoted by education systems whose values were those of the landlord rather than those of the urban businessman.'[26] Radically different definitions of education follow a change in power relationships. One of the consequences of the growing bureaucratization of society as Weber saw it was the gradual replacement of the cultivated man, or amateur, by the bureaucrat, whose power is based upon his expert knowledge.

Using a neo-Marxist approach, but one that has considerable affinity with Weber, Raymond Williams[27] has distinguished four sets of educational ideologies which relate back to the social position of those who hold them. The first of these is the ideal of the gentleman which is associated with the aristocracy or gentry. Secondly Williams describes the professional or vocational ideal of the merchant and professional. Thirdly, there is the expansionist ideal of the educational reformer, and fourthly the ideal of the working classes and other subordinate groups, which, largely outside the formal educational system, stresses relevance, choice and participation. As Young points out, however, the main weakness in this approach is that little attention is paid by Williams to the changing power relationships between groups which might account for actual changes in the curriculum. It is also difficult to associate the radical reformers with any single group in society. Clearly expansionist ideas have been held by both 'liberal' conservatives and 'conservative' radicals, and have indeed played a dominant role in the educational policies of the Labour Party. As Rodney Barker has shown, the advocates of an independent working-class education failed to get a foothold in the Party, and Labour policy remained committed to an extension of opportunities for working-class children in the existing system.[28]

Young has suggested that we need to look at the interrelationship between various social, cultural and institutional factors influencing curricular change. He commends in particular the work of Davie, who has described the attempt of the Scottish universities to retain their distinctive features, which were democratic and generalist, against assimilation to the very different traditions of Oxford and Cambridge.[29] The study by Rothblatt of nineteenth-century Cambridge describes the rather more successful efforts of the Cambridge dons to retain their traditional aristocratic connections through an opposition to 'useful' knowledge.[30]

Smith,[31] too, has drawn attention to the need to examine the relationship between educational and other structures *over time*. He suggests that both the emergence and the erosion of the English collection systems must be understood as an outcome of changing patterns of relationship among elites, and between elite groups and an increasingly organized work force. Since the last war, both obligarchic collection and the sponsorship model of selection have been fundamentally weakened as a result of the increased power of managerial elites and working-class organization. Ideologies of integration, with their desire to democratize power structures, represent a disenchantment on the part of these new groups with the old assumptions about the class structure. Smith therefore sees it to some extent as a crisis of legitimacy.

This is similar to Eggleston's argument[32] that the traditional curriculum is being challenged by new groups with a more democratic ideology. In developing a typology of orientation towards the curriculum Eggleston sees signs of a move from a traditional, determined and commitment-based curriculum towards one which is futuristic, innovatory and contract-based. One of its most significant aspects is the opening up of curriculum decision-making to students and pupils. Eggleston, however, is more concerned with the contents of the rival ideologies than with delineating the relationship between the groups involved.

It should be recalled, however, that there has recently been a reappraisal of progressive education as it has developed in the United States. The stress on cooperation, social adjustment and group work has been seen by some writers,[33] at least, as conservative rather than radical in its implications. On the other hand Swift takes a different view, and sees it in part at least as a consequence of the development of the largely unstreamed comprehensive school. It is perhaps significant that the development of the integrated curriculum is taking place in this country just as schools and teachers are beginning to face up to some of the implications of mixed-ability teaching.

It is clear, therefore, that the study of this aspect of the sociology of education has only just begun. Not only is there a dearth of empirical studies, but major theoretical problems remain unsolved. One of the most important areas still to be explored is the relationship between the stratification of knowledge, ideology, and the economy. Clearly there is no simple mechanism linking the curriculum and the economy and the relationship between the two is mediated by the system of stratification, and the structure of power. It is

Smith's view, for example, that the integrated curriculum is essentially unstable, and that what is likely to occur is a drift towards some form of *egalitarian* collection. This is largely because relationships within the macrostructure are not altered by setting up an arena of democratic cooperation within the schools. Consequently what will in effect emerge is a *de facto* contest system in which only the conditions of competition have changed.

There will also be variations between societies in the degree to which the educational system is brought into relationship with the economy, as well as in the nature of the relationship itself. Nevertheless attempts at a theory of curriculum change must account for the part played by the economy.

At the same time, attempts at curricular reform, as with other movements for change in the educational system, must take account of the enormous complexity of the relationship between education and other aspects of the social structure. Whitty, for example, has drawn attention to the dangers as well as the advantages of the social construction of knowledge approach. He argues that too narrow a concentration on the 'processes whereby particular conceptions of school knowledge are legitimated and sustained' may lead to the implication that 'any educational alternative, or redefinition of knowledge is possible'.[34] In so far as the stratification of knowledge is bound up with the system of social stratification, and with systems of rewards and power, some of the arguments for curricular change can indeed be seen in Whitty's words as 'romantic individualism'. The emphasis on cultural relativism which is a feature of Nell Keddie's Reader[35] adds a valuable sociological perspective to philosophic and psychological studies of the curriculum, but can be misleading if it ignores the structural and indeed historical context in which beliefs about knowledge occur. It is this romanticism which mars the new sociology of education and which is strikingly exemplified not only in its treatment of the curriculum but in its handling of pedagogy and evaluation.

3 Pedagogy

Bernstein[36] defines pedagogy, the second of his three message systems, as the way in which the curriculum is transmitted. Just as he develops the concept of *classification* to indicate the strength of the boundaries between the content of knowledge, so he introduces the concept of *frame* to define the relationship between teacher and taught. The strength of framing therefore refers to the degree of control teachers and taught possess over the selection, organization and pacing of the knowledge transmitted. Where the framing is weak, therefore, the child rather than the teacher controls the selection and organization of his learning and the time-scale over which he works.

Classification and framing can vary independently of one another. The progressive schools which developed in the independent sectors of secondary education during the 1920s and 1930s, schools like Dartington Hall and Summerhill, appear to have been organized around a system of very weak framing but relatively strong classification, since they were still based largely on traditional subjects. In the United States on the other hand, the progressive movement which spread through the public sector of education before the war was marked by a move towards the integrated curriculum and away from the traditional academic subjects, but there does not seem to have been any very consistent or persistent move towards a system of weak framing.

There is however evidence that the new movement in this country towards the integrated curriculum proceeds alongside a new style of pedagogy. It is probably found most extensively in the infant school where a great deal has been done to 'translate child-centre theory into every-day practice',[37] but its spread into the whole of primary education is likely to be encouraged by the endorsement given to this particular approach by the Plowden Report, which recognized 'a general and quickening trend' in that direction. The ideology of the Report clearly supports both weak framing and weak classification, in its advocacy of individual discovery, first-hand experience and opportunities for creative work, and its insistence 'that knowledge does not fall into neatly separate compartments, and that work and play are not opposite but complementary'.[38]

The movement has been noticeably slower in secondary education, although the integrated curriculum has made some small headway, particularly for the less able child. Radical changes in pedagogy, on the other hand, seem to have been confined to a relatively small number of schools, of which Countesthorpe in Leicestershire is perhaps the best known.[39] One of the central features of Countesthorpe, and similar schools, is the greater involvement of the pupils, collectively, in decision-making, and the more relaxed atmosphere within the classroom. The traditional classroom has also been replaced by a series of teaching groups of different sizes, and there is a heavy emphasis on individual learning. The emphasis is also away from traditional subjects and towards themes, such as 'work', 'education', and 'law and order'.

On the whole, sociologists have been much less interested in pedagogy than in the curriculum, so that we have few sociological studies of changes in pedagogic style, and either their causes or their consequences. There is a vast literature on teaching method, and the effectiveness of different teaching styles, but this has been conducted in the main by educationists and is rarely set in a specifically sociological framework. It will however be discussed briefly in the chapter on the classroom.

On the other hand, it seems reasonable to interpret the development of the new pedagogy in terms of the pressures which are also at work in changing the curriculum. Certainly, in the move for greater participation by pupils we can see evidence of the pressure for a more democratic form of society. Similarly the change in the mode of control on the part of the teacher reflects, and indeed to some extent follows, a change towards a greater egalitarianism within the family. This in itself may reflect, as Bernstein has suggested, a crisis in the structure of power and principles of control, or as Smith has phrased it, a disenchantment with old assumptions about the class structure.

This is reflected very clearly in the attempt, on the part of what Hargreaves has called the New Romantics, 'to erode or blur the distinction between teachers and other adults, between teachers and learners, between schools and other institutions in society'.[40] He draws attention to the crucial part played in their ideological position by the concepts of voluntarism, freedom and choice, and, as a corollary, self-directed, individualized, learning. As Hargreaves also points out, the New Romantics share with the deschoolers a 'deep-rooted faith in the individual and his potentiality for self-realization'[41] It is this essential optimism about the nature of man which justifies Hargreaves' description of their philosophy as Romantic. It also explains their faith in the 'free' school.

This aspect of the new pedagogy, which finds expression for example in the Plowden Report, has been described by Bernstein and Davies as a 'horticultural view of child nature and development'.[42] In it the child is regarded as passing, naturally, through a series of stages, and his ultimate maturity is seen as basically developmental. The analogy here, although it may be an extreme one, is the development of the seed into the flower, or the acorn into the tree. This is not, of course, to deny the importance of the environment, but the teacher in this analogy is the gardener, who provides the conditions for growth but does not fashion or mould the flower or tree.

Bernstein and Davies criticize this perspective for neglecting 'the cultural and social shaping of the roles of children of different sexes from differing class backgrounds'.[43] In a later paper, Bernstein has taken up some of these points and elaborated them in a critique of what he calls the invisible pedagogy, particularly as it is practised in the infant school.[44] He suggests that weak classification and framing are realized through invisible pedagogies. Bernstein, however, has pointed out that the invisible pedagogy had its origins in the private nursery schools and represents an ideological conflict *within* the middle class. The new middle class, who represent the invisible pedagogy, are those who are filling the expanding major and minor professional class, concerned with the servicing of persons. They are, Bernstein adds, agents of symbolic control. The assumptions of the invisible pedagogy also betray their class origins. It presupposes, for example, an elaborated form of communication, and therefore the type of family structure from which this springs and a mother who is herself an agent of 'cultural reproduction'.

When the invisible pedagogy is translated into the ordinary infant school it raises problems for the teacher, since it is an expensive style of teaching. It needs, for example, small classes and a particular style of architecture for its successful application. Furthermore, although it is potentially beneficial to the working-class child, in that its pace is more relaxed, the symbolic discontinuity between school and home may prevent this potential from being realized. Finally, the shift from invisible to visible pedagogies at later stages of the educational process is likely to be harder for the working-class child.

Similar anxieties with respect to the progress of working-class children have been expressed in relation to individualized learning. Taylor, for example, has pointed out that individual work 'amounts in a very real sense to a sharpening of streaming',[45] since it enables some children to go ahead much faster than others. Bernbaum, in his study of Countesthorpe College, also feared an increasing polarization of achievement on social class lines. Teachers complained that children who needed to do extra work were just the ones who refused to do it.[46]

The problems raised by Bernstein, and also by Taylor and Bernbaum, arise partly from inadequacies in the assumptions underlying the new pedagogy and partly from a failure to appreciate the social and cultural context in which education is set. The freedom and self-realization of the new-style classroom is, as Bernstein has pointed up, more apparent than real, since the teacher still controls the setting and evaluates the progress of the child. Moreover this is necessary while the school still serves as a selective and socializing agency for the world of work. It is for this reason that the sociology of educational knowledge is deeply concerned with the concept of evaluation.

4 Evaluation

Bernstein's third message system, evaluation, has been of much greater concern to sociologists than either pedagogy or the curriculum, probably because of its very clear and obvious relationship with selection. It is however its links with social stratification and the division of labour which have been chiefly explored in the past, and less attention has been paid to evaluation itself, and to its relationship to the nature of educational knowledge.

There are a number of ways in which forms of assessment can vary, and the first necessity is a framework in which this variation can be explored. Young,[47] for example, has drawn attention to the crucial distinction between non-literate and literate societies and the consequences for evaluation of the decline in importance of an oral tradition and oral expression. Equally significant has been the increasing bureaucratization of education and the search for objective or universalistic forms of assessment to replace the older, particularistic system of patronage.

Weber saw this development in terms of the growing significance in an industrializing society of 'expert' knowledge. This is linked in turn with the changing importance of social groupings whether these are concerned as classes, or status groups. Gusfield,[48] in an interesting paper on the British Civil Service, has argued that during the nineteenth century the demand for bureaucratic norms of recruitment served what he calls an 'invading' function. By replacing informal contact with examination success it enabled a new group without such contacts to increase its competitive advantage in the search for jobs. Ringer[49] has also suggested that the universities were an important source of social mobility for non-nobles in eighteenth-century Germany. Once established in one of the state bureaucracies, even at a relatively low level, they were able to encourage their sons to make further advances along the same route.

Bureaucratic norms of universality and objectivity are therefore closely associated with meritocratic ideologies because they seem to offer equality of educational and occupational opportunity. It is in this context that we must understand the attempt to open up secondary education and the grammar schools through the use of intelligence tests, which were perceived as more 'objective' than the older techniques of interviews and essay type examinations. In practice, of course, bureaucratic norms are equally as effective in helping existing groups to maintain their position as in helping invading social groups. Access to the necessary educational requirements is frequently monopolized by the children of existing groups since they have access, as Bourdieu has pointed out, to both economic and cultural capital. Social mobility through education tends therefore to be the result of an expansion of the middle and professional groups in society, and to occur in new or rapidly expanding occupations. Gusfield for example cites teaching, business leadership and salaried engineering as particularly open to the striver for upward mobility.

Clignet[50] has attempted to relate style of assessment to ideologies of selection. He suggests that the monolithic character of elites typical of sponsored mobility allows for a 'visible' system of certification and this is further encouraged by a centralized system of administration which gives added power to the elites. Sponsored mobility and centralization both, therefore, favour bureaucratic systems of assessment. Under contest mobility, and especially where the system is decentralized, there are many channels of mobility, and marked variation in the forms and techniques of examination. At the same time overt forms of selection, often at a particular point in time, and for a particular age-group, such as the 11 +, or A levels, give way to a process of continuous assessment. Guidance and counselling now become important, particularly to fulfil the important function of cooling-out the unsuccessful aspirants.

Bernsten similarly has suggested that the integrated curriculum with its weak classification, and the invisible pedagogy, with its weak framing, are likely to give rise to criteria of evaluation which are both multiple and diffuse. Moreover Bernstein believes that the more diffuse the criteria of assessment the more the system favours those who are already privileged.[51] Working-class parents, because they do not understand the underlying theory, may be cut off from the evaluation of their child's progress. Bourdieu[52] too sees the less specific forms of assessment laying more emphasis on those imponderable qualities which are one aspect of cultural capital.

Support for these arguments is provided by studies, in the United States, of the part played by the school-counselling service. A pioneering and highly influential case-study by Cicourel and Kitsuse[53] examined the role of the school counsellor in an upper-middle-class suburb. They found that students who were considered by counsellors to have low ability were automatically excluded from the college preparatory course. However, ability was not judged simply on test scores or grade-point averages, but included such criteria as belonging to the in-group and not getting into trouble.

A rather differently oriented study by Armor, which surveyed a range of schools, found that counsellors seemed to have more impact in working-class schools. This is in line with what we know of the greater dependence of the working-class family on advice from the school.[54]

There is some reason to suppose, therefore, that the current trend away from visible selection and written examinations and towards continuous assessment is another aspect of the general movement from sponsored to contest mobility. It should be noticed however that this only changes the form of assessment, which still remains an important function of the school. Moreover the elimination of the more visible methods of evaluation paves the way for more covert means, and these may, as Bernstein has warned, increase rather than decrease the power of the teacher over the child. The pleas of the deschoolers, and of many of the New Romantics, to free the schools from the selection process cannot therefore be achieved in this way. Indeed, as we have seen, changes in the employment market on the one hand, and the devaluation of educational qualifications on the other, continue to make the pressures on the school more rather than less important.[55] Bernstein's third message system is, therefore, of key importance, linking as it does both structural and cultural aspects of the sociology of education.

9 The school as an organization

1 *The teacher in the authority structure of the school*

To a considerable extent the study of schools as organizations remains one of the least satisfactory aspects of the sociology of education in spite of the fact that, unlike the study of the curriculum, its importance has long been recognized. The fact of its neglect, particularly by British sociologists, was noted by Jean Floud and A. H. Halsey in the Trend Report as early as 1958[1] and was re-emphasized by Hoyle as recently as 1973[2]. Although there are problems of method in studying schools as organizations, and difficulties in applying concepts derived from other types of organization to schools, both Hoyle and Davies emphasize the conceptual and theoretical weaknesses which lie at the heart of organizational analysis itself. Davies, for example, points up the bewildering choice of approaches open to the sociologist interested in organizations, and the unreconciled differences which, to a large extent, still remain between them. 'The working surface of organizational studies', he suggests, 'appears to be occupied by a number of distinct sets of protagonists, each characteristically emphasizing one level, one approach, one or a few aspects of organizational structure or process'.[3]

One particular problem noted by Davies is the conflict between the sociological and the managerial approach and the tendency, as he puts it, to slip from the empirical to the axiomatic. American studies, Hoyle suggests,[4] have frequently been carried out by educational psychologists whose focus was leadership, morale and communication rather than formal structure, goals and culture. Although British studies have not, on the whole, been in this tradition, they have tended to focus on the differentiation of pupils, pupil subcultures and the opportunity structure. In so far as this section attempts to concentrate on the authority structure of the school, it will therefore be chiefly concerned with American material and the studies on which it draws will frequently not be specifically sociological in character.

Organizations have been defined as 'social units that pursue specific goals which they are structured to serve'.[5] Typical organizations include hospitals, prisons, armies and churches as well as schools and universities. The distinctive characteristic of an organization, which distinguishes it from social structures like the family, is that it has been formally established for the *explicit* purpose of achieving certain goals. Every organization has a formally instituted pattern of authority and an official body of rules and procedures which are intended to achieve its specific goals. Alongside this formal aspect of the organization, however, are networks of informal relations and unofficial norms which arise out of the social interaction of individuals and groups working together within the formal structure.

One of the most important aspects of the formal structure of an organization is its system of administration and in a modern society the typical administrative system is the bureaucracy. 'Complex organizations in American society are bureaucratized,' Corwin argues, 'and schools are no exception.'[6] It is necessary, therefore, to consider the concept of bureaucracy and its meanings for the functioning of educational institutions. Weber is still the foremost authority on bureaucracy and, in spite of criticisms of particular aspects of his analysis, all discussions of the concept are derived from his treatment of the subject. According to Weber the ideal type of bureaucracy is characterized by a high degree of specialization; a hierarchical system of authority; explicit rules which define the responsibility of each member of the organization and the co-ordination of different tasks; the exclusion of personal considerations from official business, and impartiality in the treatment of subordinates and clients; recruitment of experts; the existence of a career.[7]

A number of writers have emphasized the problems arising from trying to make use of Weber's particular approach to bureaucracy. Crozier[8] for example has pointed up in detail the paradox that exists in Weber's work between its efficiency and the danger to human freedom implicit in its rigidity and standardization. Whereas Weber himself tended to lay more emphasis on its efficiency, a later generation of socioligists like Merton and Gouldner have been concerned to point to what they see as the dysfunctions of bureaucracy.

The question of efficiency is to a large extent an empirical one. Of more importance perhaps in the long run is the problem of defining, in more precise terms than Weber employed, what we mean by bureaucracy. Albrow,[9] for example, has argued that there is no agreed definition of bureaucracy and that the term is best treated as a signpost concept to identify the whole gamut of issues concerning the relations of individuals to abstract organizational features. Clignet, too, has pointed out that 'it is not certain that all the dimensions that apparently constitute patterns of organization are really highly interrelated'.[10] The imprecise and indeed equivocal character of the concept of bureaucracy does not however destroy its value in the study of educational organizations, always provided that its limitations are borne in mind.

Clearly, bureaucratic characteristics are present to some degree in education, just as they are in political and military organizations, churches and industry. Schools, for example, increasingly employ specialized personnel recruited on the basis of expert qualifications. They have, to varying degrees, a hierarchical system of authority involving specific lines of command from the school superintendent or Director of Education downwards. At the same time there is considerable standardization with respect to such matters as textbooks, courses and examinations, although the extent to which the teachers' behaviour in the classroom is routinized varies considerably from one educational system to another and between different parts of the same system. Moreover, wherever rules exist the teacher is expected to apply them with strict impartiality.

Corwin has suggested some of the conditions favourable to the development of bureaucracy in education. These include population expansion, urbanization, increasing mobility, the knowledge explosion and the growing economic importance of education.[11] Clignet has also pointed to the significance of the pressures for educational equality which often demands the development of uniform educational curricula and programmes.[12] The professionalization of teaching has also done much to encourage bureaucratic tendencies by its promotion of policies with respect to qualified entrants, security of tenure, career opportunities and the pressure for control by the expert rather than the layman or amateur. Yet the process of bureaucratization also carries with it consequences that run counter to the conceptions of the teacher role held not only by the teachers themselves but by many other educators. For example, the standardization inherent in a bureaucratic system comes into inevitable conflict with the ideal of individual attention to students and pupils which is basic to most current educational thinking. The hierarchical authority structure typical of bureaucracy also conflicts with the teachers' demand for professional autonomy in the classroom and a share in the decision-making process. Consequently there are strong pressures within the educational system working for what Bidwell has called de-bureaucratization. It is necessary therefore to look more closely at research on the school as an organization in order to determine the effect of these conflicting pressures on the teacher's role and the teacher's performance.

Many writers on organizational theory have pointed to the different ways in which authority is legitimated from a bureaucratic as distinct from a professional basis. In a bureaucratic system the legitimation is in terms of rank and deference, and obedience is due from those of lower to those of higher status in the organization. In professional terms, however, deference is due only to competence or expert knowledge. Consequently, the loyalty of the professional is to his professional standards, whereas that of the bureaucrat is to his superiors and to the organization itself. Moreover, whereas the bureaucrat obeys orders and carries out the tasks allotted to him, the professional fulfils his professional duties according to his own or his profession's decisions. The role of the professional in a bureaucratic organization is, therefore, of particular interest to the sociologist, involving, as it is almost certain to do, the possibilities of role conflict. At the same time Warwick[13] has warned against the danger of using too reified a notion of the distinctive characteristics of professional and bureaucratic work. He suggests that professionalization and bureaucratization are interpenetrating rather than opposing processes, and that indeed when the actor's perception of the situation is taken into account it is not always easy for the sociologist to distinguish between the two orientations.

In general, what information we have suggests that teachers often have very little control over many important decisions. Corwin, for example, argues that the participation of teachers in the decision-making process 'is usually limited to either (1) interpretation of established policy, (2) advice, or (3) the execution of established policy. The actual policy decisions are usually reserved for the chief executive.'[14] Corwin is describing the American teacher but his conclusions apply in some degree to the English situation as well. Nor are bureaucratic tendencies confined to the schools. 'In higher education the increasing specialization of work and differentiation of roles extend the need for bureaucratic co-ordination, and there is a pronounced trend toward formal codification of rules, accompanied by a weaker trend toward the fixing of responsibility in a higher and wider hierarchy of administrative positions.'[15]

A recent study by Anderson[16] showed, however, that there are differences both between schools and between departments in the degree of bureaucratization, measured by the amount of control over teachers in such matters as the selection of textbooks, the grading and testing of students and students' work. For example the number of such rules were higher, the lower the socio-economic status of the community from which the students were drawn. Anderson suggests that part of the reason for this lies in the greater complexity of both administration and teaching in such schools. There were also variations between departments, with craft departments having fewer rules than English departments, and, according to the characteristics of the teachers, with the more experienced teachers, and male teachers, having greater autonomy. Size of department is also a factor, with smaller departments having fewer rules. Anderson suggests that 'by defining the teacher's role and prescribing and proscribing certain instructional practices, rules obviate the need for class supervision'.[17] Size was also found to be a factor in bureaucratization by Samuels.[18] He found that as school districts increased in size, the more likely they were to provide teachers with standardized instructional resources.

A number of studies have also explored the extent to which teachers actually perceive a conflict between their positions as employees and their professional standards. Washburne, for example, interviewed 20 teachers who were graduate students in education and found that 'the status of teachers is given one role by the teacher and another by the bureaucracy in which he works'.[19] Sharma also found that the percentage of teachers desiring teacher participation in decision-making was greater than the percentage reporting such participation.[20] Getzels and Guba found evidence in interviews with teachers of a conflict between their professional role and the expectancy that they will submit to others.[21] A study of a rather different kind by Carpenter looked at the relationship between different kinds of organizational structure and the job satisfaction of teachers. He found that teachers in what he called 'flat' structures as distinct from 'tall' structures perceived themselves as having more professional authority and a greater sense of participation in determining school goals.[22] On the other hand, a study by Seeman found many teachers reluctant to participate in decision-making,[23] and Moeller and Charters found that teachers in highly bureaucratized schools, contrary to their initial hypothesis, had a higher sense of power than teachers in less bureaucratized systems.[24]

Undoubtedly an important factor here is the extent to which teachers actually do adhere to professional values. Corwin, for example, in a study of 28 public high schools, found that there was more tension and conflict in schools where the staff in general seemed to be more professionally oriented towards their work. Although the source of the conflict varied greatly, nearly half of the incidents described could be classified as authority problems, and Corwin estimated that one in every four involved teachers and administrators in disputes over authority. There were also however more conflicts over authority in the schools which were larger, more complex in their organization, and more standardized in their activities. A heterogeneous teaching staff also seems to increase the chance of discord.[25] Studies which have attempted to relate staff participation in decision-making and teacher satisfaction also tend to show that job satisfaction is influenced not by the actual extent of the participation in decision-making but by the teacher's conception of its significance.[26]

A further point which is made very strongly by Anderson, is that bureaucratic rules may be both functional and dysfunctional. In his study, the majority of junior high school teachers experienced most authority conflict, defined in terms of incidents of disagreement with administrators and supervisors and interest in teachers' unions, collective bargaining and grievance systems, when they were subjected to the least rules. Such teachers, Anderson argues, welcome the reduction of ambiguity provided by rules and regulations.[27] This is not so unexpected, however, when we remember that the absence of rules can imply arbitrary and capricious authority rather than professional autonomy.

It must also be noticed that the growth of bureaucratic elements in education is not the only hindrance to the development of professional autonomy. Traditionally, elementary school teaching has had

a very low status in the eyes of the community, and in spite of improvements in qualifications and education in recent years there is
strong resistance to the idea that teachers are true professionals.
Consequently we find that school teachers are frequently subjected
to a degree of community control that is quite incompatible with
professional status but which has nothing to do with bureaucratic
organization. In the United States in particular, the authority of the
teacher is still severely restricted by community pressures. Clark,
for example, has described the system of elementary and secondary
education as 'characterized by a vulnerable bureaucracy'. This vulnerability, he suggests, 'stems in part from the decentralization of
control to local lay boards, with job security of administrators
closely dependent on lay approval. The vulnerability is extended by
the correlated ideology of local lay control that has been a sacred
component of the American conception of education *governance*. In
addition, the ideologies of public school administration have
adjusted to this vulnerability, with administration often guided by
conceptions of service to lay demands, and efficient operation of the
schools in line with community dictates.'[28] Under such circumstances the decline of lay influence and the growing significance of a
professionally orientated administration could well have the effect
of raising rather than lowering the professional status of teaching.
The teachers' strike in New York in 1968 must also be seen as in part
a reaction of the teachers against the idea of local community control
rather than the professionally oriented control of the city administration.

Crozier too has pointed out other ways in which 'rules protect the
people who submit to them. Within the area delineated by the rules,
they are free to make their own contribution according to their
arbitrary whim. They can participate or take refuge in retreatist
behaviour, commit themselves to the organization's aims or reserve
their moral forces for some personal endeavour.'[29]

On the other hand, although there may be bureaucratic aspects to
the organization of schools, Bidwell has argued that in many aspects
of their functioning schools can be highly autonomous units, particularly at the class-room level.[30] Lortie, too, has pointed out that
classrooms are 'small universes of control with the teacher in command; administrators refer, ambivalently, to the "closed-door"
which the teacher can put between herself and administrative sur-
veillance.[31] He goes on to suggest that, while teachers value their

independence in the classroom, they are relatively indifferent to organizational affairs which do not impinge directly upon teaching, which is their principal concern. Interestingly, although Lortie is concerned primarily with teachers in American primary schools, strong confirmation for his conclusions comes from an English study of teachers in secondary schools. In his investigation into role conflict, Grace found that teachers gained considerable satisfaction from the sense of autonomy in their work. Many staff were prepared to accept quite readily the head teacher's policy in general matters provided their autonomy in the classroom was untouched.[32]

The alternative approach, through the concepts of leadership and morale, has been mainly concerned with the attempt to map out different types of administrative style in the search for the principles of effective leadership. Halpin for example, who has done a great deal of work in this field, believes that 'the effective leader is one who delineates clearly the relationship between himself and the members of the group and establishes well defined patterns of organization, channels of communication and ways of getting the job done, and whose behaviour at the same time reflects friendship, mutual trust, respect and warmth in the relationships between himself and the group.'[33] These two main dimensions of leadership are categorised as *goal achievement* and *group maintenance*.

More recently Halpin has turned his attention to the construction of a typology to measure the organizational climate of schools. This typology was arrived at inductively by factor analysis of respondents' answers to a set of questionnaires. The statements in the questionnaire covered eight dimensions, four on the principals' behaviour and four on teachers' response to this behaviour. The respondents were asked to what extent each statement characterized his school. The six organizational climates that form his typology vary primarily in the way in which the school principal is seen to handle his leadership function. The Open Climate, for example, is characterized by a principal who is perceived as having high consideration for his staff, a high level of what Halpin calls thrust, i.e. motivations through example, and an absence of close supervision.

At the other extreme, the Closed Climate is characterized by high aloofness, close supervision, and low consideration on the part of the principal, and a high level of disengagement on the part of the staff, who also perceive the organization of the school as hindering their task.[34]

An alternative but strikingly similar conceptualization of administrative style has been developed by Getzels and his associates, who have used a theoretical framework derived from Talcott Parsons. They describe three types of leader: the nomethic leader who is orientated towards the organization and its task at the expense of the satisfaction of the personal needs of his staff; the ideographic leader who, in contrast, tends to minimize the organizational requirements and is orientated towards personal relationships; and the transactional leader who can reconcile the fundamental conflict between the requirements of the system and the needs of the individuals within it.

Guba and Bidwell used this framework in a study of administrative style based on the expectations held by the principal of his teachers, and teacher reports on what they believed their principals expected of them.[35] This study showed that teachers' perceptions of their principals as transactional leaders was positively related to their level of confidence in their principal and in themselves, and in their satisfaction with the teaching situation. This supports the hypothesis that transactional leadership is the most effective. When, however, the measure of administrative style was based on the principals' own reports, no such correlations were found. It is difficult, therefore, to be sure that it is the behaviour of the principal which is the causal factor in the teachers' confidence and job satisfaction.

Yet a further weakness of much research in this area is the tendency to assume that teachers' job performance is related to their job satisfaction or morale, rather than to subject it to empirical verification. Since industrial studies have shown that workers' morale is not necessarily related to productivity it is at least conceivable that this is also true of teachers. It is therefore of particular interest to look at Gross's recent attempt to study leadership in education, which tries to relate administrative style both to teacher morale and to teacher performance.

The study itself was undertaken as part of a large-scale enquiry which involved a study of a stratified random-cluster sample of school principals in large American cities. Apart from the school principals, data were collected from immediate supervisors of the principals in the study, and a sample of teachers randomly selected from each of the schools. For the purposes of this particular study, however, only elementary schools and their principals were included. In order to measure the leadership style of a particular principal, the sample of teachers in his school were contacted by means of postal questionnaire and asked to describe how frequently their principal engaged in types of behaviour believed to represent executive professional leadership. The reports of teachers on a particular principal did not necessarily agree, and the actual E.P.L. (Executive Professional Leadership) score for each principal was averaged from scale scores developed from the reports of each teacher in each of the schools.

The teacher-observers were also used to assess the behaviour of the principal towards his teachers. The areas of behaviour investigated included the extent to which teachers were permitted to share in decisions, the extent of his equalitarian relationships with teachers and the amount of support teachers were given in a number of different areas. Scores on all these items were cross-tabulated with the E.P.L. score, and in each case a positive relationship was found. These may all be viewed as further aspects of the principal's leadership style.

The effects of E.P.L. were also studied by means of the teacher-observers. They were asked to report on teacher morale in their school, on the classroom performance of the teachers in their school, and the academic progress of their pupils. All of these were found to be positively related to E.P.L. Finally an attempt was made to assess some of the determinants of E.P.L. It was found for example that the stronger the professional leadership offered by the principal's immediate superiors, the greater his own E.P.L.

The authors of the study are well aware of the problems involved in attempting causal inferences, using this kind of data. Nevertheless they argue, on the basis of a very sophisticated and complex statistical procedure, including amongst other methods the use of the split sample, that 'both teachers' professional performance and morale may serve as links in a causal chain between the E.P.L. of principals and performance of their pupils'.[36]

An English study by Revans also attempts to link leadership style, teacher effectiveness and pupil's performance. In an attempt to explain differences in pupil involvement he investigated the attitudes of children towards teachers and the attitudes of teachers towards the authority of the school. He concluded that when teachers feel they have a hand in the running of the school they tend to be both liked by their pupils and seen as effective teachers. If, on the other hand, teachers see their supervisors as remote or dictatorial, they, in their turn, are seen by their pupils as unfriendly and ineffective.[37]

Leadership style is not however necessarily related to the level of bureaucracy in an organization. The study by Moeller and Charters, for example, to which reference has already been made, found not only that the two were unrelated, but that whereas teachers in highly bureaucratized schools had a higher sense of power than those in less bureaucratized schools, a climate of repressive authority was associated with a low sense of power. It may be, therefore, that leadership style, as it has been defined, has more to do with personality than with organizational structure. Clearly this is a highly complex area which deserves more attention than it has received.

2 The organization of learning

The concept of the school as an organization is, however, much wider than the study of administrative styles or teacher autonomy. In particular there are a number of aspects which relate primarily to administrative aspects of the teaching situation itself, and one of the most important of these is the organization of the teaching group. There are many ways of grouping pupils within a school, and only the most important of them can be described here. One of the most common is the system known as grading, which is customary both in the United States and in many European countries, including the U.S.S.R. It is a grouping system based upon the pupil's level of attainment and rate of progress. Under such a system pupils who fail to complete the work satisfactorily are made to repeat the grade. The teaching group in a graded school is, therefore, relatively heterogeneous since it will include pupils of widely different abilities and of different ages.

The main alternative to the graded school is the system known usually as streaming. This involves classifying children of the same age into two or more groups on the basis of some measure of ability. These groups are then used as the teaching unit, for all or most subjects, the rate of progress and the curriculum often being varied according to the level of ability of the group or class. A system of this kind, especially in a school with a selected intake, is often very homogeneous, both in age and in ability.

Setting, on the other hand, is the system of grouping pupils by ability for individual subjects and can be combined either with a system of grades or other forms of heterogeneous grouping, or with a system of streaming. It has, for example, long been common in British grammar schools for such subjects as languages or mathematics. Comprehensive schools, too, often combine streaming and setting to produce homogeneous teaching groups.

Finally there is the system known as tracking, in which pupils are allocated to particular 'sides' or 'courses'. Examples of tracking are the allocation of pupils to science or art sides in the English grammar school or to the college preparatory course in the American High School. Many comprehensive schools in Britain also organize their senior or upper school in the forms of 'sides'.

In recent years there has been considerable controversy over the merits of heterogeneous versus homogeneous groupings both in Britain and in the United States. On the whole the use of homogeneous groups, and especially the more rigid forms of streaming, tend to be associated with the system of sponsored mobility. Consequently its opponents in Britain tend to be those who oppose early selection and a selective secondary system. It is all the more surprising therefore to find so many comprehensive schools, particularly in the early years, continuing to stream. Pedley found in the early 1960s that out of 102 schools he questioned on the subject 'eighty-eight "stream" the children on entry, 11 during or at the end of the first year. The remaining three do so after two years.'[38]

Part of the reason for this was undoubtedly the strong pressure placed upon the schools to compete in academic terms with the grammar schools. In their anxiety to prove that the comprehensive school does not lower standards, the heads were loth to experiment and possibly risk the academic progress of the abler pupils. At the same time mixed-ability groups have undoubtedly been unpopular with teachers. The Headmistress of Woodberry Down, one of the London comprehensive schools, has recorded the dislike of teachers for the idea of the mixed ability group, [39] and indeed London's inspectorate, reporting on progress in London's comprehensive schools in 1961 dismissed the idea of 'teaching groups covering the whole range of ability' as impracticable.[40]

More recently, however, there has been a change in the climate of educational opinion with respect to streaming, which instead of being taken for granted as the only practicable method of teaching is now the subject of considerable controversy. This has been reflected in the number of comprehensive schools experimenting with some form of non-streaming. The survey by Benn and Simon[41] in 1968 found that 22 per cent of the schools they studied made use of mixed-ability groups during the first year, although only 4 per cent involved all pupils in a system of non-streamed classes. A rather similar picture is presented by Monks in the survey carried out by the National Foundation for Educational Research. The proportion of schools with no completely mixed ability groups was about two-thirds of the total but the number of schools using a complete system of unstreaming even in the first year was only 4.5 per cent. This fell to only 1.2 per cent in the second year and 0.9 per cent in the third year. This is probably because of the practice of using setting for certain subjects, normally mathematics and foreign languages. There is also a tendency to confine mixed ability teaching to subjects like art or physical education.[42]

The controversy over streaming has naturally stimulated research in this area but the results so far have been largely inconclusive. A very comprehensive survey on grouping in schools[43] has been highly critical of much of the research that has so far been carried out. Apart from such issues as the small samples frequently used, there has been a tendency to ignore many important variables, including the attitudes of teachers, and the methods and materials they are using in their teaching. Moreover, the findings have often been contradictory.

One study which attempted to solve some of these problems is the recent longitudinal study of streaming in primary schools carried out by the N.F.E.R.[44] This attempted to look at the effect of streaming not only on the pupils' achievement but also on their academic self-image, and social adjustment and attitude to the school. In addition, teachers' attitudes and class-room practices were also studied. As a result of this wide-ranging approach to the problem it became apparent that streaming and unstreamed schools did not merely differ with respect to their organization. The streamed school was more systematic and more traditional in its approach and more overtly authoritarian. However, some schools were unstreamed in name only, for the staff had retained their former classroom practices and teaching methods. Gains in achievement showed no pattern favouring either streamed or unstreamed schools, although the findings of earlier studies that streaming tends to produce a greater spread of scores was confirmed.

Although streaming has been less characteristic of the United States than Britain, research into the relative effectiveness of heterogeneous and homogeneous teaching groups has been undertaken fairly extensively in recent years. One of the best known is the experimental study carried out in 50 schools in New York City during the 1960s. The research was designed to create different patterns of ability grouping and to compare their effect on the pupils at the end of a two-year period, although no attempt was made to change the style of teaching and indeed teachers were requested to carry on in their usual way. As in the N.F.E.R. study, differences in ability grouping did not appear to have a great deal of influence on achievement. Extremely gifted children tended to do better in classes of their ability equals but their presence in other classes tended to have an upgrading effect on some students in some circumstances. The presence of slow learners in a class however, did not seem to have any consistent effect.[45]

One of the implications of these studies is that the effect of ability grouping on achievement may not be the same for all children, and that, at least for the exceptionally able child, streaming may sometimes be an advantage. Indeed Taylor has suggested, using recent findings from research in Sweden, that some of the earlier research on streaming may have under-represented the effect on the able child by using tests with too low a ceiling. The result, although a fair enough reflection of what had been learned in common by both streamed and unstreamed classes, does not measure any extra unexamined learning done in either of them.[46] On the other hand destreaming may well improve the chances of the average, or the less able child. This is well illustrated by a recent study by J. F. Douglas who studied the effects of unstreaming in a grammar school over a period of seven years. He found that significantly more pupils passed 5 or more O levels, but slightly at the expense of the quality of the passes of the brightest pupils.[47] Lacey has also described a similar experience in a grammar school which was previously organized on rigid lines with an Express stream taking O level in four years. The abolition of the Express stream improved the O level performance not only of boys who would have been in the lower stream but also of some of the boys in the Express stream who now had an extra year of O level work.[48]

Himmelweit has suggested that assignment to a high stream, in a similar way to passing the 11 +, can serve to encourage the child from a working-class family where there is little interest in education. She demonstrates, in a longitudinal analysis of pupils from both secondary modern and grammar schools, that the effect of family background was weakest where the system of streaming was at its strongest. Moreover, allocation to a particular stream seemed to affect a boy's ultimate performance far more than his ability or his motivation.[49]

A comparison over time of boys in a technical grammar school by Banks and Finlayson also appears to show the significant effect of streaming on educational aspirations and expectations. Although the first two years at the school were in mixed ability classes, an allocation to one of three streams was made at the beginning of the third year. It was found that those pupils who had actually raised their level of aspirations and expectations were almost all from those who had been allocated to the upper form, whereas a fall was significantly more likely among those pupils going into the lower stream.

Further evidence from this study on the effect of streaming is provided by a comparison of the O level and C.S.E. results of a group of boys of similar ability in three kinds of secondary school. Because these schools differed in the ability level of their intake, the boys studied represented the lowest ability range in the grammar school, the boys with the highest ability in the comprehensive school, and the average boy in the technical grammar school. Although the examination results as a whole reflected the ability level of the school itself, this was not so for the boys in the special study. Those in the comprehensive school, although of similar ability, did very much better than boys in either of the other two schools. Nor did this appear to relate to their family background which was less favourable for boys in the comprehensive school than in the grammar school, even when social class was controlled.

Although the design of the study, and the small number of schools, does not allow more than a tentative conclusion, and it would certainly be wrong to generalize widely to other schools, the superior performance of the boys in the comprehensive school would seem to have depended on their relative position in the streaming system which was strong both in the comprehensive and the grammar school. Whereas the boys in the study were largely in the bottom streams in the grammar school and regarded by all concerned, teachers, parents, and boys, as of little academic promise, those in the comprehensive school were in the top stream, and on whom the academic reputation of the school was likely to rest.[50]

Strong pressure for academic achievement, therefore, especially when it finds expression in a 'strong' system of streaming, would appear to concentrate expectations and resources on the most able or the most hard-working pupils at the expense of the rest. The abolition of streaming may, as we have seen, distribute both resources and academic success more evenly, although, as Himmelweit has pointed out, not without the possibility of reducing the efficiency of the school as a socializing agency for the *successful* working-class child.

Apart from the relationship between streaming and achievement, there has also been considerable interest in the way in which aspects of school organization impinge upon peer-group values and the pupil's involvement with the school.

Hargreaves,[51] for example, found that peer-group values appear to be reinforced by the separation of the boys into distinct streams. A similar point is made by Lacey[52] who argues that differentiation of the boys by the teachers is accentuated by streaming, so that an anti-group is produced, in opposition to the dominant culture of the school. A case study by King found a relationship between streaming and pupil involvement with the school, as measured both by an attitude questionnaire and by membership in clubs or societies.[53] The N.F.E.R. research on comprehensive schools by J. M. Ross and her associates also found that both perceptions of the school and club membership were related to stream.[54] A later study by King, however, on a considerably larger scale, found that involvement was related to stream in only about half the sample.[55] This discrepancy may however result from differences in the attitudes of teachers. The study by Barker Lunn, for example, found that the poorest attitudes were held by pupils taught in unstreamed schools, by teachers who believed in streaming.[56]

It seems, therefore, that the effect of streaming is to accentuate tendencies already present in the classroom situation, both in the relationship between pupils and teacher and in the relationship between peers. Until these are understood, research into streaming as such seems likely to remain inconclusive. Both of these issues are discussed in more detail later.

The tendencies working towards the bureaucratization of education have also, in general, worked towards an increase in school size. One of the main influences in this direction has been the growth in specialized knowledge, with its accompanying demand for specialized teaching and equipment. Consequently, as Conant has pointed out,[57] it has become difficult for the small high school to meet the needs of its pupils for advanced courses in mathematics, science and foreign languages, on the one hand, and non-academic training, on the other. In the British setting this problem has been less serious, since the highly selective nature of the grammar schools has meant that they could concentrate their resources on the academic needs of the abler pupils. However, the development of comprehensive schools has raised the issue in an acute form, since the schools have been expected to satisfy their critics that they could provide advanced courses to the same level as the more specialized grammar schools.

To some extent the increase in the size of the sixth form has meant that this is a less serious issue than was believed in the early years of the comprehensive school programme.[58] Taylor however has argued that the problem of sixth-form dispersion will increase as more school systems become comprehensive. In particular he points to the growing importance of technical colleges which now account for a large proportion of all A level entries, and the development of various kinds of Sixth-Form College may also serve the same purpose.[59]

If however a school can be too small to run efficiently it can conceivably also be too large, and there has been some anxiety expressed that the large school will be an impersonal, unfriendly place for teacher and pupil alike. Some evidence of an indirect kind is provided for this view by the researches at the University of Kansas under the guidance of Barker and his associates.[60] Thirteen Kansas high schools varying in size were studied intensively, and the results were seen in some respects at least to favour the small school. It was found, for example, that the pupils in the small school were more likely to participate in extracurricular activities and more likely to take a leading part in them in spite of the fact that the larger schools provided a greater number and variety of such activities. The authors suggest that part of the reason for this lies in the greater opportunity to participate, and especially to lead, in a small school. For example, the same size of school orchestra will involve a higher proportion of pupils in a small school than in a large school, and so will the school football team and the school play. An interesting small study by Willems also showed that 'marginal' high school students, i.e. those of low ability, low school achievement and low occupational level of their parents, had as much sense of obligation to attend voluntary school activities as other students if they were in small schools. In large schools however, such students had little if any sense of obligation to attend.[61] Anderson's study of bureaucracy also points up some of the disadvantages of the large school. He found, for example, that not only was size related to bureaucratization but that resistance to innovation increased significantly in large schools.[62]

On the other hand, the study by King found that school size was not itself a very significant variable. Not only did it not correlate with pupil involvement, but scales developed by King to measure such organizational attributes as standardization and formalization were not related to size of school.[63] The International Project for the Evaluation of Educational Attainment, established by UNESCO also discovered no clear and consistent relationship between attainment in mathematics and school size.[64] Ross and her associates in their study of comprehensive schools found that although pupils in small schools were more involved in school activities, pupils in large schools have just as favourable perceptions as those of pupils in small schools. They point out that much depends on the way the school is organized and the way in which extra-curricular activities are handled.[65]

Although the optimum size of school has been a matter of some debate and controversy this has not been so for size of class. Indeed it has been regarded as almost axiomatic that smaller classes are more effective teaching units than larger classes. Educators generally have worked hard to reduce the size of classes and any success is widely regarded as a significant educational reform.[66] There is no doubt too of the preference of teachers for small classes for their own benefit, as well as what they see to be the benefit of the pupils. Indeed a number of studies have shown that large classes are a major source of complaint for teachers.[67]

It is a matter of surprise therefore to find so little evidence for the view that small classes provide a more effective teaching or learning situation. One of the major British studies which has demonstrated the lack of relationship between class size and achievement is the longitudinal study of 15,000 children carried out by the National Children's Bureau. Although this study controlled carefully for such factors as size of school, length of schooling, social class and parental interest, none of the analyses carried out indicated that higher attainment or better adjustment was found in smaller rather than larger classes.[68] Moreover Little has carried the argument further by suggesting that on the basis of his own enquiries a reduction in class size below the size of 35 may well have a deleterious effect on children's reading skills.[69] Some American studies have also found no relationship between class size and achievement at either the school or college level,[70] although Eastcott cites several studies which showed the favourable effect of small classes on children in American *primary* schools.

It has been suggested that one of the reasons for the failure to find any significant relationship between class size and achievement lies in the inability of teachers to take advantage of the smaller class, and this is supported by Oakley's finding that changes in class size do not appear to influence many aspects of teacher or pupil behaviour.[71] It is also likely that the effect of class size will vary according to the teaching method in use, so that 'one would expect class size to be of minimal relevance in television teaching, of slight importance in lecturing, but of considerable importance in discussion teaching'.[72] The large class may also be a more appropriate vehicle for formal teaching methods than for an approach which emphasizes participation and discovery. The further study of class size therefore, as in the case of streaming, leads away from the formal organization of the school into the sociology of the classroom.

The financial resources available to a school and the physical facilities it can offer to its pupils may also be considered an aspect of its organizational structure, and the conventional wisdom of educators has always regarded the provision of adequate if not generous facilities as a necessary educational requirement. Recent research in the United States has, however, raised doubts as to the significance of these factors in educational performance. When the United States Office of Education commissioned Coleman to undertake a major survey into the availability of equal educational opportunity in American education and its effect on achievement, he himself did not anticipate the nature of his findings.[73] In fact, however, his sample of more than 3,000 metropolitan and rural schools showed that only a small amount of the variation in achievement can be accounted for explicitly by variations in such factors as the amount of money spent per pupil, or the number of books in the library, or physical facilities such as gymnasiums or cafeterias.

Coleman's rather startling findings have naturally not escaped criticism, and he has come under very heavy fire on a wide variety of grounds ranging from the high non-response rate to the computing of per-pupil expenditure on a district-wide basis rather than the individual school. His use of a linear regression model as his basic statistical tool has also come under attack, and, it has been suggested, biased his analysis *against* school resources.[74] At the same time other surveys have come to different conclusions. Boocock, for example, cites a study by Mollenkopt and Melville of a sample of 100 high schools, which demonstrated that per-pupil expenditure was one of the four characteristics showing the strongest relationship with various tests of achievement. A study by Goodman of 70,000 students in 103 school systems also found per-pupil expenditure to be positively associated with achievement.[75]

As with class size, therefore, we can come to no definite conclusion with respect to school resources and student performances, at least on the basis of the studies available to us at the present time. This is undoubtedly because the physical resources of a school are only one aspect of a complex set of interrelating and indeed interacting characteristics which includes not only its formal organization, but its informal social structure. Consequently, the effect of physical resources may vary in different circumstances and under differing contexts. Moreover once basic needs have been met, extra resources may well be spent on facilities which, while having no influence on achievement, may do a great deal to enhance the quality of school life.

At the same time, as Brookover[76] has recently pointed out, school resources, along with the provision of special services, have often been used to enhance the *differences* between students to the advantage of the more able or the more highly achieving pupil. We have already noted that this is likely to happen not only with streaming and setting but also with some kinds of individualized learning. This may help to explain Coleman's finding that there was greater variation in achievement *within* schools than between them.

3 The student sub-culture

Waller was one of the first to draw attention to the existence of a separate student sub-culture, but its systematic analysis has not been undertaken until more recently. Gordon, in his case study of

Wabash High School, reported that athletics for boys and popularity for girls were the chief determinants of status, rather than academic achievement, which appeared to be considerably less important as a source of prestige.[77] Coleman's findings, a few years later, and using 10 high schools varying in size and type of community, was in substantial agreement with Gordon.[78] The student subculture for both boys and girls was centred upon predominantly non-academic issues, in which athletics for boys and looks and personality for the girls were the most important ingredients. Good grades and academic achievement had relatively low status in all the schools, although it is interesting to notice that the 'leading crowd' tended to get better grades than the student body as a whole. On the other hand, Coleman was also able to show that the achievement of students of high IQ varied according to the value climate of the school. Where it supported achievement the students of high IQ were more likely to perform at a high level. Indeed in the schools with the strongest anti-intellectual bias, the students showing the highest performance were not the most intellectually able students, but those with motivation to stand out against the prevailing value climate.

Other studies, however, have come to rather different conclusions. Turner, for example, in a large questionnaire study of high-school seniors in the Los Angeles area found little evidence in most schools of 'an effective youth conspiracy against academic excellence'. There was, for example, no general relationship between endorsement of youth-culture items on a questionnaire and either level of ambition or lower-class background. Moreover, there was a higher degree of conformity to youth-culture values in response to a question asking for the kind of person one preferred to have as a friend than in response to questions asking for personal goals or admiration.[79] Similar findings are also reported by Riley, Riley and Moore.[80] Kandel and Lesser also argue that it may be misleading to speak of general peer versus parental influences, and suggest that whereas in certain areas peers may be more influential than parents, in other areas the reverse may be true. In a study of high-school students and their mothers they found that mothers were more influential than peers with regard to future educational goals.[81] Eve, in a comparison of students and their teachers, has also suggested the possibility that the 'adolescent value system is largely derived from the prevailing adult system and differs primarily only in the degree to which certain values are approved by adolescents'.[82]

An alternative line of criticism has been followed by Snyder, who argues that participation in athletics and other extra-curricular activities does not necessarily conflict with academic performance. In a longitudinal study of high school boys at the time of graduation from school and five years afterwards he found[83] that high school social participation and both high school and post-high school educational achievement were *positively* correlated. Moreover, although this appears to contradict Coleman, it is in line with Coleman's finding that the leading crowd tended to get better grades than the student body as a whole. Moreover, Spreitzer and Pugh have argued that the influence of sports involvement may be particularly strong for those boys not otherwise predisposed to attend college. They argue, on the basis of their findings, that in schools where sports achievement is valued, sports involvement tends to engender high perceived peer status, which in turn stimulates a desire for college attendance.[84]

An interesting and unusual approach to the problem of peer-group influence is to be found in the comparative studies carried out by Bronfenbrenner and his associates at Cornell University. In a small cross-national attempt to evaluate the part played by peers *vis-à-vis* adults in the socialization process, and using an ingenious experimental design, they found important differences between the United States and the u.s.s.r. In order to measure reaction to peers, the children were asked to respond to questionnaire items dealing with a series of conflict situations under three different conditions: a neutral condition in which they were told that no-one except the researchers would see their replies; an adult condition in which they were informed that their responses would be shown to parents and teachers; and a peer condition in which the children were told that the responses would be shown to the class itself. In both countries children gave more socially approved responses under the adult than under the neutral conditions, although the shift was more pronounced for Soviet children. When told that their classmates would see their answers there was a national difference in direction as well as degree. 'American pupils indicated greater readiness to engage in socially disapproved behaviour, whereas Soviet children exhibited increased adherence to adult standards. In other words, in the u.s.s.r. as against the United States, the influence of peers operated in the same direction as that of adults.'[85] In England, on the other hand, the peer group seems to operate in the same direction as in the United States, although the evidence suggests that the influence is even stronger.[86]

At the college level, studies of Vassar College students under the general direction of Nevitt Sanford have also found evidence of a student value climate. Although this climate is certainly not anti-intellectual and high marks are generally respected, 'the one reservation voiced by most students is that scholastic excellence should not be the sole virtue. If there is an ideal Vassar girl, she is the one who receives consistently high grades without devoting her whole time to the endeavour'.[87] Similarly, studies of student society in a medical school show vividly the extent to which the students themselves reinterpret the demands made on them by their teachers. For example, the students believed that 'the patients whom it is really important to study thoroughly are those who have common diseases – whether simple or complicated – for which there are available treatments a general practitioner could utilize'. They regarded anything they did not expect to do as general practitioners as a waste of time. Moreover, 'matters of this kind are widely discussed among the students and have important consequences for the way they interpret their experience in school and distribute their effort and time among their many competing interests'.[88] In a further study, this time of a State University, the same authors describe the development of what they call the grade point average perspective. Although the students take their work seriously, the criterion of academic success is the grade, rather than learning for its own sake or the acquisition of particular skills. In their attempt to make the grade, students learn how to give the instructor what he wants, and frequently present the appearance rather than the reality of knowledge.[89]

These studies taken together provide fairly impressive evidence for the significance of what Lambert, Bullock and Millham have called the informal social system of the school. They suggest that we can distinguish between systems in terms of the degree of consensus on norms, the strength of informal control, and the pervasiveness of the informal system. They argue that where the formal system is weak there will always be a strong pupil society, but where the official system is strong, the pupil society may be either weak, as in public schools, or strong, as in progressive schools. They also suggest that there are at least four different ways in which informal pupil systems can relate to the formal system, since it can be supportive, manipulative, passive, or rejecting. Their approach is useful in so far as they emphasize the complexity of the problem and the danger of 'large generalizations constructed on limited experience'.[90]

4 *Peer groups, reference groups and school achievement*

An alternative, and possibly more useful approach to the study of the peer group in an educational setting is to see it in the context not of an adolescent sub-culture but of reference group theory. Parsons has suggested that 'the individual headed for higher occupational status will choose peer groups that tend on the whole to facilitate his progress in this direction'. If he is accepted by such groups this can be, Parsons argues, 'a major factor in reinforcing the child's predispositions in terms of his own ability and its encouragement in the school, to transcend the expectations of his class origin'.[91]

Indeed, a large number of studies have pointed out that mobile working-class boys are more likely to have middle-class friends. Simpson, for example, in a questionnaire study of high school boys, found that ambitious working-class boys tended to have more middle-class friends than unambitious boys from both the middle and working classes.[92] Similarly, Ellis and Lane in a four-year panel study of working-class boys entering a high status university found that these boys had close associations with middle-class boys while they were at high school.[93] Turner, in his study of high school seniors also found a tendency for students to select as friends others with ambitions like their own.[94]

Several studies also indicate that friendship patterns are important in the decision to go to college. Thus, on the basis of longitudinal data, Alexander and Campbell found that a student was strongly influenced in his college plans by the plans of his best friend.[95] Similarly McDill and Coleman found that by the end of the senior year at high school, status in the social system of the school contributed more to variation in college plans than father's or mother's education. They argue that those in high-status cliques are oriented towards college by the rest of the clique, particularly in those schools where attendance at college is highly valued.[96]

At the opposite pole are those student groups or cliques which actively reject the goals and norms of the school systems.

Stinchcombe has explored this issue in detail in a study of a predominantly working-class high school in California. Although a case study, the data was obtained in the form of questionnaires to students. Stinchcombe believes that rebellion which he defines in such terms as truanting, and being sent out of class by a teacher, results when a student loses confidence in the relationship between present performance and future status. The student becomes hedonistic, Stinchcombe suggests, 'because he does not visualize achievement of long-run goals through current self-restraint'.[97] Cigarettes, cars, marriage, dating relationships, become symbols of identity when a satisfactory self-concept can no longer be reached through school achievement. Those who are most rebellious, Stinchcombe goes on to argue, are those who have most to lose. Consequently rebellion is actually highest among *middle-class* failures. Moreover, because girls can substitute the role of housewife as an aspiration, rebellion is higher for boys than for girls.

In Britain, too, studies have suggested that school success or failure is associated with different value climates. An early study by Hallworth, using sociometric techniques in a study of grammar-school pupils, found that cliques could be distinguished in terms of their agreement with, or their opposition to, the values of the school staff. Those cliques with opposing values contained a high proportion of both absentees and early leavers.[98]

Sugarman, in a more recent study, administered questionnaires to fourth-year pupils in two secondary modern, one grammar and one comprehensive school. He found that high teenage commitment, as measured by such criteria as smoking, going out with girls, wearing teenage fashions etc., was associated with unfavourable attitudes to school, poor conduct according to teachers' ratings, and to 'under-achievement relative to IQ as measured at the age of 11.[99] A replication of Sugarman's study a few years later in an American setting came to substantially the same conclusions.[100]

Hargreaves has successfully combined the approach of both Hallworth and Sugarman in an intensive study of the fourth-year pupils at a secondary modern school using participant observation, questionnaires and sociometric data. An analysis of the friendship and status systems of the boys revealed two value climates, the academic and what Hargreaves calls the 'delinquescent'. The academic subculture as Hargreaves describes it is characterized by hard work, a high standard of physical hygiene and dress, the avoidance of 'messing' in class, and of copying work from another pupil. The delinquescent subculture is its exact counterpart. Dress is deliberately nonconformist, ties are taboo, and long hair and jeans, both of which are against the school rules, are encouraged. At the same time 'messing' in class becomes a substitute for work, truancy is frequent and copying is the rule. Smoking in the school yard and fighting are signs of status. Moreover, a number of factors such as staff allocation, the structure of the timetable and the schools promotion/demotion system combine to associate these two subcultures with the system of school streams. As Hargreaves points out, 'the higher the stream, the greater degree of pupil commitment to school, satisfaction with school life, and conformity to the expectations of the teachers'.[101] At the same time the higher the stream, the greater is the tendency for high status within the peer group to be associated with academic values. In the lower streams by contrast, the academically orientated boys are deviants from group norms, and the boys of high status are those who conform to the delinquescent culture.

Lacey[102] in a similar intensive study of a grammar school, found very much the same process at work. He describes the way in which polarization occurs within the student body so that the school dominated normative culture comes to be opposed by what he calls the anti-group culture. This is not the delinquescent culture described by Hargreaves in a secondary modern school but represents a sphere of activity which has its centre of gravity outside the school, for example, pop concerts and coffee bars. Streaming and other types of academic differentiation help to speed up this process.

A number of other studies reinforce this picture. Ross and her associates, in their study of comprehensive schools, found that the more able and middle-class pupils were more likely to participate in both school and house teams and in non-sporting activities. Participation in teams was however more evenly spread over the pupils in mixed ability schools than in the others.[103] Sumner and Warburton have also linked an interest in aspects of contemporary teenage culture with a lack of success in school.[104] Similarly King in a study of a grammar school found that early leavers held few of the teacher-approved values, which gave a high place to scholarly and cultural activities, and a low place to 'pop' culture generally. On the other hand pupils in the top stream who were highly involved in school activities did not necessarily share the teachers' values.[105]

There is clear evidence, therefore, of polarization within the school on the basis of school achievement. Successful pupils tend to associate with one another, and to be more highly involved with the school. On the other hand, Bellaby has suggested that there may well be latent conflict between teachers and all their adolescent students. The ambitious 'may accept the need for a teacher's guidance, yet be critical of his attitudes to their dress and even, more specifically, be "supercilious" as one teacher put it about the content of the lesson and the method of teaching.'[106] Moreover his study of three comprehensive schools suggested that, although, as Stinchcombe has argued, both attitudes and conduct are related to the extent to which schooling is seen as relevant, the disciplinary regime imposed by the school determines whether those who see the school as irrelevant also feel hostile to it. The behaviour of students therefore must be seen in terms not only of their own attitudes and achievement, but in the context of the school.

5 Social context and social climate, the effect of the school

Studies of social climate, or school milieu as it is sometimes called, provide us with an alternative approach to the effect of norms and values on pupil achievement. Brookover and Erickson, however, have drawn attention to the different ways of defining and measuring the school milieu and make a useful distinction between the characteristics of the student body, which they call social *context*, and the attitudes, beliefs, values and norms that characterize the social system of the school, for which the term social *climate* should be reserved.[107] Although the two are clearly related, the nature of the relationship is a matter of empirical enquiry, and social climate cannot simply be inferred from the social context or social composition of the school.

Many useful studies have been concerned entirely with social context, which is of course much more easily measured than school climate. An early but influential study by Wilson[108] found that the level of educational and occupational aspirations varied according to the social class composition of the school. Not only, as is well established, were the levels of educational and occupational aspirations higher the more middle class the school context, but working-class boys in predominantly middle-class schools had higher aspirations than working-class boys in working-class schools. Moreover, the social context of the school also affected middle-class children. In predominantly middle-class schools as many as 93 per cent of the sons of professional workers aspired to college, but this proportion dropped to below two-thirds in predominantly working-class schools. Academic achievement was affected in the same way as aspirations and indeed the achievement of middle-class boys was affected even more than their aspiration. High achievers were also found to be less likely to want to go to college if they had attended a predominantly working-class school, and low achievers had higher aspirations in a middle-class school.

A later study by Wilson,[109] using longitudinal data, confirmed his earlier findings, and these were reinforced by Michael,[110] who also found that school context has more effect on attainment than on aspiration. Michael found, indeed, that the achievement scores of those from a high-status background in a predominantly working-class school were lower than those of a low-status background in predominantly middle-class schools.

The most comprehensive study of the effects of school context on achievement is provided by Coleman's major survey of equality of educational opportunity, which found that differences in the socio-economic composition of the student body were more highly related to school achievement than any other school characteristic.[111] At the same time the racial balance of the school was also of importance. The achievement of working-class white and black students was slightly higher in racially mixed schools, without depressing the achievement of white middle-class students, suggesting that both black and white working-class students are more dependent on their schools than middle-class students.

Spady,[112] however, in a recent review of findings on the impact of the school, has pointed out the apparent complexity of the relationship between the racial composition of the school and socio-economic status. He argues that, from the data currently available, the achievement of black students is only raised when there are many white students in the classroom, and when these white students are middle-class. Moreover, having such whites as class friends is a definite asset. There is however, some evidence that children in racially balanced classes name more other-race peers as friends.[113] Thus it appears from these studies that the presence of a large proportion of middle-class white students in the classroom benefits both black and white students, although the effect on black students is greatest for those who are themselves from middle-class families and who have high verbal ability.

The findings on school context, therefore, would seem to suggest that schools should have a balanced composition in terms of both social class and race if they are to promote equality of educational opportunity. This, however, is not always easy to achieve in practical terms. Experiences in 'bussing' in the United States have often proved difficult to implement, and the effects on the achievement of black students are difficult to measure in the short term.[114] Moreover, the evidence we have available indicates that both the proportion of white students and their social-class composition may be of crucial importance if racial mixing is to be a success.

Nor, on the other hand, have the conclusions drawn from social context studies gone uncriticised. The Coleman findings, as we have seen, have been heavily criticised on a variety of grounds. At a more general level the use of social-class backgrounds as an indirect indicator of parental aspirations in these studies may well have underestimated the effect of the family. In particular it may well be the case that working-class parents who send their children to predominantly middle-class schools differ in terms of their own values and aspirations from other parents.

Wilson was able to show that the working-class parents in his study who had children in middle-class schools were no more likely to be better educated or more highly skilled than other working-class parents, but this, while it goes some way to meet the criticisms, is not wholly satisfactory, since it does not take direct account of parental attitudes and values. The superior performance of working-class students in a predominantly middle-class school may, therefore, be the consequence of selective recruitment from within the working class, rather than an effect of the school.

An approach which attempts to avoid some of these difficulties is to measure the school climate directly, rather than to infer it from the social composition of its students. McDill and Rigsby selected 20 schools, representing a variety of educational environments and academic outputs. Six measures of school climate were devised, each assessing different aspects of intellectual achievement orientation, and both students and teachers were questioned on their perception of the school. It was found that the general intellectual tone of the school as perceived by students and teachers was modestly but systematically related both to the college plans and to the mathematics achievement of the students, even when ability, academic values and socio-economic background was controlled. Moreover the effect was greater for girls than for boys. The author suggests that, in addition to direct interaction with peers, and with teachers, the school itself can serve as a reference group for the individual. 'Just as the aspiring high school school athlete receives inspiration from the trophy case in the entrance hall, the potential scholar can be motivated by knowing that he is entering an institution that has high academic prestige'.[115] Perhaps the most significant aspect of their study was the finding that school climate was more closely related to the achievement of the students than the social context of the school, as defined by the socio-economic status of its students.

Further evidence on the effect of school climate is provided by a study by Brookover which selected several pairs of elementary schools with similar socio-economic status and racial composition but with significantly different levels of school achievement. As in the McDill, Rigsby study school climate was measured in terms of the perceptions of both students and teachers. He found that both the students' perceptions of the evaluation and expectations of others, and the teachers' evaluations and expectations of the students, were significant factors in explaining the differences between schools.[116] Both studies, therefore, imply that the effect of the social context or socio-economic composition of the school on achievement may lie in the academic climate.

British studies on differences in the effectiveness of schools are far less numerous than in the United States and have mainly been set in the context of the comprehensive school debate. There have, for example, been numerous attempts to compare the achievements of comprehensive schools with the achievements of those in grammar and secondary modern schools, but these have rarely been concerned with relating any differences between schools to particular aspects of the school itself. Douglas, however, in a longitudinal study of a large group of children from birth to 21 showed that good primary schools, that is to say, those with a good academic record and a high proportion of middle-class pupils, may offset the effect of lack of encouragement at home.[117] Himmelweit has also carried out a longitudinal study in which 600 thirteen to fourteen year old middle and working-class adolescent boys were re-interviewed 11 years later at the age of 25. The research was designed to examine the effect of *different* schools on children from comparable social backgrounds and the effect of the *same school* on children of different backgrounds and ability levels. She concluded that the type of school a child attends enables better predictions of his behaviour, outlook, values and attainments than does information about either his IQ or his family's social background, and these findings were confirmed by the adult data. Furthermore, the evaluation of his own career achievements was determined far more by reference to the achievements of his classmates than to those of his family. *Within* the school, the most important factor was the effect of streaming, which affected the boys' ultimate performance far more than his ability or motivation. However, strong anti-school values could, under some circumstances, act as a counter-balancing factor to the effect of allocation to one of the high streams.[118]

Further evidence that, in the British context at least, the effect of the school is mediated *through* the system of streaming is provided by the Banks and Finlayson study which compared the effect of three different types of school on pupils of comparable ability and family background. Unfortunately, as has been pointed out earlier, the three schools differed considerably both in their social-class composition and in the ability of their pupils, so that the number of pupils of similar range of ability and comparable home background in each school was very small. At the same time they represented very different positions within the streaming system in the three schools. When the three groups are compared however, it is not the boys from the middle-class, academically oriented, grammar school who were most successful in G.C.E. and C.S.E. examinations, but the boys from the predominantly working-class comprehensive school. However, when an explanation is sought at the level of the *stream* this apparent anomaly is resolved, since the boys in the comprehensive school were under strong pressure to succeed, whereas the boys in the grammar school were regarded by parents, teachers and boys alike as 'failures'.[119] To a large extent, then, this study duplicates, at stream level, the findings of Brookover and his associates at the level of the school. At the same time it reinforces his argument that studies on the effect of the school may be misleading in that they overlook differentiation within the school itself.[120]

Studies on social climate at the college level are more extensive than studies of the school, particularly in the United States, but contribute little more to our understanding and can therefore be examined only briefly. In addition Watts[121] has recently provided us with a detailed summary of the literature for both Britain and the United States. At the same time some of the methodological difficulties of research in this field have already been outlined in the account of the impact of college on values.

Although colleges and universities in the United States vary greatly in their output, much of this variation can be explained in terms of their student input. Further study of 'high output' institutions revealed that their students differed in such attributes as ability, home background, personality and motivation. Indeed when student input was included in the study, some institutions which now appeared under-productive were institutions which had formerly appeared to be highly productive. Watts concludes that differential institutional effects of attainment and academic motivation appear, on the evidence available, to be decidedly limited, and Astin, for example, is inclined to doubt that they exist at all.[122]

British studies, as Watts shows, are considerably less developed than those in the United States, and, when they exist, have been concerned mainly with the effects on students of different kinds of residential accommodation. Most of these studies, however, fail to control input variables satisfactorily, although Albrow's small but methodologically more sophisticated study demonstrated that residence in hall tended to increase the institution's influence on the individual student.[123] Watts, however, points out that not all halls of residence necessarily encourage norms which are constant with the goals of the institution itself. At the same time research also indicates that some institutions are more likely than others to encourage social interaction between students and between students and staff.

Institutions differ markedly in the aspirations and achievements of their students, and there is ample evidence to demonstrate the success of Oxbridge graduates in particular; but, as in the case of comparable findings in the United States, it is difficult to determine the extent to which this is a consequence of Oxbridge itself, or the ability and social class background of those who enter Oxbridge as students. There is however some evidence that the Oxbridge system pays particular attention to the socialization of students for the performance of elite roles in later life.

Abbott however, has drawn attention to the presence of structural divisions within universities which actually reinforce divisions based on previous background. She found that there were social-class differences in the pattern of participation in student societies in both the universities included in her study. Working-class students were also more likely to live in lodgings rather than in hall. She found in particular that large numbers of working-class students remained 'culturally of the working class', so that in their case the melting pot of the university was totally ineffective.[124]

There is little evidence that working-class students in Britain perform less well at universities, and indeed a number of studies have shown that ex-public school boys often perform less well than other students. The possibility that working-class students perform differently in institutions where they are in a minority does not however seem to be borne out by the evidence currently available. It may be however, that issues of this kind cannot be settled without studies which take into account the differential effects of college or university on particular groups of students, and which may indeed, as was suggested earlier, actually cancel each other out. Only in the light of such a development can questions on the effect of schools and colleges finally be answered.

6 Student protest

The explosion of student protest originating in Berkeley in 1964 has attracted considerable attention from sociologists, and, although none of the explanations so far produced are wholly satisfactory and much of the enormous literature is either polemical or speculative, the topic cannot be ignored. Nor does it altogether belong in this particular chapter; the strong political element in the situation might have placed it more appropriately in the chapter on the politics of education. On the other hand, the protest movement is also, and very clearly, an aspect of student culture, and the causes of the unrest are frequently sought in the organizational aspects of colleges and universities. For this reason it seemed reasonable to treat the topic in the form of a postscript to the present chapter.

The significance of the student protest in the United States, and to a large extent in Britain, is that it arose in a situation where students for some time have been generally apathetic towards political issues. Indeed the majority of students have remained indifferent. A Gallup Poll in 1968 found that only 20 per cent of students had participated in civil rights or political activities during 1967-8.[125] The radical activist groups are much smaller and comprise only about 1-2 per cent of the college population. The power of this small group of activists depends partly on the responsiveness of a much larger group of students who can be mobilized to support particular issues. At the L.S.E. in 1967, for example, 49 per cent of students joined in a boycott of lectures, and 36 per cent in a sit-in.[126] The involvement of a much smaller proportion of students can, however, successfully disrupt the work of an institution. At one of the Berkeley sit-ins, for example, only 3 per cent of the student body was involved.[127]

At the same time Adler has suggested that although the militant students are in a minority they are what he calls 'representative minorities' and not deviant ones. That is to say they represent a 'much larger group of students who, although not members of activist movements themselves, tend to sympathize with them or lend them their passive support.'[128]

Studies[129] of the left-wing activists in the United States have shown that they are mainly the left-wing children of left-wing or liberal, well-to-do parents. They are also, in the main, able students with intellectual interests from the humanities or the 'softer' social sciences. It has also been shown that they come from permissive rather than authoritarian families, although it is not clear whether this factor plays an independent role or whether it is a reflection of a different cultural and religious outlook.

The implications of some of these findings have recently been challenged by Kahn and Bowers[130] on the basis of a nationwide survey carried out in 1966 into the attitudes and behaviour of college students in the United States. They were concerned not with the 'hard core' activists but with students, representing about one-fifth of the respondents, who had participated in demonstrations or civil rights activities. On the whole they found that although the 'rank and file' activists were similar to the 'hard core' activists described in other studies, most of this was explained by the fact that they came predominantly from high-quality institutions, with high status and academically-able students. A study of students at the L.S.E. also found little difference between activist students and others, either in academic ability or social-class background.[131] How far these quality colleges promote activism and how far the explanation lies in selective entry is not clear, although it seems probable that both are involved. A panel analysis of undergraduate students at Berkeley, for example, suggests that exposure to a particular student subculture may have played a part in modifying students' views.[132] Bayer, in a study of 301 colleges and universities, also suggested that faculty support may also be an important factor, since highly selective institutions tended to attract and recruit faculty who themselves supported campus activism.[133]

Apart from 'quality', the size and complexity of institutions also appear to be factors in student protest. A study by Scott and El-Assal[134] found that 100 per cent of complex, large, high-quality institutions had had demonstrations, compared with only 34 per cent of simple, small, low-quality institutions, although large schools did not produce more demonstrators per 1,000 students than small schools. The increasing bureaucratization of higher education and the anonymity of the multiversity has frequently been put forward as a reason for student unrest, but it has also been argued that the relationship between student activity and organizational size is more likely to be a reflection of the gross numbers of diverse individuals brought together at one time and place. 'The larger the student body, the greater is the likelihood of there being some student who wishes to start something and of his being able to find others who will sympathize.[135]

Adler sees at least one source of student unrest in the unprecedented expansion of higher education, with a consequent overproduction of the educational system, particularly in non-technical or non-scientific fields. The economy, on the other hand, tends to develop at a much slower pace.[136] A similar point has been made by Scotford Archer, who, in a general survey of student unrest, argues that although a strong relationship between higher education and the economy does not preclude student discontent, it appears to be greatest in countries where there is least integration between the university and the economy. In so far as this is true it would explain why, within institutions, student unrest tends to be least in the most highly vocational subjects, and greatest in the humanities and social sciences.[137]

Ultimately, however, student unrest must also be seen in a political context. Glazer has argued that from the beginning the university issues played second fiddle to the political issues. He sees the significance of the student revolt at Berkeley as lying in the fact that it was 'the first student rebellion to have considered what is still wrong in a liberal democratic and permissive society.[138] Originating as part of the Civil Rights Movement, the protest gradually encompassed a wider range of issues including the war in Vietnam. In

Britain too, racial discrimination, especially in South Africa, and anti-war sentiments are the issues which have chiefly motivated students. At their most radical, however, student politics represent a revolt against liberalism, constitutional democracy and the rule of law. In their place, they put participatory democracy, the 'teach-ins' rather than the debate, the prolonged sit-in, generating a common basis for action through the elementary solidarity it produces among its participants, rather than the political meeting proceeding by institutionally prescribed rules.[139] Hirst's explanation of this change of attitude in terms of the different political experience of the two generations has something in common with Feuer's[140] more psychological version of the conflict of generations. Both see the students' movement as representing, fundamentally, a loss of faith in the authority of the older generation. On the other hand Spady and Adler take an alternative approach. They argue that the permissive socialization practices of many upper-middle-class families have produced in their children needs and expectations that are actually dysfunctional in the context of a large, highly selective and demanding university.[141]

There are however dangers in focusing on the American situation since to a large extent it is not typical. Meyer and Rubinson, for example, point to the historically exceptional position of students in the United States. They argue that, generally speaking, students are more rather than less politically active than are other groups, and that the degree of their politicization in any society depends upon the regulation and definition of student status. Thus, for example, when students are defined as responsible and mature, and as an elite with special abilities and rights, the greater student political activity can be expected to be.[142]

A very similar point is made by Weinberg and Walker who argue that it is the very lack of involvement by the American students in politics which has produced the particular characteristics of the American student revolt. In contrast, in Latin America, student politics are an aspect of national politics and the students are actively involved in party struggles.[143]

On the other hand, it may be a mistake to see student protest only in its political context. Spady and Adler, for example, contend that it is important to distinguish between that aspect of the movement which is a protest against war and social discrimination, and that which is concerned with changing the structure and operation of the university system itself.[144] Similarly Scotford Archer, in an account of students and universities in France, has compared Touraine's analysis, which is based on the students' condition in the contemporary class structure, and that of Bourdieu and Passeron who see the student movement as an aspect of the student condition in the contemporary university. Scotford Archer herself argues that the events in May 1956 seem to lie instead in the interaction between two different groups, one seeking political and social conflict, and the other seeking a greater degree of integration in the university.[145] This duality of purpose underlying student protest, and which seems to some extent to characterize all social movements, makes it unlikely that any simple explanation will prove acceptable in the long term. Indeed it serves to re-emphasize the complexity of the links between the educational system and other aspects of society, and points beyond organizational analysis to those issues which formed the substance of earlier chapters on the economy and on the political system. It is perhaps the neglect by organizational theory of some of these wider issues that has limited its application to the sociology of education.

10 The sociology of the classroom

1 *The effective teacher*

Although Waller,[1] in his pioneering study of the sociology of teaching, originally published in 1932, saw the teaching process as central in any study of the sociology of school, sociologists have neglected the classroom and have preferred to study the role of the teacher in the community or in the school instead of in the classroom. Studies of teaching have therefore been mainly the province of educationists who have on the whole tended to borrow their concepts and methods from the psychologist rather than the sociologist. Moreover, as educationists, they have been concerned with such practical considerations as 'finding better methods for selecting persons who would make "good" teachers', and 'in improving the training and assessment of students and practitioners'.[2] It is in this context that we must set the search, during the 1940s and 1950s particularly, for measures of teacher effectiveness.

Morrison and McIntyre have pointed out that the basic model underlying this research has included, on the one hand, measures of the personal qualities of teachers and, on the other hand, a criterion of effectiveness, so that the qualities of the effective teacher might emerge from the study. Personality traits and attitudes and interests have probably been the most popular teacher characteristics with researchers, although ability, type of training, and social-class origin have also featured in some research designs. The judgment of what constitutes effective teaching has usually taken the form either of assessment of pupil performance, or, perhaps rather more frequently, observer ratings of teacher performance. These observers were frequently members of the administrative structure, so that the rating scales were based on traits or qualities which superintendents or supervisors considered desirable.

It soon became evident, however that superintendents', princi-

227

pals', supervisors' and board members' ratings of teachers showed very little reliability and little relationship to one another's assessment.[3] Nor did they, in the main, show any relationship with measures of pupil performance.[4]

Pupils' ratings of teacher behaviour have also been used as an alternative measure of teacher effectiveness, but such ratings show little relationship with those of administrators,[5] who appear to approach the task of rating with quite different frames of reference. There is evidence both that administrators tend to stress poor discipline as the most important cause of teacher failure and that they tend to favour 'the more rigid conforming personalities among their teachers'.[6] Pupils, on the other hand, appear to prefer teachers whose attitudes are receptive and permissive.[7] Brookover, for example, in a study of the pupils of 66 male high-school history teachers, found that friendly helpful teachers, who were admired by the students, and in whom the students could confide, were rated more favourably as teachers by their pupils. Teachers who frequently scolded or used sarcasm, or were considered peculiar, were rated less favourably. The teachers liked by their pupils were however, *less* successful in imparting information as measured by the pupils' gains in history.[8] Moreover Bush, studying primary school pupils, found that teachers' liking for pupils was seldom reciprocated by the pupils themselves.[9] On the other hand pupils' perceptions of their teachers' feelings towards them may be very important indeed. Davidson and Lang, in an influential study, found that the more positive the children's perception of their teachers' feelings, the higher the child's own self-image, the better the child's academic achievement, and the more desirable his or her classroom behaviour as rated by the teacher.[10] This study, and its findings, point to the way towards studies of pupil-teacher *interaction* in the classroom which will be discussed later.

An alternative approach to the effective teacher, and one which was also popular in the United States during this period, is the study of teaching 'styles' and their effect on pupil morale and pupil performance which has developed out of Lippitt's original work with youth clubs in Iowa in 1939 and 1940.[11] This famous study utilized experimental groups of 11-year-old boys, who met for six weeks under a leader who employed either a democratic, an autocratic, or a *laissez-faire* leadership style. Each group was exposed to each of these leadership styles in turn, the same leaders adopting different styles. Two sets of observers kept detailed records of the behaviour of the boys in the groups. Lippitt concluded that different leadership styles produced different group and individual behaviours. Group members in a democratic social climate were more friendly to each other and showed greater initiative than they did under either authoritarian or *laissez-faire* leadership. Output, however, was highest under authoritarian leadership so long as the leader remained in the room.

Research on autocratic and democratic leadership in school situations has tended to make use of the concepts of teacher-centred and learner-centred teaching styles, and a large number of studies have been made within this general frame of reference, attempting to relate teaching style to cognitive achievement.[12] Unfortunately their findings, taken as a whole, are inconclusive. Thus, while a number of studies have reported greater learning in teacher-centred groups, others have found learner-centred groups superior, and many have found no significant differences at all. Several reasons have been put forward to explain the inconclusive and indeed contradictory results of research in this field. It has been pointed out, for example, that most of the studies show a lack of methodo-logical rigour and inadequate research design. Where, for example, students are introduced to a new method, the break from routine or 'Hawthorne effect' may in itself produce a temporary improvement in learning, irrespective of the merits of the new method. This 'Hawthorne effect', as McKeachie points out, may also affect the teachers as well as the pupils. 'How many new curricula, new courses, or new teaching methods have flowered briefly and then faded as the innovator's enthusiasm waned or as new staff members replaced the originators? Unfortunately relatively few studies have made comparisons over a period longer than one semester.'[13] Other methodological problems arise in establishing a suitable control group and in avoiding biased sampling.

Yet another problem is posed by variations in the criteria to be used in judging the effectiveness of a particular teaching style. There are many ways of measuring cognitive achievement, and the criteria in use vary from the transmission of factual knowledge to the development of problem-solving skills. There is some evidence that the techniques most suitable for transmitting knowledge may not be those most effective for developing motivation, the critical use of concepts, and skill in solving problems.

At the same time the distinction between authoritarian and democratic teaching methods not only lacks precision but is an oversimplified view of leadership style. 'To say that a style of leadership is authoritarian,' Anderson argues, 'does not adequately describe the behaviour which the leader actually exhibited.'[14] He suggests that the affective style of the leader should be separated from the amount and kind of control exercised over the group. 'For example, because we have grown used to thinking of the authoritarian leader as impersonal, cool and sometimes hostile, the possibility of a leader who maintains complete control of the decisions of the group and yet is friendly and personal does not seem very real to us.'[15]

There is indeed evidence to support Anderson's contention. Henry, for example, using an extensive programme of observation in primary school classrooms has shown convincingly how the use of techniques relying mainly on affective interaction between teacher and pupil can act as a powerful instrument of control, when the children, fearful of loss of love, are anxious to give the teacher what she wants.[16] Gordon, on the other hand, in his study of Wabash High School, gives us a picture of the pupils manipulating the teachers in order to get higher grades.[17]

Walker[18] has suggested that this strong emphasis in American educational research on the authoritarian/democratic dimensions of personality, which has no real counterpart in Britain, must be understood as an aspect of American culture. It involves on the one hand a strong moral commitment to liberal political attitudes, and on th ohter an emphasis on personality and culture which leaves little room for social structure. Waller's analysis, which emphasizes the inevitable conflict between teacher and pupil and the antagonism which is always latent in the classroom, has been largely ignored.

There have also been a number of studies which have shown that student attitudes to particular teaching styles and teaching methods vary according to the students' own personality. Student-centred instruction tends to be preferred by those students who 'reject traditional sources of authority, have strong needs for demonstrating their personal independence, and are characterized by a high desire for academic achievement.'[19] The type of student with high authoritarian needs is likely to be unhappy in the student-centred class. Convergent rather than divergent thinkers also prefer order and structure in the classroom, whereas high dependency-prone students are particularly sensitive to warmth.[20] A study by McKeachie also found that the effect of teacher warmth on students' achievement depended not only on the sex and personality of the student, but also on the sex of the instructor.[21]

There has also been some attention paid to the effect of social class differences on pupil-teacher relationships. Becker, for example, in interviews with Chicago school teachers found that lower-class children were, on the whole, considered unrewarding to teach. This was particularly true of children in slum schools. Comments were made by the teachers on such characteristics as the low level of motivation of such children, and the difficulty of maintaining control over the classroom. There were also criticisms of the habits of such children including their aggression, and their lack of cleanliness and indifference to hygiene.[22] A larger study by Kaplan into the types of pupil behaviour found disturbing or annoying by teachers reached much the same conclusions as Becker. Teachers reported that they were disturbed by such behaviour as stealing, lying, cheating, aggression and destruction of property. They also disliked inattentiveness, indifference to school work and nonconformity.[23]

There is also evidence that the career patterns of teachers in the United States are away from schools with a high proportion of working-class pupils. Becker found this to be so in Chicago in the 1950s,[24] and his findings have recently been reinforced by a much wider study by Herriott and St John. According to their survey, not only do schools with pupils of low socio-economic status contain proportionately more young and inexperienced teachers, but teachers in these schools are the least satisfied with their teaching situation. Moreover, '42 per cent of the teachers in these schools, as compared with 18 per cent in schools of highest socio-economic status, aspire to a school in a better neighbourhood'.[25]

While these studies are of teachers in the United States, there is similar evidence for Britain. Goodacre, for example, found that teachers in areas of low socio-economic status tended to assume that they had no pupils of above average intellectual ability, and so to under-estimate the ability of some of their pupils.[26] Brandis and Bernstein also found evidence that infant school teachers in a predominantly middle-class area operated with different principles of selection and control from teachers in predominantly working-class areas. In particular there was more emphasis on self-regulating behaviour in the middle-class area. The IQ of the child was highly correlated with a favourable teachers' rating in both areas, but rather more strongly in the *working-class* area. The social-class background of the child was less important than IQ in both areas, but more important in the working-class than in the middle-class area.[27]

Although the preference of teachers for middle-class children is by now well-established, the assumption that this leads to discrimination against the working-class child has been much less firmly grounded. This is largely because we had, until recently, very few studies of classrooms, and especially no studies of the pattern of interaction between teachers and working-class as distinct from middle-class pupils. This gap in our knowledge is now being filled, and one of the first areas to attract the attention of substantial numbers of researchers has been that of teacher expectations.

2 *Teacher expectations*

The possibility that teacher expectations may influence the performance of their students was raised on a number of occasions in the previous chapter. It was argued, for example, that differences in the expectations of teachers may explain at least part of the effect of school climate on achievement, as well as the effect of the socioeconomic background of the school. The consequences of streaming on performance have also been attributed to a large extent to the effect of teacher expectations. Pidgeon has argued that beliefs about the concept of intelligence and about differences between the sexes as well as school objectives and curricula can also have an influence on teachers' attitudes about what should be taught, and the kind of responses that they can expect from their pupils.[28] The studies cited earlier, and most of the evidence provided by Pidgeon, do not however examine teacher expectations directly, and the conclusions drawn about their significance are to a large extent based on inference. It is only comparatively recently that researchers have turned their attention specifically to studies of what have come to be known as teacher-expectancy effects.

The present 'flurry of research'[29] was set off by Rosenthal and Jacobson's[30] much publicized and ingenious experiment in which teachers were given the names of children in their classes who, in the year ahead, were expected to show dramatic intellectual growth. In fact these children, about 20 per cent of those in the school, had been chosen at random, and the test which purported to select the potential 'spurter' was a standard test of intelligence. When these children were re-tested later the potential 'spurters' had made significant gains in IQ in comparison with their classmates.

Although Rosenthal and Jacobson claim to have found evidence of teacher-expectancy effect, their study has since received considerable criticism on a number of important grounds. In the first place the effect for the school as a whole was largely accounted for by very large differences in only two out of eighteen classrooms, and in general effects were both small and inconsistent. There have been criticisms, too, of the test itself, and of the way in which it was administered. Moreover, the teachers themselves, two years afterwards, could not recall which children had been involved in the experiment, and did not appear, in fact, to have paid a great deal of attention to the lists of names.[31]

The attempt to replicate the Rosenthal and Jacobson study has led to inconsistent findings. Although a large number of studies, some of which have avoided the methodological weaknesses of the original research, have failed to produce any evidence of the teacher-expectancy effect others have demonstrated it successfully.[32] The successful studies tend to differ in their procedures in so far as they are more likely to employ what Brophy and Good called 'naturalistic' rather than 'experimental' methods. That is to say, the potential 'spurters' were chosen by the teachers themselves, and so the teachers actually used their own biases and expectations in terms of the actual characteristics of the children. Reviewing a number of these naturalistic studies Brophy and Good argue that although the findings are not always consistent, genuine expectation affects have been convincingly demonstrated. Some of these studies too, unlike the original Rosenthal and Jacobson research, observed the teacher in the classroom, and so were able to demonstrate differences in teacher behaviour towards children rated as 'high' and as 'low' achievers.

Although most of the research has been carried out in the U.S.A., a British study on the teaching of French to children of primary school age found that teachers' attitudes on the teaching of French to children of low ability seemed to be related to the subsequent achievement of the children concerned. High-scoring low-ability children were found to be concentrated in a small number of schools where the teachers had expressed a positive attitude.[33]

Brophy and Good argue, on the basis of the studies then available, that not all teachers 'allow their expectations to interfere with their ability to treat students appropriately'.[34] Untrained teachers, and less-experienced teachers, are more likely to show the expectancy effect, which also appears to vary with the teacher's personality and his or her role definition. Thus the teacher's beliefs about the potential for change in students is important.

Grieger has suggested a number of pupil characteristics which appear to influence teacher expectations. These include socio-economic status as expressed in dress, style of speech, etc., sex, and ability as expressed in terms of prior academic achievement. Physical attractiveness has also been shown to be important. One study, for example, asked 404 elementary school teachers to rate children on a number of characteristics on the basis of a report card and a photograph. All reports were filled out for an above average student. It was found that the child's attractiveness independently rated by twenty educators, was significantly associated with the teachers' expectations about how intelligent the child was, how interested in education his parents were, how far he was likely to progress in school, and how popular he or she would be with peers.[35]

Although, therefore, there is evidence both that some teachers at least have different expectations for different groups of students, and that these expectations can result in differences in student performance, the design of many of these studies does not help us to discover the way in which these expectations communicate themselves to the student, and influence his or her achievement. For this purpose we need to look at those studies which are concerned directly with the process of classroom interaction.

3 The dynamics of the classroom

To some extent the current and widespread interest in the class room may be seen as a logical development from previous research on the school. On the one hand organizational studies have pointed up the crucial role of the teacher in interpreting, and even re-interpreting, the formal structure of the organization, and on the other hand, studies of teacher characteristics, teaching style and teacher expectations have underlined the need to examine these in the context of pupil-teacher interaction. At the same time the growth on a large scale of discontent with the outcome of schooling has led to a renewed emphasis on what is seen not just as a failure of the school but also as a failure of the teacher; an interpretation which has been strongly reinforced by individual teachers who have described in vivid terms their disillusion with the teaching situation.[36] Attempts to introduce changes, both in the formal structure of the organization and in the curriculum, the pedagogy, and the system of evaluation have also raised in an acute form the problems raised by the implementation of innovation at the classroom level. As Walker has pointed out, this has 'created problems for the curriculum developer and the teacher educator especially, and they are the ones who have started doing research'.[37]

The earlier attempts to describe life in classrooms do however predate the recent upsurge of interest in the field, although at this stage, they still made use of predominantly psychological concepts, and were still concerned to a major extent with teaching style. The best known example of this work is probably Flanders' attempt to develop an observational technique which would provide a picture of classroom behaviour.[38] This makes use of ten categories of teacher and pupil verbal behaviour, or teacher and pupil *talk*. Teacher talk is further subdivided into indirect and direct influence, and the balance between these can provide the basis for a distinction in terms of teacher style.[39] Flanders' interaction analysis has been widely accepted as a useful tool for the observation of classrooms. The indirect rather than the direct teaching style has, for example, been shown to be related to achievement in geometry and to favourable pupil attitudes.[40] The use of interaction analysis has also proved valuable in the training of teachers.[41] This should not, however, blind us to its limitations. Perhaps the most obvious of these is its concentration upon verbal behaviour, although non-verbal interaction can also be shown to be important. To some extent this concentration on verbal behaviour can be justified by the importance of language in the classroom as well by the practical difficulty of including non-verbal behaviour in observational categories. Adams and Biddle have however demonstrated the use of video-tape in illuminating the complexities of classrooms.[42] At a more fundamental level Flanders has been criticised for his stress on the teachers' behaviour towards the entire class rather than towards individual students, for his emphasis on teacher-initiated communication, and for his disregard for the context and setting in which interaction takes place.[43]

More recently, developments in classroom observational research have brought it much closer to sociology. This is partly because of the greater concern with context and meaning, which leads the observer to the study of long-term patterns which emerge over several months. This requires the use of techniques quite different from those of interaction analysis which are designed for short periods of observation in a large number of schools. In so far as the stress is still on *observation,* however, the new approach, which Robinson has described, in the paper already cited, as an ethnography of classrooms, leans more heavily on participant observation and anthropological field-studies than on the methods of traditional sociology. At the same time some of its exponents have been influenced by the phenomenological approach to sociology. There is therefore, as Robinson makes clear, an emphasis in many studies on an understanding of the interpretative procedures used by members in their everyday world, an understanding to be reached through persistent observation and shared analysis of the events as they happen. The anthropological viewpoint is welcomed because it provides the necessary 'anthropological strangeness' to sensitize the observer to the 'taken-for-granted assumptions which sustain members' views of the world'.[44] Although this particular viewpoint is not held by everyone working in this field, there is a widely shared assumption that what is needed at the present time is 'a great many "field trips" in a great variety of schools'.[45]

There are now a number of published studies which to a greater or lesser extent fall into the category of an ethnography of classrooms, and because it is an expanding field, others are likely to be available in the near future, so that it is no longer possible to regard this as a neglected area. At the same time, there are a number of reasons why it is difficult at this stage to present what may be described as a review of findings.[46] This is partly because much of the work is still small-scale and exploratory, and partly because the emphasis is on description rather than theory, but also because the researchers involved are united more by an adherence to a particular method than by a concern for a common set of problems. In consequence, although the studies taken together illustrate the complexity of the issue, taken individually they illuminate many different aspects of life in classrooms.

One study which has thrown considerable light on both teacher expectation and teaching style was carried out by Leacock in a number of city schools in the United States. Information was collected using three different perspectives: observation in the classrooms, interviews with the teachers, and brief sessions with the pupils. At the same time the use of two major variables, income and race, allowed the introduction of a comparative perspective which is impossible in the single case study. One of the most striking findings was the light thrown on the relationship between teacher warmth and supportiveness, and achievement. A relaxed and sociable atmosphere could, and did, exist alongside low standards. Thus the two teachers in the lower-income Negro schools were by no means lacking in warmth towards the children but they shared a derogatory attitude towards them and their potentiality as a group. This emerged in practice as a lack of challenge in the classrooms. In the middle-income Negro schools, although the children were given little freedom for individual expression, the teachers set and achieved high standards of *academic* achievement. The author argues that the school, far from presenting middle-class values to working-class children, is conveying a middle-class image of how working-class children are and how they should be.[47]

A somewhat similar point is made by Keddie in her study of an English comprehensive school. She found that teachers, in spite of an ideological commitment to the integrated curriculum, had quite different conceptions of what was suitable material for the A and the C streams. For example, teachers believed that they could 'get away with' poorly prepared material for the C stream. This arose, Keddie argues, from the way in which 'ability' was used as an organizing but largely unexamined concept by the teacher. The low expectations the teacher had with respect to the C stream led to situations in which questions from C-stream pupils were dismissed as playing up or being awkward, whereas the same kind of questions gained approval from pupils in the A stream.[48]

Another issue to which Leacock devotes considerable attention, and which also is one of the main themes developed by Keddie in her paper, is the problem faced by the teacher in trying to implement a child-centred rather than a teacher-centred pedagogy. Although teachers may have accepted that teaching is concerned with 'getting something out of a child', they have great difficulty in translating this into concrete and practical terms.[49] Using many examples of actual classroom practice, Leacock shows that teachers have not had adequate training in the very different technique needed for this kind of teaching so that they are unable to carry it into effect.

A very similar point is made by Gross and his colleagues in their study of an attempt to introduce pupil-centred teaching into a traditional elementary school. Although the teachers were initially favourable towards the innovation, observations revealed that the degree of implementation was minimal. Although there were a number of reasons for this, Gross emphasizes in particular the lack of clarity about the innovation at the *behavioural* level, the lack of materials, and the lack of skills and knowledge on the part of teachers to perform the new role. One consequence of this, which is also brought out by Leacock, is that although teachers may adopt some of the formal aspects of pupil-centred learning, for example children may be free to move about the room and to choose their activities, the ability on the part of the teacher to make this a learning situation is in fact lacking.[50] Leacock also draws attention to the extent to which teachers are concerned with the moral aspect of their teaching. In all the classrooms she studied the pupils saw their teachers as being more concerned about good or bad behaviour than about academic work and performance. As a consequence she argues, obedience, respect and conscientiousness come to be seen as desirable qualities rather than ability, responsibility and initiative. Nor is she alone in her assessment. Brophy and Good point to the evidence that teachers generally prefer high achieving students who are hard working, dependable and responsive rather than independent students who aggressively pursue their own interests.[51] Similarly McPherson, in her perceptive study of a small rural elementary school, using participant observation, describes the beliefs of these, admittedly very traditional teachers, as 'docility plus effort equals success'. The successful student who was neither docile nor hard-working was seen as a threat to this belief-system, and the fact of his or her achievement was often minimized or even disbelieved. Surprisingly enough, Delamont also came to very similar conclusions in her observations in an upper-middle-class girls' school in Scotland. When the girls were asked to describe the 'good' pupil they characterized her not only as attentive and well-behaved but also lacking in intellectual independence.[52]

A number of researchers have drawn attention to the significance for classroom interaction of the 'hidden curriculum' which, Philip Jackson argues, 'each student and teacher must master if he is to make his way satisfactorily through the school'.[53] Similarly Keddie has suggested that it is the willingness of the A stream to accept the teacher's presentation on trust which makes them such acceptable pupils.[54] Peter Woods has also suggested that there are two punishment structures in schools, one formal, open and official; the other unofficial and concealed. He instances 'showing-up' as an example of an unofficial but widespread method which teachers employ to keep control over the pupil and the class.[55]

Although most observers tend to agree that teachers play the dominant role in the classroom, there are also significant differences amongst the pupils in the way in which they play the pupil role. Delamont has distinguished between what she calls the syllabus-bound student and the syllabus-free student. These have quite different personal styles which are related to both the amount and the content of pupil talk. For example, the syllabus-free students made more independent contribution in class.[56] Lundgren similarly distinguishes between active and passive pupils. Active pupils structure and initiate discussion, whereas the teachers seem unable to activate the more passive students. He also distinguishes a third group of pupils who steer the pace. The teacher uses their responses to judge when it is time to leave one topic and go on to the next.[57]

There is also evidence that teachers interact differently to pupils according to their success. Lundgren, for example, found that boys were more likely than girls to be 'active' pupils. Brophy and Good, in a review of findings in this area also found boys more active in the classroom and more likely to draw attention to themselves. They also break more classroom rules and are more often warned or criticised for misbehaviour by male as well as female teachers. At the same time, because boys, as a group, are more variable than girls, they also receive more praise.[58]

A particularly interesting, but highly complex, area of research is the attempt to discover the ways in which teachers interact with low-achieving pupils. Brophy and Good have suggested that teachers respond differently to failure, and that some teachers gear their instruction primarily towards high achievers, others towards low achievers. Similarly low achievers may provoke concern or rejection. A small early study by Hoehn, for example, found that the teachers in his sample tended to concentrate on the low achievers. On the other hand, although the teachers spent more time with them they gave them less approval.[59] A later study by Rist of a kindergarten classroom of black children in a predominantly low-income area found the differences between slow and fast learners reflected in the spatial arrangement of the classroom. Moreover the table for the fast learners was more favourably placed for observing the teacher's blackboard activities.[60]

Nash, in a study of British schools, compared the way teachers ranked individual pupils with observations of their classroom behaviour. He found evidence of discrimination against those pupils poorly regarded by the teacher, in so far as the same behaviour was treated differently depending on which pupil was involved. On the whole teachers were more indulgent towards those pupils of whom they approved.[61]

Perhaps the most interesting aspect of Nash's study was the accuracy with which the children, even in unstreamed classes, perceived their position relative to other children. The children, although all of junior school age, were easily able to see through the camouflage that teachers used to disguise this fact, and perceived the reality not only behind labels that attempted to conceal rank, but also the most determined attempts to mix the children up in a highly complicated arrangement of different teaching groups. It is, indeed, as Nash points out, not difficult for even the youngest child to infer that book two is higher than book one.

This relationship between social class and achievement may provide the basis for the way teachers interact with working-class pupils. Both Hoehn and Rist note that the low-achieving students were also of lower social status. There is however evidence, as we have seen, that teachers may actually underestimate the ability of working-class pupils.[62] On the other hand Nash found that some teachers tended to assume, quite wrongly, that slower and less likeable children came from poor homes.

Some very interesting examples of the way in which teachers interpreted the behaviour of different pupils in terms of their social background is provided by McPherson. In this small rural school the teachers, solidly lower-middle-class themselves, had very clear preferences for pupils of similar background as opposed to those from both the working *and* the upper-middle classes. The teachers knew exactly who belonged where and used this information both in interpreting behaviour and in deciding how to handle it.

Although this has been only a somewhat brief and selective review of research in classroom interaction it should have sufficed to indicate that teacher-pupil relationships are an important aspect of the sociology of learning. It seems clear that, in spite of the need for more and better studies in classrooms, the ways that teachers perform their task, and the manner of their interaction with different kinds of pupils have a profound effect on pupil behaviour. At the same time, in spite of the dominance of the teacher in the classroom, the pattern of interaction is deeply affected by pupil characteristics. Personality, ability, sex, and social background have all been found to influence not only the teacher's reaction to the pupil but also the pupil's reaction to the teacher.

4 The socialization of the teacher

Although studies of the classroom have demonstrated its importance for learning, the understanding of why teachers behave as they do is considerably less developed. Early studies of the effective teacher were, it is true, often concerned with teacher characteristics, including their educational and social background and their personality. At the same time there have been numerous studies of the reasons for becoming a teacher. [63] Yet the way that teachers are socialized for a particular role, either in their preparation or in the context of the teaching profession, has been little studied. It is the purpose of this final section to draw together the major findings in this area in order to explore their implications for the behaviour of the teacher in the classroom. Westwood has suggested that teacher training should be regarded as the period when the student develops his concept of the mature teacher's behaviour.[64] On the other hand, studies of the output of colleges and departments of education face the problems of determining criteria not only of successful student performance but also of effective teacher behaviour. Moreover such studies as we have available[65] in this country suggest that there is little correlation between the assessments made of students in college and later criteria of successful professional performance. The vagueness about what constitutes effective teaching also pervades school practice. Indeed Morrison and McIntyre go as far as to suggest that 'a growing body of research evidence supports the view that the college supervisor is largely irrelevant to what they learn from teaching practice'.[66] What students learn, and how much they learn, depends, in their view, largely on their relationship with the *class* teacher.

Studies of the effect of college on attitudes to teaching show, however, that during their training students become more progressive and liberal in their expressed attitudes. Indeed to a large extent they become more like their lecturers. Moreover, there appears to be a direct relationship between the educational quality of the college climate and the amount of change taking place in student attitudes.[67] On the other hand, all the evidence suggests that these new attitudes are short-lived.

A number of studies have demonstrated that after a few months of teaching the new teachers' attitudes are closer to those of his school colleagues than to those of the college.[68] Moreover, this process may begin while they are still students. Finlayson and Cohen, in a comparison of student and head-teacher expectations for teachers' behaviour in four role sectors, found that a consistent pattern of change towards less authoritarian classroom behaviour was found to reach its peak in the second-year students' responses. The third-year students were closer to the head teachers and more authoritarian in expectations than the second-year students. The authors suggest that it is during the second year that students are most detached from the everyday workings of school, and more likely therefore to come under the influence of the liberal views of college lecturers. During the third year of training, however, the students are in closer contact with the schools and in consequence they seek 'to narrow the gap in the conception of what is thought to be desirable teacher behaviour by the college and what they see will be expected of them in schools'.[69]

Clearly therefore the school itself is acting as an important and indeed perhaps more important socializing agency than the college, and it is surprising that we have so few studies of how this takes effect. From what we know of the process of socialization, and particularly secondary socialization, it would appear however that teacher colleagues, as well as head teachers, may be expected to play a significant part. It is at this day-to-day level therefore, as Corwin has pointed out, that 'teaching roles and expectations are forged out and compromised'.[70] This will include the learning not only of official values and objectives but of informal goals, ideologies and prodedures. Newcomers may be taught, for example, that even though it is officially outlawed, corporal punishment is customarily used in some schools. Webb has described some of the methods used to bring a new colleague into line. 'If a teacher lets playground chaos into his class, it may spill over into a colleague's, so threatening him with increased fatigue. Ridicule is used to stop this threat. (Hell of a row from your room this morning, Mr Penguin. Thought you'd left them for a minute, and the little blighters were taking advantage. Just going to go in and step on them, when I saw you were there.)[71]

McPherson has also presented a detailed and vivid picture of the socialization of the new teacher. Like the school described by Webb this is a traditional school, and the emphasis is on the teacher as disciplinarian. Keeping order was assumed to be necessary as a precondition of learning, so that the main problem faced by the young teacher was controlling the class. Some teachers stood out as role-models for the group, and these were the ones who were able to maintain order without losing dignity or resorting to sarcasm. However, by no means all teachers were able to live up to this ideal. The significance of classroom order is well exemplified by the practice of leaving classroom doors open during the day to demonstrate the teacher's control over her class. A closed door unless there were special circumstances was a sign to the other teachers that this control had broken down.[72]

Although the expectations of colleagues are clearly of importance, the pupils themselves play a powerful role. Waller has presented the pupil-teacher relationship as one of inevitable conflict. The reason for this antagonism, Waller suggests, arises because teachers need to force pupils to learn. 'If students could be allowed to learn only what interested them, to learn in their own way, and to learn no more and no better than it pleased them to do, if good order were not considered a necessary condition of learning, if teachers did not have to be taskmasters but merely helpers and friends, then life would be sweet in the classroom.'[73] Moreover because of the antagonism which is always latent in the classroom, if the teacher lays down control the initiative passes to the class itself, and the fact that this sometimes happens, and the fear of the teacher that it will happen, is amusingly and tellingly illustrated by Waller's entertaining case-studies. Woods also draws attention to the continuous assaults by pupils on the power and status of the teachers. The process of 'playing up' and 'trying out' is a typical and well-known phenomenon in schools, and teachers are on the whole regarded as fair game.[74] Other observers have noted the different ways in which students try, successfully, to manipulate teachers.[75]

The prevalence of liberal and progressive attitudes in teacher education may make it harder for the new teacher to adjust to the harsh realities of life in classrooms. Whiteside, Bernbaum and Noble have suggested that entrants to the teaching profession often have an idealized conception of the teaching role. The new teacher 'they assume and hope will, through his skill and endeavour, reproduce in his pupils his own enthusiasm for his subject'. When this fails to happen they are shocked and discouraged.[76] The nature of the act of teaching also adds its constraints to the situation. Brophy and Good point out that confronted with a class of students the teacher is all too often frantically trying to keep pace with events over which he has only partial control. The necessary absorption in the present makes it difficult for teachers to monitor their own behaviour.

Undoubtedly part of the attraction of child-centred pedagogy arises from the promise it appears to offer of overcoming the conflict inherent in the teaching situation, and getting the pupil on the teacher's side. The New Romantics in particular are attracted by the idea, implicit in the new pedagogy, of pupil and teacher learning together. Undoubtedly, the successful implementation of the new pedagogy would introduce important changes in the teacher's role, but the nature of these changes has not yet been fully explored.

The ambiguities in the teacher's role can also be seen as contributing to the teacher's behaviour in the classroom. McPherson has pointed to the elusive character of success in teaching, which leads to an emphasis on its more obvious manifestations in good behaviour and examination success. Kelsall and Kelsall have also drawn attention to the conflicts and insecurities arising from the diverse obligations attached to the teacher's role; and also from the tendency, in consequence, to impose on teachers unattainable standards.[77] The autonomy the teacher enjoys in the classroom is indeed important, but should not lead to the neglect of the pressures which arise from outside the school, and which shape the teacher's role in many different ways. As we have seen the teacher may frustrate the implementation of innovations like destreaming and the integrated curriculum, but the innovating teacher may well face equally formidable obstacles ranging from angry parents to prescribed textbooks.[78]

There is, furthermore, a profound ambiguity in the very concept of child-centred learning, which lies behind many of the problems which, as we have seen, impede the transition from the teacher-dominated to the child-dominated classroom. Although the idea of *involving* pupils in their own learning does not in itself appear to raise any fundamental difficulties, the attempt to carry this through in practice involves the teacher in apparently insuperable problems with respect to his or her own role in the classroom. This relates primarily to the *amount* of direction which is to be permitted to the teacher, and the degree of freedom which is to be allowed the pupil both over his or her own behaviour and over the direction of his learning. In so far as the teacher is still expected to teach and the pupil to 'learn', the consequence of an unthinking acceptance of the new pedagogy is all too likely to result, as Bernstein has pointed out, in the replacement of overt by covert systems of control, and the growing significance of the hidden curriculum.

The conclusion to this chapter, therefore, is a re-emphasis on what may be described as the message of the book as a whole. It is not possible to isolate one aspect of the sociology of education from the subject as a whole, nor a consideration of problems at the micro-level, such as the classroom, without also considering those at the macro-level, such as the relationship between education and politics or education and the economy. Nor ultimately, can the sociology of education be separated from sociology itself.

Notes

Chapter 1. Introduction

1 Corwin, R. G. *A Sociology of Education,* New York: Appleton-Century-Crofts, 1965, p. 56.
2 Brim, O. *Sociology in the Field of Education,* New York: Russell Sage Foundation, 1958.
3 Corwin, R. G. *op. cit.,* ch. 3.
4 Conant, J. B. *The Education of American Teachers,* New York: McGraw-Hill, 1963, p. 131.
5 Brookover, W. B. and Erickson, E. L. *Sociology of Education,* Illinois: The Dorsey Press, 1975, p. 10.
6 Corwin, R. G. *op. cit.,* p. 65.
7 For an account of the development of sociology in teacher education see Reid, I. and Wormald, E. *Sociology and Teacher Education,* Sociology Section of the Association of Teachers in Colleges and Departments of Education, 1974.
8 Tropp, A. 'The English Case' in Hansen, D. A. and Gerstl, J. E. (eds) *On Education: Sociological Perspective,* New York: Wiley, 1967, p. 287.
9 Floud, J. 'Sociology and Education', *The Sociological Review Monograph,* no. 4, July 1961, p. 60.
10 Williamson, B. 'Continuities and Discontinuities in the Sociology of Education' in Flude, M. and Ahier, J. *Educability, Schools and Ideology,* London: Croom Helm, 1974, p. 7.
11 *Ibid.,* p. 10.
12 Davies, I. 'The Management of Knowledge' in Young, M. F. D. (ed.) *Knowledge and Control: New Directions for the Sociology of Education,* London: Collier Macmillan, 1971, p. 273.
13 Durkheim, E. *Education and Sociology,* Glencoe, Illinois: Free Press, 1956, p. 71.
14 Floud, J. and Halsey, A. H. 'The Sociology of Education. A Trend Report and Bibliography' in *Current Sociology,* vol. VIII (3), 1958, p. 168.
15 *Ibid.,* p. 171.
16 Consider, for example, his relegation of conflict to pathological types of the division of labour. Durkheim, E. *The Division of Labour in Society,* Glencoe, Illinois: Free Press, 1933.

247

[17] Ideology includes both popularly accepted ideas about the nature of society and popularly approved values and goals for the society. See Johnson, H. M. *Sociology: A Systematic Introduction,* London: Routledge & Kegan Paul, 1961, pp. 587-8.

[18] Gouldner, A. *The Coming Crisis of Western Sociology,* New York, London: Basic Books, 1970, p. 439.

[19] See for example Eggleston, J. *Contemporary Research in the Sociology of Education,* London: Methuen, 1974, Editorial introduction.

[20] Berger, P. and Luckmann, T. *The Social Construction of Reality,* London: Allen Lane, The Penguin Press, 1967.

[21] Esland, G. M. 'Teaching and Learning as the Organization of Knowledge' in Young, M. F. D. (ed.) *Knowledge and Control: New Directions for the Sociology of Education, op. cit.* pp. 70-115.

[22] Banks, O. 'The "New" Sociology of Education', *Forum,* vol. 17, 1974.

[23] Young, M. F. D. 'An Approach to the Study of Curricula as Socially Organized Knowledge' in Young, M. F. D. (ed.) *Knowledge and Control: New Directions for the Sociology of Education,* London: Collier Macmillan, 1971.

[24] Davies, I. 'The Management of Knowledge', *ibid.*

[25] See the interesting critique by Whitty, G. 'Sociology and the Problem of Radical Educational Change' in Flude, M. and Ahier, J. (eds) *Educability, Schools and Ideology, op. cit.*

[26] Floud, J. and Halsey, A. H. 'The Sociology of Education: A Trend Report and Bibliography', *Current Sociology,* vol. VIII, 1958, p. 186.

[27] Floud, J. 'Sociology and Education' *op. cit.* p. 64.

[28] Gross, N. 'The Sociology of Education' in Merton, R. K. (ed.) *Sociology Today,* New York: Basic Books, 1959, p. 131.

[29] Davies, B. 'On the contribution of organizational analysis to the study of educational institutions' in Brown, R. (ed.) *Knowledge, Education and Cultural Change,* London: Tavistock, 1973.

[30] Hoyle, E. 'Organizational Analysis in the Field of Education', *Educational Research,* vol. VII, 1965.

[31] Hoyle, E. 'The Study of Schools as Organizations.' in Butcher, H. J. and Pont, H. B. (eds) *Educational Research in Britain,* vol. 3, University of London Press, 1973, p. 34.

Chapter 2. Education and the Economy

[1] Schelsky, H. 'Technical Change and Educational Consequences', in Halsey, A. H., Floud, J. and Anderson, C. A. (eds) *Education, Economy and Society,* New York: The Free Press, 1961, p. 33.

[2] Blau, P. M. 'Parameters of Social Structure', *American Sociological Review,* vol. XXXIX, 1974, pp. 627-9.

[3] See particularly Schultz, T. W. *The Economic Value of Education,* Columbia University Press, 1963.

[4] See for example Woodhall, M. *Economic aspects of education,* Slough, Berkshire: N.F.E.R., 1972, for a good discussion of this and related issues.

5 Roberts, K. 'Economy and Education: Foundations of a General Theory', *Comparative Education,* vol. 7, 1971, pp. 3-14.

6 See, for example, Banks, O. *Parity and Prestige in English Secondary Education,* London: Routledge & Kegan Paul, 1955.

7 Taylor, W. *The Secondary Modern School,* London: Faber & Faber, 1963, pp. 53-4.

8 Banks, O. *op. cit.*

9 Neave, G. *How They Fared,* London: Routledge & Kegan Paul, 1975.

10 Counts, G. S. *Education and American Civilization,* New York Teachers' College, 1952, p. 454.

11 Halsey, A. H. 'The Changing Functions of Universities', in Halsey, Floud, Anderson, *op. cit.,* p. 457.

12 Anderson, C. Arnold. 'Access to Higher Education and Economic Development', in Halsey, Floud, Anderson, *op. cit.,* pp. 253-5.

13 Ben-David, J. 'Professions in the Class System of Present-day Societies', *Current Sociology,* vol. XII (3), 1963-4, pp. 256-61.

14 *Ibid.,* p. 261.

15 Layard, R., King, J. and Moser, C. *The Impact of Robbins,* Harmondsworth, Middlesex: Penguin, 1969, p. 24, Table 3.

16 For a variety of reasons future expansion is likely to take place in the polytechnics.

17 The Hudson Report, *The United Kingdom in 1980,* London: Associated Business Programmes Ltd, 1974, pp. 90-91.

18 Berendzen, R., 'Population changes and higher education' in *Educational Record,* 1974, vol. 55, pp. 115-25. See also Bowers, R. H. 'Higher education: a growth industry?', *ibid.,* pp. 147-58.

19 *Report on Higher Education* (Robbins Report), London: H.M.S.O., Cmnd 2154 - V, 1963, p. 171.

20 Riesman, D. 'The Academic Procession', in Halsey, Floud, Anderson, *op. cit.,* pp. 477-501. See also Ashby, E. *Any Person, Any Study. An Essay in Higher Education in the United States,* London: McGraw-Hill, 1971.

21 Robbins Report, *op. cit.,* Appendix 5, Table 3, p. 9.

22 Folger, J. K. and Nam, C. B. *The Education of the American Population,* Washington, D.C.: U.S. Bureau of the Census, U.S. Govt Printing Office, 1967, pp. 175-6. See also Folger, J. K., Astin H. S. and Bayer, A. E., *Human Resources and Higher Education,* New York: Russell Sage Foundation, 1970.

23 Berg, I. *Education and Jobs: The Great Training Robbery,* Harmondsworth, Middlesex: Penguin, 1970, pp. 144, 183.

24 Roberts, K. *op. cit.,* p. 4.

25 Hofstadter, Richard, and Metzger, Walter P. *The Development of Academic Freedom in the United States,* Columbia University Press, 1955, p. 6.

26 Ashby, Sir Eric *Technology and the Academics,* London: Macmillan; New York: St. Martin's Press, 1958, ch. III.

27 Ben-David, J. *op. cit.,* p. 275.

28 Rothblatt, S. *The Revolution of the Dons,* London: Faber & Faber, 1968, pp. 90-91.

29 Ashby, Sir Eric 'On Universities and the Scientific Revolution', in Halsey, Floud, Anderson, *op. cit.,* p. 466.

30 Cotgrove, S. *Technical Education and Social Change,* London: Routledge & Kegan Paul, 1958, p. 27.
31 Quoted in Musgrave, P. W. *Technical Change, the Labour Force and Education,* Oxford: Pergamon, 1967, pp. 62, 200.
32 Landes, D. S. *The Unbound Prometheus,* London: Cambridge University Press, 1969, p. 340.
33 *Ibid.,* p. 346.
34 Sanderson, M. *The Universities and British Industry, 1850-1970,* London: Routledge & Kegan Paul, 1972.
35 See for example Rothblatt, S. *op. cit.,* pp. 266-8.
36 Sanderson, M. (ed.) *The Universities in the Nineteenth Century,* London: Routledge & Kegan Paul, 1974.
37 Sanderson, M. *The Universities and British Industry, 1850-1970, op. cit.,* p. 312.
38 Banks, O. *Parity and Prestige in English Secondary Education, op. cit.,* ch. 12.
39 For details of changes in Government policy since 1945 see Cotgrove, S. *op. cit.,* ch. 12.
40 Committee on Manpower Resources for Science and Technology, *The Flow into Employment of Scientists, Engineers and Technologists.* H.M.S.O. Cmnd 3760, 1968, p. vii.
41 Rudd, E. and Hatch, S. *Graduate Study and After,* London: Weidenfeld and Nicolson, 1968.
42 Council for Scientific Policy, *Enquiry into the Flow of Candidates in Science and Technology into Higher Education,* London: H.M.S.O., Cmnd 3541, 1968.
43 *Ibid.*
44 Pont, H. B. 'The Arts Science Dichotomy', in *Educational Research in Britain* Vol. II Butcher, H. J. and Pont, H. B. (eds), University of London Press, 1970.
45 Richmond, P. E. 'Science Teaching' in Butcher, H. J. and Pont, H. B. (eds), *Educational Research in Britain,* vol. III. University of London Press, 1973.
46 See Prandy, K. *Professional Employees, a Study of Scientists and Engineers.* London: Faber and Faber, 1965, chapters 1 and 2.
47 Reported in Pont, H. B. *op. cit.*
48 Hutchings, D. *The Science Undergraduate: A Study of Science at Five English Universities,* Oxford: University of Oxford Department of Education, 1967.
49 McPherson, A. F. 'The Dainton Report: A Scottish Dissent', *Universities Quarterly,* vol. 22(3), 1968, pp. 254-73, and 'Swing from Science or Retreat from Reason', *Universities Quarterly,* vol. 24 (1), 1969, pp. 29-43.
50 Neave, G. *op. cit:*
51 Keeves, J. P. 'Differences Between the Sexes in Mathematics and Science Courses' in *International Review of Education,* Special Number: The Education of Women, vol. XIX, 1973, pp. 47-63.
52 Gannicott, K. G. and Blaug, M. 'Manpower Forecasting since Robbins – a Science Lobby in Action' from *Higher Education Review,* Autumn 1969, reprinted in *Decision Making in British Education,* G. Fowler (ed.) *et al.,* London: Heinemann, 1973, p. 276.
53 *Ibid.,* p. 270
54 See for example Greenaway, G. 'The Impact of Educational Policies' in *Patterns of Change in Graduate Employment,* Greenaway, H. and Williams, G., London: Society for Research into Higher Education, 1973.

[55] Woodhall, M., *Economic Aspects of Education, op. cit.* p. 61.

[56] Collins, R. 'Where are Educational Requirements for Employment Highest?' in *Sociology of Education,* 1974, vol. 47, pp. 419–442.

[57] Ben-David, J. *op. cit.,* pp. 274–5.

[58] Prandy, K. *op. cit.,* p. 20.

[59] *Ibid.,* p. 57.

[60] Cotgrove, S., 'Education and Occupation', *British Journal of Sociology,* vol. XIII, 1962, pp. 34–5. See also Lee, D. 'Industrial Training and Social Class', *Sociological Review,* vol. XIV, 1966, p. 271.

[61] See for example Venables, E. 'The Further Education of the Young·Worker', *Educational Review,* vol. XIII, 1960–61.

[62] Ben-David, J. *op. cit.,* p. 270.

[63] Stewart, C. 'The Place of Higher Education in a Changing Society', in Sanford, N. (ed.) *The American College,* New York: Wiley, 1962, p. 930.

[64] Ben-David, J. *op. cit.,* p. 273.

[65] The Minister of Higher Education in the U.S.S.R. in 1959, quoted in Grant, N. *Soviet Education,* Harmondsworth, Middlesex: Penguin, 1964, p. 23.

[66] *Ibid.,* p. 34. See also Bereday, G. *et al. The Changing Soviet School,* London: Constable, 1960.

[67] King, E. J. (ed.) *Communist Education,* London: Methuen, 1963, p. 177.

[68] This is accentuated by recent attempts to introduce the so-called polytechnic principle into education.

[69] Grant, N. *op. cit.,* pp. 124–6.

[70] Coleman, J. S. (ed.) *Education and Political Development,* Princeton University Press, 1965, p. 522.

[71] Hurd, G. E. and Johnson, T. J. 'Education and Development', *Sociological Review,* vol. XV, 1967, p. 59.

[72] Hoselitz, B. F. 'Investment in Education', in Coleman, J. S. *op. cit.,* pp. 542–3.

[73] Bowman, M. J. and Anderson, C. A. 'Concerning the Role of Education in Development', in Geertz, C. (ed.) *Old Societies and New States: The Quest for Modernity in Asia and Africa,* New York: Free Press, 1963, pp. 247–79.

[74] Aran, L., Eisenstadt, S. N. and Adler, C. 'The Effectiveness of Educational Systems in the Processes of Modernization', *Comparative Education Review,* 1972, vol. 16, pp. 30–43.

[75] Cipolla, C. M. *Literacy and Development in the West,* Harmondsworth, Middlesex: Penguin, 1969, p. 102.

[76] Dore, R. P. *Education in Tokagawa Japan,* London: Routledge & Kegan Paul, 1965, ch. 10. See also Shipman, M. D. *Education and Modernization,* London: Faber & Faber, 1971.

[77] Adams, D. and Bjork, R. M. *Education in Developing Areas,* New York: David McKay & Co., 1969, p. 38.

[78] Thabault, R. *Education and change in a village community,* London: Routledge & Kegan Paul, 1971, p. 70.

[79] *Ibid.,* pp. 229–33.

[80] Coleman, J. S., *op. cit.,* p. 29.

[81] Cowan, L. G., O'Connell, J. and Scanlon, D. G. (eds) *Education and Nation Building in Africa,* New York: Praeger, 1965, p. 31.

[82] Coleman, J. S. *op. cit.,* p. 73.

[83] *Ibid.,* p. 187.

[84] Foster, P. J. *Education and Social Change in Ghana,* London: Routledge & Kegan Paul, 1965.

[85] Hurd, G. E. and Johnson, T. J. *op. cit.,* p. 62.

[86] Foster, P. J. 'The Vocational School Fallacy in Development Planning', in Anderson, C. A. and Bowman, M. J. (eds) *Education and Economic Development,* Chicago: Aldine, 1965, pp. 142-66.

[87] Kazamias, A. M. *Education and the Quest for Modernity in Turkey,* London: Allen & Unwin, 1966, pp. 153-4.

[88] *Ibid.,* p. 266.

[89] Inkeles, A. and Holsinger, D. B. *Education and Individual Modernity in Developing Countries,* Leiden: E. J. Brill, 1974.

[90] Katz, M. B. *Class, Bureaucracy and Schools: The Illusion of Educational Change in America,* New York, Washington, London: Praeger, 1971.

Chapter 3. Education and social mobility

[1] Blau, P. 'Parameters of Social Structure', *American Sociological Review,* vol. XXXIX, 1974, pp. 627-8.

[2] Taken from Folger, J. K. and Nam, C. B. *op. cit.,* p. 170, Table 6-3.

[3] Taken from 1961 Census, England and Wales, *Education Tables,* London: H.M.S.O., 1966, pp. 17-20.

[4] Glass, D. V. (ed.) *Social Mobility in Britain,* London: Routledge & Kegan Paul, 1954, ch X, pp. 291-307.

[5] Centers, R. 'Education and Occupational Mobility', *American Sociological Review,* vol. XIV, February 1949, pp. 143-4

[6] Blau, P. M. and Duncan, O. D. *The American Occupational Structure,* New York, London, Sydney: Wiley, 1967, p. 403.

[7] Havighurst, R. J. 'Education and Social Mobility in Four Societies' in Halsey, Floud, Anderson, *op. cit.,* p. 238.

[8] Husén, T. *The Learning Society,* London: Methuen, 1974.

[9] Anderson, Arnold C. 'A Skeptical Note on Education and Mobility', in Halsey, Floud, Anderson, *op. cit.,* pp. 164-79.

[10] Boudon, R. *Education, Opportunity and Social Inequality,* New York: Wiley, 1973, p. 136.

[11] Jencks, C. *Inequality: A Reassessment of the Effect of Family and Schooling in America,* New York, London: Basic Books, 1972, p. 191.

[12] *Ibid.,* pp. 221-6.

[13] See, for example, the Symposium Review in *Sociology of Education,* vol. XLVI, 1973, pp. 427-70. See also 'Perspectives on *Inequality',* *Harvard Educational Review,* vol. XLIII, 1973, pp. 92-164.

[14] Miller, S. 'On the Uses, Misuses and Abuses of Jencks's *Inequality',* *Sociology of Education,* vol. 46, 1973, p. 428.

[15] The Acton Society Trust, *Management Succession,* 1956.

[16] Although some of them may have acquired technical qualifications by means of part-time education.

[17] Lee, D. J. 'Class Differentials in Educational Opportunity and Promotion from the Ranks', *Sociology,* vol. II (3), 1968.

[18] Folger, J. F. and Nam, C. B. 'Trends in Education in Relation to the Occupational Structure', *Sociology of Education*, vol. XXXVIII, 1964.

[19] Turner, R. H. 'Modes of Social Ascent through Education. Sponsored and Contest Mobility', in Halsey, Floud, Anderson, *op. cit.*, pp. 121–39.

[20] Although after 1933 a Means Test was introduced and Free Places became Special Places.

[21] See for example Kalton, G. *The Public Schools*, London: Longman, 1966.

[22] Halsey, A. H. 'Theoretical advance and empirical challenge' in Hopper, E. I. (ed.) *Readings in the Theory of Educational Systems*, London: Hutchinson, 1971.

[23] McConnell, T. R. and Heist, P. 'The Diverse College Student Population', in Sanford, N. (ed) *The American College*, New York: Wiley, 1962, p. 232.

[24] Ashby, E. 'The Great Reappraisal' in *Universities Facing the Future*, World Year Book of Education, 1972/3, London: Evans Bros Ltd, 1972, p. 29.

[25] Medsker, L. L. and Tillery, D. *Breaking the Access Barriers: A Profile of Two-year Colleges*, New York: McGraw-Hill, 1971.

[26] See also the earlier study Clark Burton, R. *The Open Door College: A Case Study*, New York: McGraw-Hill, 1960.

[27] *Report of the Committee on Higher Education* (Robbins Report), London: H.M.S.O., Cmnd 2154-V, 1963, vol. 1, pp. 38–9.

[28] *Statistics of Education*, 1973, vol. 5, Finance and Awards, H.M.S.O.

[29] See the discussion in Miller, G. W. *Success, Failure and Wastage in Higher Education*, London: Harrap & Co. Ltd, 1970, pp. 11–18.

[30] *Report of the Central Advisory Council for Education* (Crowther Report), London: H.M.S.O., 1959, pp. 354–60.

[31] Simon, B. and Joan (eds) *Educational Psychology in the U.S.S.R.*, London: Routledge & Kegan Paul, 1963, p. 15.

[32] *Ibid.*, p. 18.

[33] Bereday, G. *et al. The Changing Soviet School*, London: Constable, 1960, pp. 362–3.

[34] Grant, N. *Soviet Education*, Harmondsworth, Middlesex: Penguin, 1964, p. 44.

[35] Figueroa, J. J. 'Selection and Differentiation in Soviet Schools', in King, E. J. (ed.) *Communist Education*, London: Methuen, 1963.

[36] Grant, N. in *Students, University and Society*, (ed. M. Scotford-Archer) London: Heinemann, 1972, pp. 80–102.

[37] See for example the survey of five countries in Western Europe by King, E. J. Moor, C. H. and Mundy, J. A. *Post-compulsory Education: a New Analysis in Western Europe*, London: Sage Publications, 1974.

[38] Neave, G. *op. cit.*

[39] Hopper, E. I. 'A Typology for the Classification of Educational Systems' in Hopper, E. I. (ed.) *op. cit.*

[40] Davies, I., 'The Management of Knowledge: A Critique of the Use of Typologies in Educational Systems', in Hopper, E. I. (ed.) *op. cit.*

[41] Smith, D. 'Selection and Knowledge Management in Education Systems', in Hopper, E. I. (ed.) *op. cit.*

[42] It is not possible to set out all the arguments here, but there is a detailed discussion in Smith's paper, *ibid.*

[43] *Ibid.*, p. 150.

[44] Smith's model is discussed further in chapter 6.

NOTES

45 Little, A. and Westergaard, J. 'The Trend of Class Differentials in Educational Opportunity in England and Wales', *British Journal of Sociology*, vol. xv, 1964, Table 1, p. 304.

46 *Development of Secondary Education: Trends and Implications*, Paris: Organization for Economic Co-operation and Development, 1969. See also the data from France in Clignet, R. *Liberty and Equality in the Educational Process*, New York: Wiley, 1974.

47 Halsey, A. H. 'Sociology and the Equality Debate', *Oxford Review of Education*, vol. 1, 1957, pp. 14-15.

48 Scotford-Archer, M. and Giner, S. *Contemporary Europe: Class, Status and Power*, London: Weidenfeld & Nicolson, 1971, p. 401.

49 Watts, A. G. *Diversity and Choice in Higher education*, London: Routledge & Kegan Paul, 1972, pp. 56-64.

50 Hordley, I. and Lee, D. J. 'The Alternative Route: Social Change and Opportunity in Technical Education', *Sociology*, vol. IV, 1970.

51 See also Kemeny, P. J. 'The Affluent worker project: Some Criticisms and a Derivative Study', *The Sociological Review*, vol. xx, 1972.

52 Donaldson, L. 'Social Class and the Polytechnics', *Higher Education Review*, vol. 4, 1971.

53 Pratt, J. 'Open University', *Higher Education Review*, vol. 3, 1971.

54 Couper, M. and Harris, C. 'C.A.T. to University. The Changing Student Intake', *Educational Research*, vol. xII, 1970.

55 Burgess, T. and Pratt, J. 'Policy and Practice: the Colleges of Advanced Technology,' London: Allen Lane, The Penguin Press, 1970.

56 Pratt, J. and Burgess, T. *Polytechnics: a Report*, London: Pitman, 1974.

57 Folger, J. K. and Nam, C. B. *The Education of the American Population, op. cit.*, p. 47.

58 *Ibid.*, p. 56.

59 Adapted from Folger, J. K., Astin, H. S., and Bayer, A. E. *Human Resources and Higher Education*, New York: Russell Sage Foundation, 1970, p. 310.

60 Bowen, H. R. 'Higher Education: A Growth Industry?', *Educational Record*, vol. 55, 1974.

61 Sewell, W. H. 'Inequality of Opportunity for Higher Education', *American Sociological Review*, vol. xxxvi, 1971. See also Trent, J. W. and Medsker, L. L. *Beyond High School: a Study of 10,000 High School Graduates*, Berkeley: University of California Center for Research and Development in Higher Education, 1967.

62 Folger, J. K., Astin, H. S. and Bayer, A. E. *Human Resources and Higher Education, op. cit.*, pp. 312-21.

63 Quoted in Birenbaum, W. 'From Class to Mass in Higher Education', *Higher Education Review*, vol. 6, 1973.

64 Katz, J. M., Gold, D. F. and Jones, E. T. 'Equality of Opportunity in a Democratic Institution', *Education and Urban Society*, vol. v, 1973.

65 Yanowitch, M. and Dodge, N., 'Social class and education: Soviet findings and reactions', *Comparative Education Review*, 1968, vol. xII (3), and Mathews, M. 'Class Bias in Russian Education', *New Society*, 19th December, 1968. See also Lane, D. *The end of inequality?*, Harmondsworth, Middlesex: Penguin, 1971.

66 See for example Vaughan, M. 'Poland' in Scotford-Archer, M. and Giner, S. (eds) *Contemporary Europe,* London: Weidenfeld & Nicolson, 1971. See also Fiszman, J. R. *Revolution and Tradition in People's Poland,* Princeton University Press, 1972.

67 Fiszman, J. R., *op. cit.,* p. 48.

68 Sewell, W. H. 'Community of Residence and College Plans', *American Sociological Review,* vol. xxix, 1964.

69 Carnegie Commission on Higher Education, *The Capitol and the Campus: State Responsibility for Post-secondary Education,* New York: McGraw-Hill, 1971.

70 See for example Wise, A. E. *Rich Schools, Poor Schools: The Promise of Equal Educational Opportunity,* University of Chicago Press, 1967.

71 Taylor, G. and Ayres, N. *Born and Bred Unequal,* London: Longman, 1969.

72 These studies will be examined in more detail in a later chapter.

73 Boaden, N. *Urban Policy-making: Influences on County Boroughs in England and Wales,* Cambridge University Press, 1971.

74 Byrne, E. M. *Planning and Educational Inequality: A Study of the Rationale of Resource Allocation,* Slough: N.F.E.R., 1974.

75 Coleman, J. S. *et al. Equality of Educational Opportunity,* Washington D.C., U.S. Department of Health, Education and Welfare, U.S. Govt Printing Office: 1966.

76 Folger, J. K. and Nam, C. B. *op. cit.,* pp. 45-6.

77 *Ibid.*

78 Wolfe, D. 'Educational Opportunity, Measured Intelligence and Social Background' in Halsey, Floud, Anderson *op. cit.,* p. 236.

79 Henderson, A. D. and Henderson, J. G. *Higher Education in America,* San Francisco, Jossey-Bass, 1974, p. 55. See also Sewell, W. H. 'Inequality of Opportunity for Higher Education', *American Sociological Review,* vol. xxxvi, 1971, p. 797.

80 Robbins Report on Higher Education, *op. cit.,* p. 43.

81 Committee of Vice-Chancellors and Principals, *Equal Opportunities for Men and Women,* London, 1974.

82 Boocock, S. S. *An Introduction to the Sociology of Learning,* Boston: Houghton Miflin, 1972, pp. 80-81.

83 *Opportunity for Women in Higher Education,* Report of the Carnegie Commission, New York: McGraw-Hill, 1974.

84 Keeves, J. 'Differences Between the Sexes in Mathematics and Science Courses', *International Review of Education,* vol. xix, 1973. See also Clignet, R. *Liberty and Equality in the Educational Process,* New York: Wiley, 1974, pp. 232-7.

85 Lane, D. *The end of inequality?* Harmondsworth, Middlesex: Penguin, 1971, p. 89.

86 See Riordan, J. 'Survey shows Russians share western problem', *Times Higher Education Supplement,* 6 September, 1974.

87 Sewell, W. H. 'Inequality of Opportunity for Higher Education', *American Sociological Reivew,* vol. xxxvi, 1971.

88 Little, A. and Westergaard, J. 'The Trend of Class Differentials in Educational Opportunity in England and Wales', *British Journal of Sociology,* vol. xv, 1964, pp. 307-8.

89 Eggleston, J. 'Some Environmental Correlates of Extended Secondary Education in England', *Comparative Education,* vol. iii, 1967.

90 Benn, C. 'School Style and Staying On', *New Society*, 24 June 1971.
91 Neave, G. *How They Fared, op. cit.*, pp. 72-6.
92 Ford, J. *Social Class and the Comprehensive School*, London: Routledge & Kegan Paul, 1979.
93 Neave, G. *op. cit.*
94 Boudon, R. *Education, Opportunity and Social Inequality*, New York: Wiley, 1974.
95 See for example the discussion in Clignet, R. 'Liberty and Equality in the Educational Process', *op. cit.*, pp. 256-8, and in Bell, D. *The Coming of Post-Industrial Society*, London: Heinemann, 1974, pp. 416-19.
96 Quoted in Husén, T. *The Learning Society, op. cit.*, p. 71.
97 Halsey, A. H. 'Theoretical Advance and Empirical Challenge' in Hopper, E. I. (ed.) *Readings in the Theory of Educational Systems, op. cit.*, pp. 276-277.
98 Boudon, R. *op. cit.*, p. 136.
99 Stern, D. 'Some Speculations on School Finance and a More Equalitarian Society', *Education and Urban Society*, vol. v, 1973, p. 230.
100 Although there is some evidence that this is declining faster than is the gap in schooling. See Milner, M. Jnr, 'Race, Education, and Job Trends, 1960-1970' in *Sociology of Education*, vol. 46, 1973.
101 Treiman, D. J. and Terrell, K. 'Sex and the Process of Status Attainment: a Comparison of Working Women and Men', *American Sociological Review*, vol. XL, 1975.
102 Wootton, B. quoted in Silver, H. *Equal Opportunity in Education*, London: Methuen, 1973, p. xxxi.
103 See also Halsey, A. H. 'Sociology and the Equality Debate', *Oxford Review of Education*, vol. I, 1975.

Chapter 4. Family background, values and achievement

1 Parsons, T. 'The School Class as a Social System', in Halsey, Floud, Anderson, *op. cit.*, p. 435.
2 See Stinchcombe, A. L. 'Environment: the Cumulation of Effects is yet to be understood', *Harvard Educational Review, vol.* XXXIX, 1969, pp. 511-22.
3 Vernon, P. E. 'Development of Current Ideas about Intelligence Tests' in Meade, J. E. and Parkes, A. S. (eds) *Biological Aspects of Social Problems*, London: Oliver and Boyd, 1966, p. 5.
4 *Ibid.*, p. 13.
5 *Ibid.*, p. 5.
6 Jenson, A. P. 'How Much Can We Boost I.Q. and Scholastic Achievement?' *Harvard Educational Review*, vol. XXXIX (I), 1969.
7 See for example, the subsequent controversy in *Harvard Educational Review*, vol. XXXIX, 1969.
8 Vernon, P. E. *op. cit.*, p. 7. See also the useful discussion in Husén, T. *Social Background and Educational Career*, Paris: O.E.C.D., 1972, pp. 52-5.

⁹ Folger, J. K., Astin, H. S. and Bayer, A. E. *Human Resources and Higher Education, op. cit.*, p. 310.

¹⁰ *Ibid.*, p. 320.

¹¹ Sewell, W. H. 'Inequality in Opportunity for Higher Education', *American Sociological Review*, vol. XXXVI, 1971, p. 795.

¹² Report of the Central Advisory Council for Education (England), *15 to 18*, London: H.M.S.O., vol. I, p. 9.

¹³ *Report of the Committee on Higher Education* (Robbins Report), *op. cit.*, Appendix 1, p. 42.

¹⁴ Floud, J. 'Social Class Factors in Educational Achievement', in Halsey, A. H. *Ability and Educational Opportunity*, Paris: O.E.C.D., 1961, p. 94.

¹⁵ Havighurst, R. J. *et al. Growing up in River City*, New York: Wiley, 1962, pp. 60–61, 104.

¹⁶ Dyer, for example, estimated that only one-tenth of the total cost to students is in the form of aid including loans. Dyer, H. S. 'Admissions-College and University' in Ebel, R. L. (ed.) *Encyclopedia of Educational Research*, 4th edition, London: Collier Macmillan, 1969, p. 27.

¹⁷ See the studies described by Nash, G. 'Students Financial Aid', in Ebel, R. L. (ed.) *op. cit.*, pp. 1346–7.

¹⁸ *Ibid.*, p. 1347.

¹⁹ Berdie, R. F. *After High School What?*, University of Minnesota Press, 1954.

²⁰ Report of the Central Advisory Council for Education (England), *15 to 18*, London: H.M.S.O., vol. II, p. 19 *et seq.*

²¹ *Ibid.*, p. 20.

²² Report of the Central Advisory Council for Education (England), *Children and their Primary Schools* (Plowden Report), London: H.M.S.O., 1967, vól. II, Appendix 4, p. 184.

²³ *Ibid.*, Appendix 9, p. 369.

²⁴ *Children and their Primary Schools* (Plowden Report), *op. cit.*, vol. II, Appendix 3.

²⁵ See Douglas, J. W. B. *The Home and the School*, London: MacGibbon & Kee, 1964, and Davie, R., Butler W. and Goldstein, H. *From Birth to Seven*, Slough: N.F.E.R., 1972.

²⁶ Report of the Central Advisory Council for Education (England), *Half our Future*, London: H.M.S.O., 1963, pp. 24–5. See also Sexton, P. *Education and Income*, New York: Viking Press, 1961, on the situation in the United States.

²⁷ Davie, R. *et al., op. cit.*

²⁸ Floud, J., Halsey, A. H. and Martin, I. M. *Social Class and Educational Opportunity*, London: Heinemann, 1956, pp. 89, 145.

²⁹ Hyman, H. H. 'The Value-System of Different Classes', in Bendix, R. and Lipset, S. (eds) *Class Status and Power*, London: Routledge & Kegan Paul, 1954.

³⁰ Sewell, W. H., Haller, A. O. and Straus, M. A. 'Social Status and Educational and Occupational Aspirations', *American Sociological Review*, vol. XXII, 1957.

³¹ Sewell, W. H. and Shah, V. P. 'Social Class, Parental Encouragement and Educational Aspirations', *American Journal of Sociology*, vol. LXXIII, 1968.

³² Sewell, W. H., Haller, A. O., Portes, A. 'The Educational and early Occupational Attainment Process', *American Sociological Review*, vol. XXXIV, 1969. See also Haller, A. O. and Portes, A. 'Status Attainment Processes', *Sociology of Education*, vol. 46, 1973.

[33] Floud, Halsey, Martin, *op. cit.*, p. 82.

[34] Douglas, J. W. B. *op. cit.*, p. 52. See also Douglas, J. W. B. *et al. All our Future*, London: Peter Davies, 1968.

[35] *Children and their Primary Schools* (Plowden Report), *op. cit.*, vol. II, pp. 118–23.

[36] Turner, R. *The Social Context of Ambition*, San Francisco: Chandler, 1964, p. 47.

[37] Boudon, R. *op. cit.*

[38] Turner, R. *op. cit.*, p. 47.

[39] Empey, L. T. 'Social Class and Occupational Aspirations', *American Sociological Review*, vol. XXI, 1956.

[40] Simmons, R. G. and Rosenberg, M. 'Functions of Children's Perceptions of the Stratification System', *American Sociological Review*, vol. XXXVI, 1971.

[41] *Children and their Primary Schools* (Plowden Report), *op. cit.*, vol. II, pp. 121–2.

[42] Scanzoni, J. 'Socialization, Achievement, and Achievement Values', *American Sociological Review*, vol. XXXII, 1967. This article summarizes a number of recent studies. See also Weiner, M. and Murray, W. 'Another Look at the Culturally Deprived and their Levels of Aspiration', *Journal of Educational Sociology*, 1963.

[43] Stephenson, R. M. 'Stratification, Education and Occupational Orientation', *British Journal of Sociology*, vol. IX, 1958

[44] Caro, F. G. and Pihlblad, C. T. 'Aspirations and Expectations', *Sociology and Social Research*, vol. XLIX, 1965.

[45] Banks, O. and Finlayson, D. *Success and Failure in the Secondary School*, London: Methuen, 1973, ch. 3.

[46] Hopper, E. I. 'Educational Systems and Selected Consequences of Patterns of Mobility and Non-mobility in Industrial Societies' in Hopper, E. I. (ed.) *Readings in the Theory of Educational Systems, op. cit.*, p. 305.

[47] Elder, G. H., Jnr, 'Life Opportunity and Personality: Some Consequences of Stratified Secondary Education in Great Britain', *Sociology of Education*, vol. XXXVIII, 1965.

[48] See for example Jackson, B. and Marsden, D. *Education and the Working Class*, London: Routledge & Kegan Paul, 1962.

[49] Himmelweit, H. T. and Swift, B. 'A Model for the Understanding of School as a Socializing Agent' in P. Mussen *et al.* (eds) *Trends and Issues in Developmental Psychology*, New York: Holt Rinehart & Winston, 1969.

[50] Neave, G., *op. cit.*, p. 142.

[51] Kandel, D. and Lesser, G. S. 'School, Family and Peer Influence on Educational Plans of Adolescents in the U.S. and Denmark', *Sociology of Education*, vol. XLIII, 1970.

[52] Schwarzweller, H. K. and Lyson, T. A. 'Social Class, Parental Interest and the Educational Plans of American and Norwegian Rural Youth', *Sociology of Education*, vol. XLVII, 1974.

[53] Kluckhohn, F. R. and Strodtbeck, F. L. *Variations in Value Orientations*, Chicago: Row, Peterson, 1961, p. 4.

[54] Kluckhohn, F. R. *op. cit.*, p. 17.

[55] Schneider, L. and Lysgaard, S. 'The Deferred Gratification Pattern: a Preliminary Study', *American Sociological Review*, vol. XVIII, 1953, pp. 142–9.

[56] Kahl, J. A. 'Some Measurements of Achievement Orientation', *American Journal of Sociology*, vol. LXX, 1965.

[57] Straus, M. A. 'Deferred Gratification, Social Class and the Achievement Syndrome', *American Sociological Review*, vol. XXVII, 1962.

[58] Turner, R. *The Social Context of Ambition, op. cit.*, p. 213.

[59] *Ibid.*, p. 214.

[60] Scanzoni, J. H. *Opportunity and the Family*, London: Collier Macmillan, 1970, pp. 173–4.

[61] Kahl, J. A. ' "Common-Man" Boys', in Halsey, Floud, Anderson, *op. cit.*, p. 349 *et seq*.

[62] Rosen, B. C. 'The Achievement Syndrome: a Psycho-cultural Dimension of Social Stratification', *American Sociological Review*, vol. XX, April 1956, pp. 203–11.

[63] Swift, D. F. 'Social Class and Achievement Motivation', *Educational Research*, vol. VIII (2), 1966, p. 93.

[64] Jayasuriya, D. L., from an unpublished PH.D. thesis, University of London, 1960, reported in Sugarman, B. H. 'Social Class and Values as Related to Achievement and Conduct in School', *Sociological Review*, vol. XIV, 1966, p. 290.

[65] Sugarman, B. H. *ibid.*

[66] Banks, O. and Finlayson, D. *Success and Failure in Secondary School, op. cit.*, pp. 134–5.

[67] Craft, M. 'Talent, Family Values and Education in Ireland' in J. Eggleston (ed.) *Contemporary Research in the Sociology of Education*, London: Methuen, 1974.

[68] See for example Crandall, V. C. 'Achievement Behaviour in Young Children' in Rosen, B. C. *et al.* (eds) *Achievement in American Society*, Cambridge, Mass.: Schenkman Publishing Co., 1969, and Boocock, S. S. *An Introduction to the Sociology of Learning*, Boston: Houghton Miflin, 1972, pp. 74–5.

[69] Rosen, B. C. 'The Achievement Syndrome: a Psycho-cultural Dimension of Social Stratification', *op. cit.*

[70] Strodtbeck, F. L. 'Family Integration, Values and Achievement' in Halsey, Floud, Anderson (eds) *Education, Economy and Society, op. cit.*

[71] Routh, G. *Occupation and Pay in Great Britain, 1906-1960*, London: Cambridge University Press, 1965. See also Goldthorpe, J. H. *et al.* 'The Affluent Worker and the Thesis of Embourgeoisement', *Sociology*, vol. I, 1967, pp. 12–31.

[72] Inkeles, A. 'Industrial Man: the Relation of Status to Experience Perception and Value', *American Journal of Sociology*, vol. LXV, 1960. See also Lyman, E. L. 'Occupation Differences in the Value Attached to Work', *American Journal of Sociology*, vol. LXVI, 1961.

[73] Squibb, P. G. 'Education and Class', *Educational Research*, vol. 15, 1973. See also Lane, M. 'Educational Choice, *Sociology*, vol. VI, 1972.

[74] See, for example, Gouldner, A. W. *Patterns of Industrial Bureaucracy*, London: Routledge & Kegan Paul, 1955, pp. 177–36; and Katz, F. M. 'The Meaning of Success: Some Differences in Value Systems of Social Classes', *Journal of Social Psychology*, vol. LXII, 1964.

[75] Goldthorpe, J. H. *et al, op. cit.*

[76] See, for example, the descriptions of working-class parents in Jackson, B. and Marsden, D. *Education and the Working Class*, London: Routledge & Kegan Paul, 1962, p. 88.

[77] Brookover, W. B. and Erickson, E. L. *Sociology of Education*, Illinois: The Dorsey Press, 1975, chapters 11-12, pp. 259-322.

[78] See, for example, Floud, Halsey, Martin, *op. cit.*; Cohen, E. C. 'Parental Factors in Educational Mobility', *Sociology of Education*, vol. XXXVIII, 1965.

[79] Smelser, W. T. 'Adolescent and Adult Occupational Choice as a Function of Socioeconomic History', *Sociometry*, vol. XXVI, 1963.

[80] Cohen, E. C. *op. cit.* See also Kraus, I. 'Aspirations among Working-Class Youth', *American Sociological Review*, vol. XXIX, 1964, p. 869.

[81] Floud, Halsey, Martin, *op. cit.*, p. 88.

[82] Kohn, M. L. 'Social Class and Parental Values', *American Journal of Sociology*, vol. LXIV, 1959.

[83] Cohen, E. C. *op. cit.*, p. 422.

[84] Swift, D. F. 'Social Class and Achievement Motivation', *op. cit.*, p. 93.

[85] Cohen, E. C. *op. cit.*

[86] Kahl, J. A. ' "Common Man" Boys', *op. cit.*

[87] Harrington, M. 'Parents' Hopes and Children's Success', *New Society*, 26 November 1964, p. 9.

[88] Proshansky, H. and Newton, P. 'The Nature and Meaning of Negro Self Identity', in Deutsch, M., Katz, I. and Jensen, A. R. (eds) *Social Class, Race, and Psychological Development*, New York: Holt, Rinehart & Winston, 1968, p. 178.

[89] Deutsch, M. and Brown, B. R. 'Social Influences in Negro-White Intelligence Differences' in Deutsch, M. (ed.) *The Disadvantaged Child*, New York, London: Basic Books, 1967, p. 298.

[90] Prohansky, H. and Newton, P. *op. cit.*

[91] See for example Gist, N. P. and Bennett, W. S. Jnr 'Aspirations of Negro and White Students', *Social Forces*, vol. 42, 1963, and Kandel, D. B. 'Race, Maternal Authority and Adolescent Aspirations', *American Journal of Sociology*, vol. LXXVI, 1971.

[92] Turner, R. *The Context of Ambition*, *op. cit.*, p. 39.

[93] See for example King, R. 'Unequal Access in Education – Sex and Social Class', *Social and Economic Administration*, vol. 5, 1971.

[94] Clignet, R. *Liberty and Equality in the Educational Process*, *op. cit.*, p. 23.

[95] See for example Rossi, A. S. 'Women in Science: Why so Few?' in Rosen, B. C. *et al. Achievement in American Society*, *op. cit.*

[96] Sewell, W. H. 'Inequality of Opportunity for Higher Education', *American Sociological Review*, vol. XXXVI, p. 804.

[97] *Report of the Committee on Higher Education* (Robbins Report), London: H.M.S.O., Cmnd 2154-I, 1963, Appendix 1, p. 237.

[98] Douglas, J. W. B., Ross, J. M. and Simpson, H. R. *All Our Future*, *op. cit.*, p. 34.

[99] See for example Rossi, A. and Calderwood, A. *Academic Women on the Move*, New York: Russell Sage Foundation, 1974.

[100] Luria, Z. 'Recent Women College Graduates: A Study of Rising Expectations', *American Journal of Orthopsychiatry*, vol. 44, 1974.

[101] Lueptow, L. B. 'Parental Status and Influence and the Achievement Orientations of High School Seniors', *Sociology of Education*, vol. XLVIII, 1975.

[102] Hutchinson, D. and McPherson, A. F. 'Competing Inequalities: the Sex and Social Class Structure of the First-year Scottish University Student Population, 1962-1972', *Centre for Educational Sociology*, University of Edinburgh, May 1975 (mimeographed).

Chapter 5.   The family, the socialization process and achievement

1 Bronfenbrenner, U. 'Socialization and Social Class Through Time and Space' in Maccoby, Newcombe and Hartley, *Readings in Social Psychology*, 3rd ed., New York: Holt, 1958.

2 Kohn, M. L. 'Social Class and the Exercise of Parental Authority', *American Sociological Review*, vol. xxiv, 1959.

3 Kohn, M. L. 'Social Class and Parent-child Relationship: an Interpretation', *American Sociological Review*, vol. lxviii, 1963.

4 McKinley, D. G. *Social Class and Family Life*, Glencoe, Illinois: The Free Press, 1964, p. 54.

5 Kohn, M. L. and Carroll, E. E. 'Social Class and the Allocation of Parental Responsibilities', *Sociometry*, 1960.

6 Devereux, E. C. Jnr, Bronfenbrenner, U. and Rodgers, R. R. 'Child Rearing in England and the United States, a Cross-national Comparison', *Journal of Marriage and the Family*, vol. xxxi (2), 1969.

7 Newson, J. and E. *Patterns of Infant Care in an Urban Community*, London: Allen & Unwin, 1963. See also Newson, J. and E. *Four Years Old in an Urban Community*, London: Allen & Unwin, 1968.

8 Kerckhoff, A. C. *Socialization and Social Class*, New Jersey: Prentice-Hall, 1972.

9 Bernstein, B. B. *Class, Codes and Control*, vol. i, London: Routledge & Kegan Paul, 1971, ch. 8.

10 This research is reported in Brandis, W. and Henderson, D. *Social Class, Language and Communication*, London: Routledge & Kegan Paul, 1970. See also Cook, J. *Social Control and Socialization*, London: Routledge & Kegan Paul, 1972.

11 Wootton, A. J. 'Talk in the Homes of Young Children', *Sociology*, vol. 8, 1974.

12 Ford, J., Young, D. and Box, S. 'Functional Autonomy, Role Distance and Social Class', *British Journal of Sociology*, vol. 18, 1967.

13 Newson, J., Newson, E. and Barnes, P. 'Child-rearing Practices' in Butcher, H. J. and Pont, H. B. (eds) *Educational Research in Britain*, vol. 3, University of London Press, 1973, p. 70.

14 Erlanger, H. S. 'Social Class and Corporal Punishment in Child-rearing: a Re-assessment', *American Sociological Review*, vol. xxxix, 1974.

15 Bernstein, B. *Class, Codes and Control*, vol. i, *op. cit.*, p. 162.

16 Toomey, D. M. 'Home-centred Working-class Parents' Attitudes Towards Their Sons' Education and Careers', *Sociology*, vol. iii, 1969.

17 Rosen, B. C. and d'Andrade, R. 'The Psycho Social Origin of Achievement Motivation', *Sociometry*, vol. xxii, 1959.

18 Rosen, B. C. 'Socialization and Achievement Motivation in Brazil', *American Sociological Review*, vol. xxvii, 1962.

19 Milner, E. 'A Study of the Relationships between Reading Readiness in Grade One School Children and Patterns of Parent-Child Interaction', *Child Development*, 1951.

20 Drews, E. M. and Teahan, J. E. 'Parental Attitudes and Academic Achievement', *Journal of Clinical Psychology*, 1957.

21 Morrow, W. R. and Wilson, R. C. 'Family Relations of Bright High-Achieving and Under-Achieving High School Boys', *Child Development*, 1961.

[22] See, for example, the studies quoted in Drews and Teahan, *op. cit.*

[23] Douvan, E. and Adelson, J. 'The Psychodynamics of Social Mobility in Adolescent Boys', *Journal of Abnormal and Social Psychology,* vol. LVI, 1958,

[24] Becker, W. C. 'Consequences of Different Kinds of Parental Discipline' in Hoffman, M. and Hoffman, L. W. (eds) *Review of Child Development Research,* New York: Russell Sage Foundation, 1964, vol. I, p. 177.

[25] Rosen, B. C. 'Family Structure and Value Transmission', *Merrill-Palmer Quarterly,* vol. X, 1964.

[26] Strodtbeck, F. L. 'Family Integration, Values and Achievement', in Halsey, Floud, Anderson, *op. cit.,* pp. 315–47.

[27] Katkovsky, W., Crandall, V. C. and Good, S. 'Parental Antecedents of Children's Beliefs in Internal-External Control of Reinforcements in Intellectual Achievement Situations', *Child Development,* 1967.

[28] Elder, G. 'Parental Power Legitimation and its Effect on the Adolescent', *Sociometry,* 1963.

[29] Banks, O. and Finlayson, D. *Success and Failure in the Secondary School, op. cit.*

[30] Greenberg, J. W. and Davidson, H. H. 'Home Background and School Achievement of Black Urban Ghetto Children', *American Journal of Orthopsychiatry,* vol. 42, 1972.

[31] Anderson, C. Arnold, 'Successes and Frustration in the Sociological Study of Education', *Social Science Quarterly,* vol. 55, 1974, p. 286.

[32] Banks, O. and Finlayson, D. *op. cit.,* p. 181.

[33] Boocock, S. S. *An Introduction to the Sociology of Learning, op. cit.,* ch. 5.

[34] Maccoby, E. (ed.) *The Development of Sex Differences,* Stanford University Press, 1966.

[35] Sexton, P. *The Feminized Male,* London: Pitman, 1970.

[36] Kagan, J. and Moss, H. *From Birth to Maturity,* New York: Wiley, 1962.

[37] Boocock, S S. *op. cit.,* p. 64.

[38] Lawton, D., 'Language, Social Class and the Curriculum' in Butcher, H. J. and Pont, H. B. (eds) *Educational Research in Britain,* vol. 3, 1973, *op. cit.,* p. 1969.

[39] *Ibid.,* p. 170.

[40] The development of Bernstein's ideas over time in this area can be followed in *Class, Codes and Control, vol. I, Theoretical Studies towards a Sociology of Language, op. cit.,* especially parts I and II.

[41] Bernstein's theories are highly complex, and this represents only a fairly crude summary.

[42] Bernstein, B. 'A Socio-linguistic Approach to Socialization: With Some Reference to Educability' in *Class, Codes and Control, vol. I, op. cit.,* p. 151.

[43] Lawton, D. *Social Class, Language and Education,* London: Routledge & Kegan Paul, 1968, pp. 92-6, and 103-43.

[44] Hawkins, P. R. 'Social Class, the Nominal Group and Reference' in Bernstein, B. (ed.) *Class, Codes and Control, vol. II:* Applied Studies Towards a Sociology of Language, London: Routledge & Kegan Paul, 1973.

[45] Hess, R. D. and Shipman, V. C. 'Early Experience and the Socialization of Cognitive Modes in Children', *Child Development,* 1965.

[46] Schatzman, L. and Strauss, A. 'Social Class and Modes of Communication', *American Journal of Sociology,* vol. LX, 1955.

47 Deutsch, M. 'The Role of Social Class in Language Development and Cognition', *American Journal of Orthopsychiatry*, vol. xxxv, 1965. See also Deutsch, M. (ed.) *The Disadvantaged Child, op. cit.*

48 Ward, Martha C. *Them Children: a Study in Language Learning*, New York: Holt, Rinehart & Winston, 1971.

49 Pap, M. and Pléh, C. 'Social Class Differences in the Speech of Six-year-old Hungarian Children,' *Sociology*, vol. 8, 1974.

50 There is a very fair account in Grimshaw, A. 'On Language in Society, Part I', *Contemporary Sociology*, vol. 2, 1973.

51 Labov, W. 'The Logic of Non-standard English' in Williams, F. (ed.) *Language and Poverty: Perspectives on a Theme*, Chicago: Markham Publishing Co., 1970. See also the account in Grimshaw, A. *ibid.* The critique by Harold Rosen draws heavily on Labov. See Rosen, H. *Language and Class: A Critical Look at the Theories of Bernstein*, Bristol: Falling Wall Press, 1972.

52 An early critic was Riessman, F. *The Culturally Deprived Child*, New York: Harper & Row, 1962. See also Keddie, N. (ed.) *Tinker, Tailor . . . The Myth of Cultural Deprivation*, Harmondsworth, Middlesex: Penguin, 1973.

53 A useful account of the American programmes is given in Halsey, A. H. *Educational Priority*, vol. I, London: H.M.S.O., 1972, Ch. 2.

54 See for example McDill, E. L., McDill, M. S. and Spreke, J. T. *Strategies for Success in Compensatory Education: An Appraisal of Evaluation Research*, Baltimore: Johns Hopkins, 1969.

55 Hunt, J. McV. 'Has Compensatory Education Failed? Has It Been Attempted?' in *Equal Education Opportunity*, Cambridge, Mass.: Harvard University Press, 1969, p. 297.

56 Halsey, A. H. *Educational Priority*, vol. I, *op. cit.*, p. 116.

57 Bernstein, B. 'A Critique of the Concept of Compensatory Education' in *Class, Codes and Control*, vol. I, *op. cit.*, p. 192.

58 Keddie, N. *Tinker, Tailor . . . the Myth of Cultural Deprivation, op. cit.*, p. 19.

59 See for example Wolf, E. P. and Wolf, L. 'Sociological Perspectives on the Education of Culturally Deprived Children', *School Review*, vol. LXX, 1962.

60 Morton, D. C. and Watson, D. R. 'Compensatory Education and Contemporary Liberalism in the U.S.: a Sociological View' in Raynor, J. and Harden, J. *Equality and City Schools: Readings in Urban Education*, vol. 2, London: Routledge & Kegan Paul, 1973.

61 Halsey, A. H. *Educational Priority*, vol. I, *op. cit.*, p. 19.

62 *Ibid*, p. 117.

63 *Ibid.* p. 189.

64 Anderson, C. Arnold 'Successes and Frustration in the Sociological Study of Education', *Social Science Quarterly*, vol. 55, 1974.

65 Goody, J. and Watt, I. 'The Consequences of Literacy' in Goody, J. (ed.) *Literacy in Traditional Societies*, Cambridge University Press, 1969, p. 44.

Chapter 6. The politics of education

1 Bourdieu, P. 'Cultural Reproduction and Social Reproduction', in Brown, R. (ed.) *Knowledge, Education and Cultural Change*, London: Tavistock, 1973, p. 71.

2 Bourdieu, P. 'The School as a Conservative Force: Scholastic and Cultural Inequalities' in Eggleston, J. (ed.) *Contemporary Research in the Sociology of Education*, London: Methuen, 1974, p. 32.

3 *Ibid.*, p. 42.

4 Cosin, B. R. (ed.) *Education: Structure and Society*, Harmondsworth, Middlesex: Penguin, 1972, p. 174.

5 Althusser, L. 'Ideology and Ideological State Apparatuses' in Cosin, B. R. *ibid.* p. 260.

6 *Ibid.*, p. 261.

7 Johnson, R. 'Educational Policy and Social Control in Early Victorian England', *Past and Present*, vol. 49, 1970.

8 See for example Sloan, D. 'Historiography and the History of Education' in Kerlinger, F. (ed.), *Review of Research in Education*, American Educational Research Association, 1973.

9 Katz, M. B. *Class, Bureaucracy and Schools*, New York: Praeger, 1971, p. 32.

10 *Ibid.*, p. 36.

11 *Ibid.*, p. 123.

12 Spring, J. *Education and the Rise of the Corporate State*, Boston: Beacon, 1972.

13 Lucas, C. J. 'Historical Revisionism and the Retreat from Schooling', *Education and Urban Society*, vol. VI, 1974, p. 360.

14 Swift, David W. *Ideology and Change in the Public Schools: Latent Functions of Progressive Education*, Columbus, Ohio: Merrill, 1971.

15 Scotford-Archer, M. and Vaughan, M. 'Domination and Assertion in Educational Systems', in Hopper, E. I. (ed.) *Readings in the Theory of Educational Systems*, LondonHutchinson University Library, 1971.

16 Collins, R. 'Functional and Conflict Theories of Educational Stratification, *American Sociological Review*, vol. XXXVI, 1971.

17 Smith, D. 'Power, Ideology and Transmission of Knowledge', in Hopper, E. I. (ed.) *Readings in the Theory of Educational Systems, op. cit.*

18 See the discussion in Zeigler, H. and Peak, W. 'The Political Function of the Educational System' in Hopper, E. I. (ed.) *op. cit.*, pp. 218-9.

19 Barker, R. *Education and Politics, 1900-1951: A Study of the Labour Party*, Oxford: Clarendon Press, 1972.

20 *Ibid.*, p. 40.

21 *Ibid.*, p. 71.

22 See for example the argument in Marsden, D. *Politicans, Equality and Comprehensives*, Fabian Tract 411, 1971. See also Banks, O. *Parity and Prestige in English Secondary Education, op. cit.*

23 Talbott, J. E. *The Politics of Educational Reform in France, 1918-1940*, Princeton University Press, 1969.

24 Hopper, E. I. 'A Typology for the Classification of Educational Systems', in Hopper, E. I. (ed.), *op. cit.*, p. 95.

25 Reller, T. L. and Morphet, E. L. *Comparative Educational Administration*, New Jersey: Prentice-Hall, 1962.

26 Brand, J. A. 'Ministry Control and Local Autonomy in Education', *Political Quarterly*, vol. 36, 1965.

27 Berrill, K. 'Autonomy v. Accountability', *Times Higher Education Supplement*, 14 June 1974, p. 13.

[28] Crozier, M. *The Bureaucratic Phenomenon,* University of Chicago Press, 1964, p. 237.

[29] *Ibid.,* p. 234.

[30] Clignet, R. *Liberty and Equality in the Educational Process, op. cit.,* p. 88.

[30] *Ibid.,* pp. 126-7.

[31] Berube, M. R. and Gittell, M. (eds) *Confrontation at Ocean-Hill-Brownsville,* New York: Praeger, 1969.

[33] Smith, D. 'Power, Ideology and the Transmission of Knowledge', in Hopper, E. I. (ed.), *op. cit.*

[34] Mushkin, S. J. 'Financing Secondary School Expansion in O.E.C.D. Countries', *Sociology of Education,* vol. XXXVIII, 1964-5.

[35] See for example, Kirst, M. W. 'The Growth of Federal Influence on Education', in Gordon C. Wayne, (ed.) *The Uses of Sociology,* University of Chicago Press, 1974.

[36] See, for example, Edmonds, E. I. *The School Inspector,* London: Routledge & Kegan Paul, 1962.

[37] Kirst, M. W. *op. cit.,* p. 449.

[38] See, for example, Henderson, A. D. and J. G. *Higher Education in America,* San Francisco: Jossey-Bass, 1974, p. 202.

[39] Blondel, J. 'The State and the Universities', *Sociological Review Monograph No. 7. Sociological Studies in British University Education,* 1963, p. 36.

[40] Moos, M. and Rourke, F. E. *The Campus and the State,* Baltimore: Johns Hopkins Press, 1959.

[41] Smith, D. *op. cit.*

[42] This is also true at the level of the organization and of the classroom. The issues raised at these levels will be discussed in subsequent chapters.

[43] See for example Brookover, W. B. and Erickson, E. L. *Sociology of Education,* Illinois: The Dorsey Press, 1975, pp. 179-83.

[44] Crain R. L. *The Politics of School Desegregation,* Chicago: Aldine, 1968.

[45] Brookover, W. B. and Erickson, E. L. *op. cit.,* p. 181.

[46] Bidwell, C. E. 'The School as a Formal Organization', in March, J. G. (ed.) *Handbook of Social Organization,* Chicago: Rand McNally, 1965, pp. 972-1022.

[47] Seely, J. R., Sim, R. A. and Loosley, E. W. *Crestwood Heights: a Study of the Culture of Suburban Life,* New York: Basic Books, 1956.

[48] Vidich, A. J. and Bensman, J. *Small Town in Mass Society* (Garden City, New York), New York: Doubleday, 1960, p. 179.

[49] For a good short account of the background see Brookover, W. B. and Erickson, E. L. *op. cit.,* pp. 131-8.

[50] Crain, R. L. *op. cit.*

[51] The same conclusion was reached in a study by King, C. E. and Mayer, R. R. 'The Exercise of Community Leadership for School Desegregation', *Urban Education,* vol VII, 1972.

[52] See for example Dye, T. R. 'Urban School Segregation: A Comparative Analysis' in Gittell, M. and Hevesi, A. G. (eds) *The Politics of Urban Education,* New York: Praeger, 1969. Also Pettigrew, T. 'Continuing Barriers to Desegregated Education in the South', *Sociology of Education,* vol. XXXVIII, 1965.

[53] Rubin, Lilian B. *Bussing and Backlash: White against White in an Urban School District,* University of California Press, 1972, p. 51.

54 Swanson, B. E. 'Factoring Subcommunity Variables' in Drabick, L. W. *Interpreting Education,* New York: Appleton-Century-Crofts, 1971.

55 Rogers, D. 'Obstacles to School Desegregation in New York City: A Benchmark Case' in Gittell, M. and Hevesi, A. G. (eds) *The Politics of Urban Education, op. cit.*

56 Gross, N. *Who Runs Our Schools?,* New York: Wiley, 1958.

57 Bidwell, C. *op. cit.,* pp. 1010–11.

58 Vidich, A. J. and Bensman, J. *op. cit.*

59 Gans, H. J. *The Levittowners,* London: Allen Lane, The Penguin Press, 1967, p. 89.

60 *Ibid.,* p. 97.

61 Minar, D. W. 'The Community Basis of Conflict in School System Politics', *American Sociological Review,* vol. XXXI, 1966.

62 Kerr, N. D. 'The School Board as an Agency of Legitimation', *Sociology of Education,* vol. XXXVIII, 1964.

63 McCarty, D. J. and Ramsey, C. E. *The School Managers - Power and Conflict in American Public Education,* Westport, Connecticut: Glenwood Publishing Co., 1971.

64 Gross, N., Mason, W. and McEachern, A. W. *Explorations in Role Analysis: Studies of the School Superintendent's Role,* New York: Wiley, 1958.

65 Bidwell, C. E. *op. cit.*

66 Crain, R. L. *op. cit.*

67 Rogers, D. *op. cit.*

68 Baron, G. and Tropp, A. 'Teachers in England and America', in Halsey, Floud, Anderson, *op. cit.,* pp. 545–57.

69 Peschek, D. and Brand, J. 'Policies and Politics in Secondary Education: Case Studies in West Ham and Reading', *Greater London Papers No. 11,* London School of Economics, 1966, p. 47. See also Mays, J. B. *Education and the Urban Child, op. cit.,* pp. 49–55.

70 Peschek, D. and Brand, J. *op. cit,* p. 101.

71 Sharrock, Anne *Home/School Relations,* London: Macmillan & Co. Ltd, 1970, ch. 6.

72 Saran, R. *Policy-making in Secondary Education,* Oxford: Clarendon Press, 1973.

73 Similar changes of policy also occurred elsewhere at this time. See Banks, O. *Parity and Prestige in English Secondary Education, op. cit.,* p. 147.

74 Boaden, N. *Urban Policy-making: Influences on County Boroughs in England and Wales,* Cambridge University Press, 1971, pp. 45–58.

75 Byrne, D. S. and Williamson, W. 'Some Intra-regional Variations in Educational Provision and their Bearing upon Educational Attainment in the Case of the North-east', *Sociology,* vol. VI, 1972.

76 Byrne, E. M. *Planning and Educational Inequality: A Study of the Rationale of Resource Allocation,* Slough: N.F.E.R., 1974.

77 Batley, R., O'Brien, O. and Parris, H. *Going Comprehensive,* London: Routledge & Kegan Paul, 1970.

78 Lee, J. M. *Social Leaders and Public Persons,* Oxford University Press, 1963.

79 Batley, R. *et al., op. cit.*

80 Byrne, Eileen M. *op. cit.*

81 Peschek, D. and Brand, J. *op. cit.*
82 Kogan, M. and Van der Eyken, W. *County Hall - The Role of the Chief Education Officer*, Harmondsworth, Middlesex: Penguin, 1973, p. 42.
83 Saran, R. *op. cit.*, p. 255.
84 Baron, G. and Tropp, A. *op. cit.*, p. 550.
85 See the letter from Margaret Cole, *New Society*, 15 August 1968, p. 245.
86 Although pro-Duane, the book by Leila Berg demonstrates this very well. See Berg, L. *Risinghill, Death of a Comprehensive School*, Harmondsworth, Middlesex: Penguin, 1968.
87 Brittan, S. *The Treasury under the Tories, 1951-1964*, Harmondsworth, Middlesex: Penguin, 1964.
88 Kazamias, A. M. *Politics, Society and Secondary Education in England*, University of Pennsylvania Press, 1966, ch. 5.
89 Eaglesham, E. J. R. *The Foundation of Twentieth-century Education in England*, London: Routledge & Kegan Paul, 1967, pp. 90-92.
90 Boyle, E. and Crosland, A. *The Politics of Education*, Harmondsworth, Middlesex: Penguin, 1971.
91 This is also the situation in China today.
92 Zeigler, H. and Peak, W. 'The Political Functions of the Educational System' in Hopper, E. I. (ed.) *Readings in the Theory of Educational Systems, op. cit.*
93 Vaughan, M. and Scotford-Archer, M. *Social Conflict and Educational Change in England and France, 1781-1848*, Cambridge University Press.
94 Cannon, C. 'The Influence of Religion on Educational Policy 1902-1944' *British Journal of Educational Studies*, vol. xii, 1963-4.
95 Butler, R. A. 'The Politics of the 1944 Education Act' in Fowler, G., Morris, V. and Ozga, J. *Decision-making in British Education*, London: Heinemann, 1973.
96 Passin, H. 'Japan', in Coleman, J. S. *Education and Political Development*, Princeton University Press, 1965, p. 308.
97 *Ibid.*, p. 310.
98 *Ibid.*, pp. 243-4.
99 Coleman, J. S. *op. cit.*, pp. 254-71.
100 Khrushchev, N. S. 'Memorandum approved by the Presidium of the Central Committee of the Communist Party of the Soviet Union', September 1958, quoted in Grant, N. *Soviet Education, op. cit.*, pp. 101-2.
101 Grant, N. *op. cit.*, p. 25.
102 Clawson, R. W. 'Political Socialization of Children in the u.s.s.r.', *Political Science Quarterly*, vol. 88, 1973.
103 Hess, R. D. and Torney, J. V. *The Development of Political Attitudes in Children*, New York: Doubleday, 1968.
104 *Ibid.*, p. 248.
105 Zeigler, H. and Peak, W. *op. cit.*, p. 218. See also Merelman, R. M. 'The Adolescence of Political Socialization', *Sociology of Education* vol. xlv, 1972.
106 Lipset, S. M. *Political Man*, London: Heinemann, 1960, p. 56.
107 Miller, S. M. and Riessman, F. 'Working Class Authoritarianism? A Critique of Lipset', *British Journal of Sociology*, vol. xii, 1961. For a more recent critique see Jackman, M. R. 'Education and Prejudice or Education and Response - Set', *American Sociological Review*, vol. xxxviii, 1973.

[108] Lipset, S. M. *op. cit.,* p. 174.

[109] Feldman, K. A. and Newcomb, T. A. *The Impact of College on Students,* San Francisco: Jossey Bass, 1973.

[110] Selvin, H. C. and Hagstrom, W. O. 'Determinants of Support for Civil Liberties', *British Journal of Sociology,* vol. II, 1960.

[111] Stern, G. G. 'Measuring Noncognitive Variables in Research on Teaching' in Gage, N. L. (ed.) *Handbook of Research on Teaching,* Chicago: Rand McNally, 1963, p. 431.

[112] Newcomb, T. A. *Personality and Social Change: Attitude Formation in a Student Community,* New York: Dryden Press, 1943.

[113] Newcomb, T. M., Koenig, K. E., Flacks, R., Warwick, D. P. *Persistence and Change: Bennington College and its Students after Twenty-five Years,* New York: Wiley, 1967.

[114] Clignet, R. *Liberty and Equality in the Educational Process, op. cit.,* pp. 91–5.

[115] Lister, I. 'The Challenge of Deschooling' in Lister I. (ed.) *Deschooling,* London: Cambridge University Press, 1974, p. 2.

[116] Illich, I. *Deschooling Society,* Harmondsworth, Middlesex: Penguin, 1973. The other important deschooler is Everett Reimer: see Reimer, E. *School is Dead: An Essay on Alternatives in Education,* Harmondsworth, Middlesex: Penguin, 1971.

[117] Hargreaves, D. H. 'Deschoolers and New Romantics' in Flude, M. and Ahier, J. *Educability, Schools and Ideology, op. cit.,* p. 186.

[118] See also Gintis, H. 'Towards a Political Economy of Education' in Lister, I. (ed.) *Deschooling, op. cit.*

[119] Fay, M. A. 'Ivan Illich: a Charismatic Hero in a Disenchanted World', *Higher Education Review,* vol. 6, 1974.

[120] Huberman, M. 'Learning, Democratizing and Deschooling' in Lister, I. (ed.) *Deschooling, op. cit.*

Chapter 7. The teaching profession

[1] Brookover, W. B. and Gottlieb, D. *A Sociology of Education,* New York: American Book Co., 1964, pp. 299–300.

[2] Tropp, A. *The School Teachers,* London: Heinemann, 1957, p. 8.

[3] The Newcastle Commission Report, for example, pointed out that 'boys who would otherwise go out to work at mechanical trades at twelve or thirteen years of age, are carefully educated at the public expense'. Reported in Tropp, A. *ibid.,* p. 72.

[4] Bamford, T. W. *The Rise of the Public Schools,* London: Nelson, 1967, p. 120.

[5] *Ibid.,* p. 55.

[6] *Ibid.,* p. 150.

[7] Tropp, A. *op. cit.,* p. 40.

[8] *Ibid.,* p. 194.

[9] Thabault, R. 'The Professional Training of Teachers in France', *Year Book of Education,* London: Evans Bros, 1963, pp. 244–5.

[10] Fiszman, J. R. *Revolution and Tradition in People's Poland,* Princeton University Press, 1972.

[11] Stiles, L. J. *et al. Teacher Education in the United States,* New York: Ronald Press, 1960.

[12] See, for example, Conant, J. B. *The Education of American Teachers,* New York: McGraw-Hill, 1963.

[13] Rothblatt, S. *Revolution of the Dons, op. cit.,* p. 227.

[14] Ringer, F. K. *The Decline of the German Mandarins. The German Academic Community 1890-1933,* Cambridge, Mass.: Harvard University Press, 1969, p. 45.

[15] Davie, G. E. *The Democratic Intellect: Scotland and her Universities in the Nineteenth Century,* Edinburgh University Press, 1961.

[16] McPherson, A. 'Selections and Survivals. A Sociology of the Ancient Scottish Universities', in Brown, R. (ed.) *Knowledge, Education, and Cultural Change,* London: Tavistock, 1973.

[17] Light, D. Jnr 'The Structure of the Academic Profession', *Sociology of Education,* vol. XLVII, 1974.

[18] Halsey, A. H. and Trow, M. A. *The British Academics,* London: Faber & Faber, 1971, p. 458.

[19] *Ibid.,* p. 496.

[20] Fulton, O. and Trow, M. A. 'Research Activity in American Higher Education', *Sociology of Education,* vol. XLVII, 1974.

[21] *Report of the Committee on Higher Education* (Robbins Report), *op. cit.,* Appendix 3, p. 92.

[22] *Ibid.,* pp. 117-9.

[23] Whitburn, J. 'Newer Poly teachers more academic', *Times Higher Education Supplement,* 31 May 1974.

[24] Fulton, O. 'The C.A.T.s in transition', in Halsey, A. H. and Trow, M. A. *The British Academics, op. cit.,* Appendix A.

[25] Berelson, B. *Graduate Education in the United States,* New York: McGraw-Hill, 1960.

[26] Caplow, T. and McGee, R. J. *The Academic Marketplace,* New York: Basic Books, 1958.

[27] Knapp, R. H. 'Changing Functions of the College Professor', in Sanford, N. (ed.) *The American College, op. cit.,* p. 290.

[28] Floud, J. and Scott, W. 'Recruitment to Teaching in England and Wales', in Halsey, Floud, Anderson, *op. cit.,* pp. 527-44.

[29] *Ibid.,* Table II (adapted), p. 54.

[30] Lomax, D. 'Teacher Education' in Butcher, H. J. and Pont, H. B. *Educational Research in Britain,* vol. 3, *op. cit.,* 1973.

[31] Kelly, S. G. *Teaching in the City,* Dublin: Gill & McMillan, 1969.

[32] Bernbaum, G. 'Headmasters and Schools: Some Preliminary Findings', *Sociological Review,* vol. XXI, 1973.

[33] See Brookover, W. B. and Erickson, E. L. *Sociology of Education,* Illinois: The Dorsey Press, 1975, pp. 211-13.

[34] Betz, M. and Garland, J. 'Intergenerational Mobility Rates of Teachers', *Sociology of Education,* vol. XLVII, 1974.

[35] Carlson, R. O. 'Variations and Myth in the Social Status of Teachers', *Journal of Educational Sociology,* vol. XXXV, November 1951, pp. 104-18.

[36] Brookover, W. B. and Gottlieb, D. *op. cit.,* p. 310.

[37] Becker, H. S. 'The Career of the Chicago Public School Teacher', *American Journal of Sociology*, vol. LVII, p. 952.

[38] Herriott, R. E. and St John, W. H. *Social Class and the Urban School*, New York: Wiley, 1966, pp. 70-74.

[39] Knapp, R. H. *op. cit.*, p. 297.

[40] Crane, D. 'Social Class Origin and Academic Success: the Influence of Two Stratification Systems on Academic Careers', *Sociology of Education*, vol. XLII, 1969.

[41] Halsey, A. H. 'Theoretical Advance and Empirical Challenge' in Hopper, E. I. (ed.) *Readings in the Theory of Educational Systems, op. cit.*

[42] Halsey, A. H. and Trow, M. A. *The British Academics, op. cit.*

[43] Glass, D. V. (ed.) *Social Mobility in Britain, op. cit.*, p. 34.

[44] Lieberman, M. *Education as a Profession*, New Jersey: Prentice-Hall, 1956, p. 480.

[45] Conant, J. B. *op. cit.*, ch. I.

[46] Tropp, A. *op. cit.*, p. 262.

[47] Blyth, W. A. L. *English Primary Education*, London: Routledge & Kegan Paul, 1965, vol. I, pp. 158-9.

[48] Quoted in Krug, E. A. *The Shaping of the American High School*, New York: Harper & Row, 1964, p. 289.

[49] *Ibid.*, p. 187.

[50] Lieberman, M. *op. cit.*, p. 134.

[51] Folger, J. K. and Nam, C. B. *Education of the American Population, op. cit.*, p. 92.

[52] *Ibid.*, p. 130.

[53] Reported in Brookover, W. B. and Gottlieb, D. *op. cit.*, p. 133.

[54] Folger, J. K. and Nam, C. B. *Education of the American Population, op. cit.*, p. 82.

[55] Hans, N. 'Status of Women Teachers', *Year Book of Education, 1953*, quoted in Lieberman, M. *op. cit.*, p. 244, Table 15.

[56] Simpson, R. L. and Simpson, I. H. 'Women and Bureaucracy in the Semi-professions', in Etzioni, A. (ed.) *The Semi-professionals and their Organization*, New York: The Free Press, 1969.

[57] Brookover, W. B. and Gottlieb, D. *op. cit.*, pp. 312-13.

[58] Folger, J. K. and Nam, C. B. *Education of the American Population, op. cit.*, pp. 88-90.

[59] Smith, D. M. and Cooper, B. 'A Study of Moonlighting by Public School Teachers' in Pavalko, R. M. (ed.) *Sociology of Education: A Book of Readings*, Itasca, Illinois: Peacock, 1968.

[60] See the detailed discussion of teachers' salaries in Manzer, R. A. *Teachers and Politics*, Manchester University Press, 1970, pp. 109-43.

[61] Fiszman, J. R. *Revolution and Tradition in People's Poland, op. cit.*

[62] Wilson, B. 'The Teacher's Role - a Sociological Analysis', *British Journal of Sociology*, vol. XIII, 1962, pp. 15-32.

[63] Conant, J. B. *op. cit.*, p. 7.

[64] Parry, N. and J. 'The Teachers and Professionalism: the Failure of an Occupational Strategy' in Flude, M. and Ahier, J. *Educability, Schools and Ideology, op. cit.* See also Tropp, A. *op. cit.*

[65] For example there has been no feminization in either Britain or the United States. There are few women academics, particularly in the higher posts.

⁶⁶ Ostroff, A. 'Economic Pressure and the Professor', in Sanford, N. (ed.) *The American College, op. cit.,* p. 448.

⁶⁷ Knapp, R. H. *op. cit.,* p. 308.

⁶⁸ Lazarsfeld, P. P. and Thielens, W. Jnr *The Academic Mind,* Glencoe, Illinois: Free Press, 1958, p. 28.

⁶⁹ Bibby, J. 'Rewards and Careers', *Higher Education Review,* vol. III, 1970.

⁷⁰ Lieberman, M. *op. cit.*

⁷¹ Quoted in Kelsall, R. H. and Kelsall, H. *The School Teacher in England and the United States,* Oxford: Pergamon, 1969, p. 164.

⁷² Rosenthal, A. *Pedagogues and Power: Teacher Groups in School Politics,* Syracuse University Press, 1969.

⁷³ See Berube, M. R. and Gittell, M. *op. cit.*

⁷⁴ Rosenthal, A. *Pedagogues and Power: Teacher Groups in School Politics, op. cit.,* p. 174.

⁷⁵ Cole, S. *The Unionization of Teachers: a Case Study of the U.F.T.,* New York: Praeger, 1969.

⁷⁶ Chaney, J. S. 'An analysis of school teacher strikes in the U.S.', *Urban Education,* vol. VIII, 1973.

⁷⁷ Tropp, A. *op. cit.,* ch. IV.

⁷⁸ Banks, O. *Parity and Prestige in English Secondary Education, op. cit.,* ch. 2.

⁷⁹ Gosden, P. H. *The Evolution of a Profession,* Oxford: Blackwell, 1972.

⁸⁰ Tropp, A. *op. cit.*

⁸¹ Manzer, R. A. *Teachers and Politics, op. cit.,* p. 158.

⁸² Peschek, D. and Brand, J. *op. cit.,* pp. 41-5.

⁸³ See Halsey, A. H. 'Politics and the Academics', *The Times Higher Education Supplement,* 11 October 1974.

⁸⁴ Roy, W. *The Teachers' Union. Aspects of Policy and Organization in the N.U.T. 1950-1966,* Kettering, Northants: The Schoolmaster Publishing Co., 1968.

⁸⁵ Finer, S. E. *Anonymous Empire,* London: Pall Mall, 1958, pp. 65-6.

⁸⁶ See for example Burke, V. *Teachers in Turmoil,* Harmondsworth, Middlesex: Penguin, 1971.

⁸⁷ Manzer, R. A. *op. cit.,* p. 118.

⁸⁸ Grace, G. R. *Role Conflict and the Teacher,* London: Routledge & Kegan Paul, 1972.

⁸⁹ Deem, R. 'Professionalism, Unity and Militant Action: The Case of Teachers', *Sociological Review,* in press.

⁹⁰ Clark, J. M. *Teachers and Politics in France,* Syracuse University Press, 1967.

⁹¹ Brookover, W. B. and Erickson, E. L. *A Sociology of Education, op. cit.,* p. 204.

Chapter 8. The sociology of educational knowledge

¹ Young, M. F. D. 'Knowledge and Control' in Young, M. F. D. (ed.) *Knowledge and Control: New Directions for the Sociology of Education, op. cit.*

² Bourdieu, P. 'Systems of Education and Systems of Thought' in Young, M. F. D. *ibid.*

³ Bernstein, B. 'On the Classification and Framing of Educational Knowledge' in Young, M. F. D. *ibid.*

⁴ Young, M. F. D., *op. cit.*

⁵ Taylor, P. H., Reid, W. A. and Holley, B. J. *The English Sixth Form*, London: Routledge & Kegan Paul, 1974.

⁶ See for example Warwick, D. 'Ideologies, Integration and Conflicts of Meaning' in Flude, M. and Ahier, J. *Educability, Schools and Ideology, op. cit.*

⁷ See the account by Nisbet, J. 'The Schools Council: The United Kingdom' in *Case Studies of Educational Innovation - Vol. I. At the Central Level,* Centre for Education Research and Innovation, Paris: O.E.C.D., 1973.

⁸ Young, M. F. D. 'On the Politics of Educational Knowledge', *Economy and Society*, vol. I, 1972. See also the Marxist critique by Holly D. *Beyond Curriculum,* London: Hart-Davis McGibbon, 1973.

⁹ Hoyle, E. 'How Does the Curriculum Change?' in Hooper, R. (ed.) *The Curriculum: Context, Design and Development,* Edinburgh: Oliver and Boyd, 1971.

¹⁰ See Banks, O. *Parity and Prestige in English Secondary Education, op. cit.*

¹¹ Shipman, M. 'Curriculum for Inequality' in Hooper, R. (ed.) *The Curriculum, Context, Design and Development, op. cit.,* p. 105.

¹² Byrne, E. M. *Planning and Educational Inequality: A Study of the Rationale of Resource Allocation,* Slough: N.F.E.R., 1974.

¹³ *Ibid.* pp. 37-40.

¹⁴ Saario, T. N., Jacklin, C. N. and Tittle, C. K. 'Sex Role Stereotyping in the Public Schools', *Harvard Educational Review*, vol. XLIII, 1973

¹⁵ Sexton, P. *The Feminized Male,* London: Pitman Publishing Co., 1970.

¹⁶ Bourdieu, P. 'Intellectual Field and Creative Project' in Young, M. F. D. (ed.) *Knowledge and Control: New Directions for the Sociology of Education, op. cit.,* pp. 180-85.

¹⁷ Bourdieu, P. 'Cultural Reproduction and Social Reproduction' in Brown, R, (ed.) *Knowledge, Education, and Cultural Change, op. cit.*

¹⁸ Bourdieu, P. 'The School as a conservative force: scholastic and cultural inequalities' in Eggleston, J. *Contemporary Research in the Sociology of Education,* London: Methuen, 1974.

¹⁹ Bourdieu, P. and Saint-Martin, M. de 'Scholastic excellence and the values of the educational system', *ibid.*

²⁰ Ben-David, J. 'Professions in the Class System of Present-day Societies', *Current Sociology* vol. XII, 1963-4, p. 294.

²¹ Bernstein, B. 'On the Classification and Framing of Educational Knowledge' in Young, M. F. D. (ed.) *Knowledge and Control, op. cit.*

²² Smith, D. 'Codes, Paradigms and Folk Norms', *Sociology,* vol. X, 1976.

²³ Shipman, M. D. with Bolan, D. and Jenkins, D. *Inside a Curriculum Project,* London: Methuen, 1974.

²⁴ Anderson, J. G. *Bureaucracy in Education,* Baltimore, Maryland: Johns Hopkins, 1968.

²⁵ Weber, M. *Essays in Sociology* translated and edited by Gerth Hand Mills, C. W., London: Routledge & Kegan Paul, 1952.

²⁶ Wilkinson, R. H. 'The Gentleman Ideal and the Maintenance of a Political Elite' in Musgrave, P. W. (ed.) *Sociology, History and Education,* London: Chatto & Windus, 1962.

27 Williams, R. *The Long Revolution*, London: Chatto & Windus, 1961.
28 Barker, R. *Education and Politics 1900-1951*, Oxford University Press, 1972.
29 Davie, G. E. *The Democratic Intellect, op. cit.*
30 Rothblatt, S. *The Revolution of the Dons, op. cit.*
31 Smith, D. *op. cit.*
32 Eggleston, J. 'Decision-making on the School Curriculum: A Conflict Model', *Sociology*, vol. VII, 1973.
33 For example Katz and Spring, see chapter 6.
34 Whitty, G. 'Sociology and the Problem of Radical Educational Change' in Flude, M. and Ahier, J. *Educability, Schools and Ideology, op. cit.*, pp. 113-4.
35 Keddie, N. (ed.) *Tinker, Tailor ... The Myth of Cultural Deprivation, op. cit.* See also the critique of cultural relativisim as applied to knowledge in Lawton, D. *Class, Culture and the Curriculum*, London: Routledge & Kegan Paul, 1975.
36 Bernstein, B. 'On the Classification and Framing of Educational Knowledge' in Young, M. F. D. (ed.) *Knowledge and Control, op. cit.*
37 Richmond, W. K. *The Free School*, London: Methuen, 1973, p. 107. See also Featherstone, J. *The British Infant Schools*, in Gross, R. and B. *Radical School Reform*, Harmondsworth, Middlesex: Penguin, 1972.
38 *Children and their Primary Schools* (Plowden Report), *op. cit.*, vol. I, pp. 187-8.
39 Bernbaum, G. 'Countesthorpe College, Leicester' in *Case Studies of Educational Innovation* - vol. III, *At the School Level*, Centre for Educational Research and Innovation, Paris: O.E.C.D., 1973. This volume also contains material on experimental schools in other countries. See also Richmond, W. K. *The Free School, op. cit.*
40 Hargreaves, D. H. 'Deschoolers and the New Romantics' in Flude, M. and Ahier, J. *Educability, Schools and Ideology, op. cit.*, p. 198.
41 *Ibid.*, p. 187.
42 Bernstein, B. and Davies, B. 'Some Sociological Comments on Plowden' in Peters, R. S. (ed.) *Perspectives on Plowden*, London: Routledge & Kegan Paul, 1969, p. 56.
43 *Ibid.*, p. 71.
44 Bernstein, B. *Class and Pedagogies: Visible and Invisible* (mimeographed), June 1973.
45 Taylor, L. C. *Resources for Learning*, Harmondsworth, Middlesex: Penguin, 1971, p. 55.
46 Bernbaum, G. 'Countesthorpe College, Leicester', *op. cit.*
47 Young, M. F. D. 'Curricula as Socially Organized Knowledge', *op. cit.* pp. 37-8.
48 Gusfield, J. R. 'Equalitarianism and Bureaucratic Recruitment' *Administrative Science Quarterly*, vol. II, 1957.
49 Ringer, F. K. *The Decline of the German Mandarins, op. cit.*, pp. 15-16.
50 Clignet, R. *Liberty and Equality in the Educational Process, op. cit.*, ch. 10.
51 See especially *Class and Pedagogies: Visible and Invisible, op. cit.*
52 Bourdieu, P. 'School as a Conservative Force' in Eggleston, J. *Contemporary Research in the Sociology of Education, op. cit.*, p. 40.
53 Cicourel, A. V. and Kitsuse, J. I. *The Educational Decision Makers*, Boston, Mass.: Bobbs Merrill, 1963.
54 Armor, D. J. *The American School Counselor*, New York: Russell Sage Foundation, 1969.

[55] See for example Taylor, W. *The Secondary Modern School,* London: Faber & Faber, 1963.

Chapter 9. The school as an organization

[1] Floud, J. and Halsey, A. H. 'The Sociology of Education: A Trend Report and Bibliography,' *Current Sociology,* vol. VIII, 1958.

[2] Hoyle, E. 'The Study of Schools as Organizations' in Butcher, H. J. and Pont, H. B. *Educational Research in Britain,* vol. III, *op. cit.*

[3] Davies, B. 'On the Contribution of Organizational Analysis to the Study of Educational Institutions' in Brown, R. (ed.) *Knowledge, Education and Cultural Change,* London: Tavistock, 1973, p. 251.

[4] Hoyle, E. *op. cit.*

[5] Etzioni, A. *Modern Organizations,* Englewood Cliffs, N.J.: Prentice-Hall, 1964, p. 4.

[6] Corwin, R. G. *A Sociology of Education, op. cit.,* p. 38.

[7] Blau, P. M. *Bureaucracy in Modern Society,* New York: Random House, 1956, pp. 29-30.

[8] Crozier, M. *The Bureaucratic Phenomenon,* University of Chicago Press, ch. 7.

[9] Albrow, M. *Bureaucracy,* London: Macmillan, 1970, p. 125.

[10] Clignet, R. *Liberty and Equality in the Educational Process, op. cit.,* p. 184.

[11] Corwin, R. G. *op. cit.,* ch. 5.

[12] Clignet, R. *op. cit.,* p. 183.

[13] Warwick, D. *Bureaucracy,* London: Longman, 1974, pp. 99-100.

[14] Corwin, R. G. *op. cit.,* p. 275.

[15] Clark, Burton R. 'Sociology of Education', in Faris, Robert E. L. (ed.) *Handbook of Modern Sociology,* Chicago: Rand McNally, 1964, p. 759.

[16] Anderson, James G. *Bureaucracy in Education,* Baltimore, Maryland: Johns Hopkins, 1968.

[17] *Ibid.,* p. 166.

[18] Samuels, J. J. 'Infringements on teachers' autonomy', *Urban Education,* vol. V, 1970.

[19] Washburne, C. 'The Teacher in the Authority System', *Journal of Educational Sociology,* vol. XXX, 1956-7.

[20] Sharma, C. L. 'Who Should Make Decisions?', *Administrator's Notebook 3* (April 1955), pp. 1-4, reported in Corwin, *op. cit.,* p. 276.

[21] Getzels and Guba, 'The Structure of Roles and Role Conflict in the Teaching Situation', *Journal of Educational Sociology,* vol. XXIX, 1955-6.

[22] Carpenter, H. H. 'Formal Organizational Structural Factors and Perceived Job Satisfaction of Classroom Teachers', *Administrative Science Quarterly,* vol. XVI, 1971.

[23] Seeman, M. *Social Status and Leadership: the Case of the School Executive,* Columbus: Bureau of Educational Research, Ohio State University, 1960.

[24] Moeller, Gerald H. and Charters, W. W. 'Relation of Bureaucratization to Sense of Power Among Teachers', *Administrative Science Quarterly,* vol. X, 1965-6.

[25] Corwin, R. G. *Militant Professionalism: A Study of Organizational Conflict in High Schools,* New York: Appleton, Century, Crofts, 1970.

26 See for example Charters, W. W. Jnr 'The Social Background of Teaching' in Gage, N. L. (ed.) *Handbook of Research on Teaching*, Chicago: Rand McNally, 1963.

27 Anderson, James G. *op. cit.*

28 Clark, Burton R. *op. cit.*, p. 760.

29 Crozier, M., *op. cit.*, p. 206.

30 Bidwell, C. E., 'The School as a Formal Organization' in March, J. G. (ed.) *Handbook of Social Organization*, Chicago: Rand McNally, 1965.

31 Lortie, D. C. 'The Balance of Control and Autonomy in Elementary School Teaching' in Etzioni, A. (ed.), *The Semi-professionals and Their Organization, op. cit.*, p. 9.

32 Grace, G. L. R., *Role Conflict and the Teacher*, London: Routledge & Kegan Paul, 1972, pp. 64-70.

33 Halpin, A. W., *The Leadership Behaviour of School Superintendents*, Midwest Administrative Center, University of Chicago, 1956.

34 Halpin, A. W. and Croft, D. *The Organizational Climate of Schools*, Midwest Administrative Center, University of Chicago, 1963.

35 Guba, E. G. and Bidwell, C. E. *Administrative Relationships*, Midwest Administrative Center, University of Chicago, 1957.

36 Gross, N. and Herriott, R. E. *Staff Leadership in Public Schools*, New York: Wiley, 1965.

37 Quoted by Hoyle, E. 'The Study of Schools as Organizations' in Butcher, H. J. and Pont, H. B. *Educational Research in Britain*, vol.III, University of London Press, 1973, p. 50.

38 Pedley, R. *The Comprehensive School*, Harmondsworth, Middx.: Penguin, 1963, p. 88.

39 Chetwynd, H. R. *Comprehensive School, the Story of Woodberry Down*, London: Routledge & Kegan Paul, 1960.

40 *London Comprehensive Schools: a Survey of Sixteen Schools*, London County Council, 1961, p. 32.

41 Benn, C. and Simon, B. *Half Way There*, London: McGraw-Hill, 1970.

42 Monks, T. G. *Comprehensive Education in England and Wales*, Slough: N.F.E.R., 1968, pp. 102-9.

43 Yates, A. *Grouping in Education*, New York: Wiley, 1966.

44 Lunn, J. C. Barker, *Streaming in the Primary School*, Slough: N.F.E.R., 1970.

45 Passow, A. H., Goldberg, M. and Justman, J. *The Effects of Ability Grouping*, Teachers College Press, University of Columbia, 1966.

46 Taylor, L. C. *Resources for Learning*, Harmondsworth, Middlesex: Penguin, 1971, pp. 53-4.

47 Douglas, J. F. 'A Study of Streaming at a Grammar School', *Educational Research*, vol. xv, 1973.

48 Lacey, C. 'Destreaming in a "Pressured" Academic Environment', in Eggleston, J. *Contemporary Research in the Sociology of Education. op. cit.*

49 Himmelweit, H. T. and Swift, B. 'A Model for the Understanding of the School as a Socializing Agent', in Mussen P. *et al.* (eds), *Trends and Issues in Developmental Psychology*, New York: Holt, Rinehart & Winston, 1969.

[50] Banks, O. and Finlayson, D. *Success and Failure in the Secondary School,* London: Methuen, 1973.

[51] Hargreaves, D. H. *Social Relations in a Secondary School,* London: Routledge & Kegan Paul, 1967.

[52] Lacey, C. *Hightown Grammar,* Manchester University Press, 1970.

[53] King, R. *Values and Involvement in a Grammar School,* London: Routledge & Kegan Paul, 1969.

[54] Ross, J. M., Bunton, W. J., Evison, P. and Robertson, T. S. *A Critical Appraisal of Comprehensive Education,* Slough: N.F.E.R., 1972.

[55] King, R. *School Organization and Pupil Involvement,* London: Routledge & Kegan Paul, 1973.

[56] Lunn, J. C. Barker *op. cit.*

[57] Conant, J. B. *The American High School Today,* New York: McGraw-Hill, 1959.

[58] See for example Ross, J. M. *et. al., op. cit.,* pp. 65-6, and p. 173.

[59] Taylor L. C. *Resources for Learning, op. cit.,* pp. 44-6.

[60] Barker, R. G. *et al. Big School - Small School,* a report to the Office of Education, U.S. Department of Health Education and Welfare, University of Kansas, Midwest Psychological Field Station, 1962.

[61] Willems, E. P. 'Sense of Obligation to High School Activities as Related to School Size and Marginality of Student', *Child Development,* vol. XXXVIII, 1967.

[62] Anderson, James G. *op. cit.*

[63] King, R. *School Organization and Pupil Involvement, op. cit.*

[64] Husén, T. (ed.) *International Study of Achievement in Mathematics. A Comparison of Twelve Countries,* New York: Wiley, 1967.

[65] Ross, J. M. *et al., op. cit.,* pp. 173-4.

[66] Eastcott, L. R. 'The Impact of Class Size on the Quality of Teaching and Learning - A Review', *Australian Journal of Education,* vol. XVII, 1973.

[67] See the discussion in Kelly, J. *Teaching in the City,* Dublin: Gill and McMillan, 1969.

[68] Davie, R. *et. al. From Birth to Seven,* London: Longman, 1972.

[69] Quoted in Eastcott, L. R. *op. cit.*

[70] See the evidence cited in Boocock, S. *An Introduction to the Sociology of Learning, op. cit.,* p. 156.

[71] Oakley, K. A. 'Stability of Teacher Behaviour in Conditions of Varying Class Size', *British Journal of Educational Psychology,* vol. XL, 1970.

[72] McKeachie, W. J. *Procedures and Techniques of Teaching. A Survey of Experimental Studies,* in Sanford, N. (ed.) *The American College,* New York: Wiley, 1962, p. 36.

[73] See for example Hodgson, G. 'Inequality: Do Schools Make a Difference?' in Silver, H. (ed.) *Equal Opportunity in Education,* London: Methuen, 1973.

[74] For a brief but helpful review of these criticisms see Heller, R. W. 'The Coleman Report Revisited', *Urban Education,* vol. IV, 1969.

[75] Boocock, S. *An Introduction to the Sociology of Learning, op. cit.,* pp. 195-7.

[76] Brookover, W. B. *et al.* 'Quality of Educational Attainment, Standardized Testing, Assessment, and Accountability' in Gordon, C. Wayne *Uses of the Sociology of Education,* National Society for the Study of Education, University of Chicago Press, 1974.

[77] Gordon, C. Wayne *The Social System of the High School*, Glencoe, Illinois: Free Press, 1957.

[78] Coleman, J. S. *The Adolescent Society*, Glencoe, Illinois: Free Press, 1961.

[79] Turner, R. *The Social Context of Ambition*, New York: Chandler, 1964, p. 223.

[80] Riley, M. W., Riley, J. Jnr and Moore, M. E. 'Adolescent Values and the Riesman Typology', in Lipset, S. M. and Lowenthal, L. (eds) *Culture and Social Character*, Glencoe, Illinois: Free Press, 1961, pp. 370-88.

[81] Kandel, D. B. and Lesser, G. S. 'Parental and Peer Influences on Educational Plans of Adolescents', *American Sociological Review*, vol. XXXIV, 1969.

[82] Eve, R. A. ' "Adolescent Culture", Convenient myth or reality? A Comparison of Students and their Teachers', *Sociology of Education*, vol. XLVIII, 1975.

[83] Snyder, E. E. 'A Longitudinal Analysis of the Relationship Between High School Student Values, Social Participation and Educational-Occupational Achievement', *Sociology of Education*, vol. XLII, 1969.

[84] Spreitzer, E. and Pugh, M. 'Interscholastic Athletics and Educational Expectations', *Sociology of Education*, vol. XLVI, 1973.

[85] Bronfenbrenner, U. 'Response to Pressure from Peers versus Adults amongst Soviet and American School Children', *Cornell Soviet Studies Reprint No. 16*, Committee on Soviet Studies, Cornell University, p. 5.

[86] *Ibid.*, p. 1.

[87] Bushnell, J. H. 'Student Culture at Vassar' in Sanford, N. (ed.) *op. cit.*, p. 507.

[88] Hughes, E., Becker, H. and Geer, B. 'Student Culture and Academic Effort', *ibid.*, p. 527.

[89] Becker, H. S., Geer, B. and Hughes, E. *Making the Grade. The Academic Side of College Life*, New York: Wiley, 1968.

[90] Lambert, R., Bullock, R. and Millham, S. 'The Informal Social System' in Brown, R. (ed.) *Knowledge, Education and Cultural Change, op. cit.*, p. 301.

[91] Parsons, T. and White, A. 'The Link Between Character and Society' in *Culture and Social Character*, Lipset, S. M. and Lowenthal, L. (eds), *op. cit.*, pp. 127-8.

[92] Simpson, R. L. 'Parental Influence, Anticipatory Socialization and Social Mobility', *American Sociological Review*, vol. XXVII, 1962.

[93] Ellis, R. A. and Lane, W. C. 'Structural Support for Upward Mobility', *American Sociological Review*, vol. XXVIII, 1963.

[94] Turner, R. *The Social Context of Ambition, op. cit.*, p. 118.

[95] Alexander, C. N. Jnr and Campbell, E. Q. 'Peer Influences on Adolescent Aspirations and Attainments', *American Sociological Review*, vol. XXIX, 1964.

[96] McDill, E. C. and Coleman, J. 'Family and Peer Influences in College Plans of High School Students', *Sociology of Education*, vol. XXXVIII, 1965.

[97] Stinchcombe, A. L. *Rebellion in the High School*, Chicago: Quadrangle Books, 1964, pp. 5-6.

[98] Hallworth, H. J. 'Sociometric Relations Among Grammar School Boys and Girls', *Sociometry*, vol. XVI, 1953.

[99] Sugarman, B. 'Involvement in Youth Culture, Academic Achievement, and Conformity in School', *British Journal of Sociology*, vol. XVIII, 1967.

[100] Polk, K. and Pink, W. 'Youth Culture and the School', *British Journal of Sociology*, vol. XXII, 1971.

[101] Hargreaves, D. H. *Social Relations in a Secondary School, op. cit.*, p. 67.

[102] Lacey, C., *Hightown Grammar, op. cit.*

[103] Ross *et al., A Critical Appraisal of Comprehensive Education, op. cit.*

[104] Sumner, R. and Warburton, F. W. *Achievement in Secondary School,* Slough: N.F.E.R., 1972.

[105] King, R., *Values and Involvement in a Grammar School,* London: Routledge & Kegan Paul, 1969.

[106] Bellaby, P. 'The Distribution of Deviance' in Eggleston, J. *Contemporary Research in the Sociology of Education, op. cit.,* pp. 180-81.

[107] Brookover, W. B. and Erickson, E. L. *Sociology of Education, op. cit.,* pp. 359-61.

[108] Wilsón, A. B. 'Residential Segregation of Social Classes and Aspirations of High School Boys', *American Sociological Review,* vol. XXIV, 1959.

[109] Wilson, A. B. 'Social Class and Equal Educational Opportunity' in *Equal Educational Opportunity,* Harvard University Press, 1969.

[110] Michael, J. 'High School Climate and Plans for Entering College', *Public Opinion Quarterly,* 1961.

[111] Coleman, J. S. *et. al. Equality of Educational Opportunity,* U.S.O.E., G.P.O., 1966.

[112] Spady, W. C. 'The Impact of School Resources on Students' in *Review of Research in Education,* Kerlinger, F. N. (ed.), American Education Research Association, Itasca, Illinois: Peacock Publishers, 1973.

[113] Koslin, S., Koslin B., Pargament, H. and Waxman, H. 'Classroom Balance and Students' Interracial Attitudes', *Sociology of Education,* vol. XLV, 1972.

[114] Jencks, C. and Brown, M. 'The Effects of Segregation on Student Achievement', *Sociology of Education,* vol. XLVIII, 1975.

[115] McDill, E. L. and Rigsby, Leo C. *Structure and Process in Secondary, Schools, The Academic Impact of Educational Climates,* London: Johns Hopkins, 1973, p. 105.

[116] Reported in Brookover, W. B. and Erickson, E. L. *Sociology of Education, op. cit.*

[117] Douglas, J. W. B. *The Home and the School,* London: Macgibbon Kee, 1964.

[118] Himmelweit, H. T. and Swift B. 'A Model for the Understanding of School as a Socializing Agent', *op. cit.*

[119] Banks, O. and Finlayson, D. *Success and Failure in the Secondary School, op. cit.*

[120] See also Nelson, J. I. 'High School Context and College Plans: the Impact of Social Structure on Aspirations', American Sociological Review, vol. XXXVII, 1972.

[121] Watts, A. G. *Diversity and Choice in Higher Education,* London: Routledge & Kegan Paul, 1972.

[122] See for example, Astin, A. W. 'The Methodology of Research on College Impact', *Sociology of Education,* vol. XLIII, 1970.

[123] Albrow, M. C. 'The Influence of Accommodation upon 64 Reading University Students', *British Journal of Sociology,* vol. XVII, 1966.

[124] Abbott, J. *Student Life in Class Society,* Oxford: Pergamon, 1971.

[125] Bell, D. and Kristol, I. *Confrontation: The Student Rebellion and Universities,* New York: Basic Books, 1969.

[126] Blackstone, T., Gales, K., Hadley, R. and Lewis, W. *Students in Conflict, L.S.E. in 1967,* London: Weidenfeld & Nicolson, 1970.

[127] Lipset, S. M. and Altbach, P. G. 'Student Politics and Higher Education in the United States' in Lipset, S.M. (ed.). *Student Politics,* New York: Basic Books, 1967.

[128] Adler, C. 'The Student Revolt: the Special Case of a Youth Culture' in Gordon, C. Wayne (ed.) *Uses of the Sociology of Education, op. cit.*, p. 127.

[129] See the summary in Lipset, S.M. 'The activists: a Profile', in Bell, D. and Kristol, I. *op. cit.*, pp. 45-57.

[130] Kahn R. and Bowers, W.J. 'The Social Context of the Rank-and-File Student Activist: A Test of Four Hypotheses', *Sociology of Education*, vol. XLIII, 1970.

[131] Blackstone, T. *et. al., op. cit.*

[132] Finney, H. C. 'Political Dimensions of College Impact on Civil-libertarianism and the Integration of Political Perspectives. A Longitudinal Analysis', *Sociology of Education*, vol. XLVII, 1974.

[133] Bayer, A. E. 'Institutional Correlates of Faculty Support of Campus Unrest', *Sociology of Education*, vol. XLV, 1972.

[134] Scott, J. W. and El-Assal, M. 'Multiversity, University Size, University Quality and Student Protest: An Empirical Study', *American Sociological Review*, vol. XXXIV, 1969.

[135] Peterson, R. E. 'The Student Left in American Higher Education' in *Daedalus*, vol. XCVII, 1968, pp. 311-12.

[136] Adler, C. 'The Student Revolt: The Special Case of a Youth Culture', *op. cit.*

[137] Scotford-Archer, M. *Students, University and Society*, London: Heinemann, 1972, pp. 1-35.

[138] Glazer, N. ' "Student Power" in Berkeley' in Bell, D. and Kristol, I. *op. cit.*, p. 5.

[139] Hirst, P. Q. 'Some Problems of Explaining Student Militancy', Brown, R. (ed.) *Knowledge, Education and Cultural Change, op. cit.*

[140] Feuer, L. S. *The Conflict of Generations*, New York: Basic Books, 1969, p. 528.

[141] Spady, W. C. and Adler, C. 'Youth, Social Change, and Unrest: A Critique and Synthesis' in Gordon, C. Wayne (ed.) *Uses of the Sociology of Education, op. cit.*

[142] Meyer, J. W. and Rubinson, R. 'Structural Determinants of Student Political Activity: A Comparative Interpretation', *Sociology of Education*, vol. XLV, 1972.

[143] Weinberg, I. and Walker, K. 'Student Politics and Political Systems', *American Journal of Sociology*, vol. LXXV, 1969.

[144] Spady, W. G. and Adler, C. 'Youth, Social Change and Unrest: A Critique and Synthesis', *op. cit.*

[145] Scotford-Archer, M. *Students, University and Society, op. cit.*

Chapter 10. The sociology of the classroom

[1] Waller, W. *The Sociology of Teaching*, New York: Wiley, 1965.

[2] Morrison, A. and McIntyre, D. *Teachers and Teaching*, 2nd edition, Harmondsworth, Middlesex: Penguin, 1973, p. 13.

[3] Withall, J. and Lewis, W. W. 'Social Interaction in the Classroom' in Gage, N. L. (ed.) *Handbook of Research on Teaching*, Chicago: Rand McNally, 1963, p. 689.

[4] Morrison, A. and McIntyre, D. *op. cit.*, pp. 54-9. See also Getzels, J. W. and Jackson, P. W. 'The Teacher's Personality and Characteristics' in Gage, N. L. (ed.) *Handbook of Research on Teaching, op. cit.*

[5] Stern, G. G. 'Measuring Non-cognitive Variables in Research on Teaching' in Gage, N. L. (ed.) *op. cit.*

[6] Withall, J. and Lewis, W. W. *op. cit.*, p. 688.

7 Stern, G. G. *op. cit.*

8 Quoted in Brookover, W. B. and Gottlieb, D. A. *A Sociology of Education,* New York: American Book Co., 2nd ed., 1964, p. 431.

9 Bush, R. N. *The Teacher-Pupil Relationship,* New York: Prentice-Hall, 1954.

10 Davidson, H. and Lang, G. 'Children's Perceptions of their Teachers', *Journal of Experimental Education,* 1960-61.

11 White, R. K. and Lippitt, R. *Autocracy and Democracy: An Experimental Inquiry,* New York: Harper, 1960.

12 For a summary of these studies and their results see Anderson, R. C. 'Learning in Discussion' in Charters, W. W. Jnr and Gage, N. L. (eds) *Readings in the Social Psychology of Education,* Boston: Allyn & Bacon, 1963, pp. 153-62.

13 McKeachie, W. J. 'Procedures and Techniques of Teaching: A Survey of Experimental Studies' in Sanford, N. (ed.) *op. cit.,* p. 1123.

14 Anderson, R. C. *op. cit.,* p. 159.

15 *Ibid.,* p. 159.

16 Henry, J. 'Docility, or Giving Teacher What She Wants', *Journal of Social Issues,* vol. XI, 1955.

17 Gordon, C. Wayne *The Social System of the High School, op. cit.*

18 Walker, R. 'The Sociology of Education and Life in Classrooms', *International Review of Education,* vol. XVIII, 1972.

19 Stern, G. G. *op. cit.,* p. 428.

20 Brophy, J. E. and Good, T. L. *Teacher-Student Relationships,* New York: Holt, Rinehart & Winston, 1974, pp. 246-52.

21 McKeachie, W. J. and Yi-quang, L. 'Sex Differences in Student Response to College Teachers: Teachers' Warmth and Teachers' Sex', *American Educational Research Journal,* vol. VII, 1971.

22 Becker, H. S. 'Social Class Variations in Pupil-Teacher Relationships', *Journal of Educational Sociology,* vol. XXV, 1952.

23 Kaplan, L. 'The Annoyances of Elementary School Teachers', *Journal of Educational Research,* vol. XLV, 1952.

24 Becker, H. S. 'The Career of the Chicago Public School Teacher', *American Journal of Sociology,* vol. XI, 1952.

25 Herriott, R. E. and St John, N. H. *Social Class and the Urban School, op. cit.*

26 Goodacre, E. J. *Teachers and their Pupils' Home Background,* Slough, N.F.E.R., 1968.

27 Brandis, W. and Bernstein, B. *Selection and Control: Teachers' Ratings of Children in the Infant School,* London: Routledge & Kegan Paul, 1974.

28 Pidgeon, D. A. *Expectation and Pupil Performance,* Slough: N.F.E.R., 1970.

29 Brophy, J. E. and Good, T. L. Teacher-Student Relationships, *op. cit.,* p. 115.

30 Rosenthal, R. and Jacobson, L. *Pygmalion in the Classroom,* New York: Holt, Rinehart & Winston, 1968.

31 Grieger, R. M. 'Pygmalion Revisited: A Loud Call for Caution', *Interchange,* vol. II, 1971.

32 These studies are summarized in Grieger, R. M. *ibid.* See also Brophy, R. E. and Good, T. L. *Teacher-Student Relationships, op. cit.,* pp. 42-115.

33 Burstall, C. *French from Eight: A National Experiment,* Slough: N.F.E.R., 1968.

34 Brophy, R. E. and Good, T. L. *op. cit.,* p. 119.

[35] Clifford, M. M. and Walster, E. 'The Effect of Physical Attractiveness on Teacher Expectations', *Sociology of Education*, vol. XLVI, 1973.

[36] For an early example see Kozol, J. *Death at an Early Age*, Harmondsworth, Middlesex: Penguin.

[37] Walker, R. 'The Sociology of Education and Life in School Classrooms' *op. cit.*, p. 37.

[38] For a description of this and other techniques see Medley, D. M. and Mitzel, H. E. 'Measuring Classroom Behaviour by Systematic Observation' in Gage, N. L. (ed.) *op. cit.*

[39] There is a useful summary of these categories in Morrison, A. and McIntyre, D. *Teachers and Teaching, op. cit.*, p. 30.

[40] See for example Flanders, N. A. 'Some Relationships Among Teacher Influence, Pupil Attitudes and Achievement' in Biddle, B. J. and Elena, W. J. (eds) *Contemporary Research in Teacher Effectiveness*, New York: Holt, Rinehart & Winston, 1964.

[41] Flanders, N. A. *Analysing Teacher Behaviour*, New York: Addison-Wesley, 1970.

[42] Adams, R. S. and Biddle, B. J. *Realities of Teaching: Explorations with Video-tape*, New York: Holt, Rinehart & Winston, 1970.

[43] See for example the criticisms by Robinson, P. E. 'An Ethnography of Classrooms' in Eggleston, J. (ed.) *Contemporary Research in the Sociology of Education, op. cit.*

[44] Robinson, P. E. *ibid*, p. 263.

[45] Leacock, E. B. quoted in Robinson, P. D. *ibid*, p. 263.

[46] For a more comprehensive account than is possible here see Delamont, S. *Interaction in the Classroom*, London: Methuen, 1976.

[47] Leacock, E. B. *Teaching and Learning in City Schools*, New York: Basic Books, 1969.

[48] Keddie, N. 'Classroom Knowledge', in Young, M. F. D. (ed.) *Knowledge and Control, op. cit.*

[49] See also Sarason, S. B., Davidson, K. S. and Blatt, B. *The Preparation of Teachers*, New York: Wiley, 1962.

[50] Gross, N. *et al. Implementing Organizational Innovation*, New York: Harper & Row, 1971.

[51] Brophy, J. E. and Good, T. L. *Teacher-Student Relationships, op. cit.*, pp. 330-37.

[52] Delamont, S. *Interaction in the Classroom, op. cit.*

[53] Jackson, P. W. *Life in Classrooms*, New York: Holt, Rinehart & Winston, 1968, pp. 33-4.

[54] Keddie, N. 'Classroom Knowledge', *op. cit.*

[55] Woods, P. 'Showing Them Up' in Chanan, G. and Delamont, S. (eds) *Frontiers of Classroom Research*, Slough: N.F.E.R., 1975.

[56] Delamont, S. *op. cit.*

[57] Lundgren, W. P. 'Pedagogical Roles in the Classroom' in Eggleston, J. (ed.) *Contemporary Research in the Sociology of Education, op. cit.*

[58] Brophy, J. E. and Good, T. L. *Teacher-Student Relationships, op. cit.*

[59] Hoehn, A. J. 'A Study of Social Status Differentiation in the Classroom Behaviour of Nineteen Third-grade Teachers', *Journal of Social Psychology*, vol. XXXIX, 1954.

60 Rist, R. C. 'Social Distance and Social Inequality in a Ghetto Kindergarten Classroom', *Urban Education*, vol. VII, 1972.
61 Nash, R. *Classrooms Observed*, London: Routledge & Kegan Paul, 1973.
62 See Goodacre, E. J. *Teachers and Their Pupils' Home Background*, *op. cit.*
63 Summaries of this research are to be found in Morrison, A. and McIntyre, D. *op. cit.* See also Kelsall, R. and Kelsall, H. M. *The School Teacher in England and the United States*, *op. cit.*
64 Westwood, L. J. 'The Role of the Teacher', *Educational Research*, vols 9 and 10, 1967.
65 Lomax, D. 'Teacher Education', in Butcher, H. J. and Pont, H. B. *Educational Research in Britain*, vol. III, *op. cit.*
66 Morrison, A. and McIntyre, D. *op. cit.*, p. 70.
67 See for example Lomax, D. *op. cit.*
68 See for example Morrison, A. and McIntyre, D. *op. cit.*
69 Finlayson, D. S. and Cohen, L. 'The Teachers' Role: a Comparative Study of the Conceptions of College of Education Students and Head Teachers', *British Journal of Educational Psychology*, vol. XXXVII, 1967, p. 29.
70 Corwin, R. G. *A Sociology of Education*, *op. cit.*, pp. 301-40.
71 Webb, J. 'The Sociology of a School', *British Journal of Sociology*, vol. XIII, 1962, p. 269.
72 McPherson, G. H. *Small Town Teacher*, Harvard University Press, 1972.
73 Waller, W. *The Sociology of Teaching*, *op. cit.*, p. 355.
74 Woods, P. 'Showing them up', in Chanan, G. and Delamont, S. *op. cit.*
75 See for example McPherson, G. H. *op. cit.*, pp. 105-110.
76 Whiteside, M. L., Bernbaum, G. and Noble, G. 'Aspirations, Reality – Shock and Entry into Teaching', *Sociological Review*, vol. XVII, 1969.
77 Kelsall, R. K. and Kelsall, H. *The School Teacher in England and the United States*, *op. cit.*
78 For a very good account of this kind of restriction see Kozol, J. *Death at an Early Age*, *op. cit.*

Index

INDEX